THE
OTHER
SIDE
OF
THE
WALL

Translated from the Hebrew by
LEONARD GOLD

Philadelphia   5743 • 1983
The Jewish Publication Society of America

THE OTHER SIDE OF THE WALL

THREE NOVELLAS

NATHAN SHAHAM

Originally published in Hebrew under the title
Kirot Etz Dakim
Copyright © 1977 by Am Oved
Publishers, Ltd., Tel Aviv
English translation copyright © 1983
by The Jewish Publication Society of America
First English edition   All rights reserved
Manufactured in the United States of America

Library of Congress Cataloging in Publication Data

Shaham, Nathan.
The other side of the wall.
Translation of: Kirot-'ets dakim.
Contents: S/S Cairo City—The other side of the
wall—The salt of the earth.
I. Title.
PJ5054.S3K5713   1983   892.4'36   83–65
ISBN 0-8276-0223-5

Designed by Adrianne Onderdonk Dudden

CONTENTS

THE
OTHER
SIDE
OF
THE
WALL

S/S
CAIRO
CITY

Geneva, Thursday, August 24, 1939

It is morning. There is a small desk near the window. A crucifix hangs on the wall. The tops of chestnut trees, the roof of the next house, and a strip of faraway blue are framed in the window. Alper has already gone out. Using some pretext, I got out of attending the sessions of the Congress again today. Madame Garni seems worried. "Is Monsieur ill?" Her tone is maternal. There's a summer flu going around and she's afraid of catching it. Who will take care of Monsieur Perrier if she gets sick? Since I am perfectly well I try to reassure her in my high-school French. "It's only a slight headache." "Monsieur came in very late last night, did he not?" A smile of sly complicity crosses her face. She is in love with love, with lovers, with anything having to do with the tender emotions.

My mind races along at terrifying speed, but my hand is leaden. I want to write you about first things first and last things last, but it all comes together in a mad jumble inside my head. Details and fragments of details whirl by and then snap to attention before my eyes in no apparent order.

My thoughts return to the train just as a person visits the grave of a dear one. The moment of separation on the platform stands out like a marker over my own grave. You are inside the carriage, your curls blowing in the wind, your features dissolving in a blur. You seem to have been taken from me by force, as if someone else had bought your ticket, put you on the train, and made you go. The wheels send forth their metallic clatter. The locomotive sighs, but finds the strength to carry on. That is the message of its huffing and puffing. Son of Man, as trains depart, even so do they return!

And yet, I was beside myself with worry and grief. How is one to describe grief? I can only paint a picture. Color it yellow-gray, with spreading purple splotches. Many daring notions flashed through my mind during those seconds: why not run after the train, jump on as it pulls out, take you in my arms, pull the emergency brake, get off with a happy smile, pay the fine with the last of our money, and plunge into a new adventure without a penny to our names? I once saw a scene like that in some silly movie. But hasn't each of us the urge, at least once in a lifetime, to live a fairy-tale scene from a dumb movie, to have the guts to make a rash decision and stay with it to the end?

Our feet are smarter than we are. And weaker. I stood among the throng for a while, until finally there was nothing to do but turn and go.

I took one last look at the empty track and something snapped inside me. As if my life had been split into two distinct parts. The track was the demarcation line, its parallel rails underscoring the importance of the break. The end. A new chapter. Things had happened too quickly. Our lips had barely touched the rim of the chalice. We thought we would have a few more days. We might have learned everything we need to know about ourselves. I use the term "to know" in its original sense. But these things have an internal rhythm all their own and cannot be hurried. I am not speaking about my emotions. These are as plain to me as is humanly possible. I am speaking about the life-force pent up in this thing that hangs by a thread.

Late in the afternoon the shocking news reached us. Two hours later there was a hasty consultation, and by nighttime we were standing on the station platform, silent and confused. In a far-off city two gentlemen in black toppers signed a paper, and on that very day the event became part of our lives. And just because I condemned the pact so vehemently Alper accused me of wanting to live outside of history.

There were also some thoughts that I should have been ashamed of. I thought that it might not be such a good idea for you to return to Poland. I looked at your trim ankles and your tiny feet, and it occurred to me that you were not exactly the person to bring deliverance to the confused kids of the youth movement. That is, if war does break out, as they are saying it will. But I couldn't even pin the blame for your going on our own people. They are not the ones who told you to go. They only meant the movement representatives from Eretz Yisrael. But they didn't tell you not to go, either. They only looked at you with affection and in Yitzhak's eyes there were even tears of happiness when you got up and announced that you were going back to Poland. You were free to understand the necessity. A choice is given, but at the same time one does what is expected. Only three weeks ago you were elected to the movement Executive and already you have a sense of noblesse oblige. I, of course, couldn't say a word. After all, you are not the only one going back to Poland. Froyka has a wife and child in Aretz* and he is flying to Warsaw tomorrow. I even felt a moment of elation. I was proud that people like us put the good of the majority before our own personal well-being. But today I recall that feeling without pride. One day I shall surely live to regret the fact that with my own hands I lifted your German knapsack onto the train.

I am standing on the platform, shocked into silence. The train pulls farther and farther into the distance. Your face is at the window, your features growing blurred.

The lives of lovers slowly fill up with symbols all their own. The train will now become a part of our own little thesaurus of symbols. The very word "train" will bear a tremendous emotional charge. At the train we came to terms with our emotions. At the train we experienced our first kiss. The one that tore us asunder.

With my eyes closed, I can relive the trip between Warsaw and Berlin minute by minute. Your hand is in mine and we are silent. German villages pass by the window as if startled out of their sleep, a deep peasant sleep, and they are carried far off to an unknown destination. The whole world is being swept backward and only we remain stationary, as if the very certainty that has come over us now fixes us in our place forevermore. Nothing was said. But there was no need to. Even the SS man with his piercing, cruel baby face was caught in the web of emotion and smiled as he raised his eyes from your passport.

And the kiss in the tunnel. At first it was just a silly joke, but our lips were painfully serious. The rattling of the cars seemed to wind up a spring inside of me. I was ready for that trip through the dark tunnel to last forever. When we emerged into the light I looked into your face. It betrayed a

*Literally, "land," intimate reference to the Land of Israel.

[6]

slight embarrassment and glowed with an apple redness. I saw at once that the miracle had occurred. One simple word says it all.

As I came away from the station some strangers invited me to share their cab. They were touched by what they had seen. I thanked them politely. "I don't live far from here," I lied. I walked a long way by the lake. I couldn't believe that you had gone. Only a few hours earlier we had been sitting together at the Rialto watching the "Carmel Newsreel." When they showed the fishing at Tel Amal I told you about the wild beauty of the Sahna, and I promised to take you there when you got to Aretz. A short time later we were on the *Général Dufour*, cruising without a care through lovely Lac Léman. We even had a small family quarrel there—we ought to be ashamed—over two and a half francs. I insisted on paying for you out of my own pocket, and you wouldn't let me tax my budget. And since Jews are not supposed to enjoy anything without making the appropriate blessing, we pretended that we were listening to speeches about the Israel Maritime League, and this in order to justify irresponsible pleasure-cruising right in the middle of the Congress. It's hard to believe that this was only last night.

I look at my watch. Not even twenty-four hours have elapsed. I wandered about the streets until sunrise. I cannot remember what I did for all those hours. Toward morning a light drizzle forced me to seek shelter. Two policemen on bicycles stopped me. Their dog, who was trained to detect alcohol, let out a low whine. And yet I hadn't touched a drop. But maybe his natural sense taught him to detect other kinds of intoxication, as well.

O, enchanted drunkenness,
Marvelous confounding of the senses.

I myself wrote a takeoff of that love poem. Now I can find no better words. Such things are best expressed in banalities.

If you try to be too clever you only miss the mark.

When the rain stopped I moved on. The city was silent and empty. Only a few people could be seen in the street. Workers, early risers. And it took me by surprise that people could still find purpose in getting up for work. I won't speak about the pain again. If you have felt it on your own there isn't much to say. If you have not felt it there is nothing to say. For the first time I saw the square in front of the Grand Théâtre without a living soul. It was like a city under curfew. I once experienced a similar feeling in the lower town of Haifa. A bomb had exploded in the marketplace and the streets had emptied. I looked out into the empty streets with an expectancy that I did not understand. It was evident that a disaster had occurred, but it was not yet clear where or if anybody was wounded.

In the square in front of the theater there was only one wounded person. I wanted to believe that two had been injured by that particular explosion.

What a foolish, petty heart! If I were really concerned for your happiness I would have to wish you peace and tranquillity. Yet I was afraid that you might be riding along in that train toward some new excitement without a thought for me. Unashamedly, I wished that you, too, might shed a tear and that your eyes, looking out of the window, would see, not the passing scenery, but the streets of Geneva and my ecstatic face.

Here I must sign off. I must hurry if the letter is to get off today. Toward morning I got to my room. It was my luck that Alper sleeps soundly, so that in the morning he had no embarrassing questions. He got up, woke me, and proposed that I go with him to the tenth session of the Congress. He seemed disappointed when I complained of a headache. He gave me a questioning look, not because he didn't believe me this time, but because he's a Galitzianer, and left. As soon as the door closed behind him, I jumped out of bed and sat down to write you.

I will end here. I have one more thing to ask of you. Please go to my father's house. Tell him you saw me in Genf. Don't say Genève or Geneva, he won't know where that is. (In the Hebrew newspapers in Eretz Yisrael for some reason they write Geneva.) Tell him that I send my love. You can tell him whatever crosses your mind. I am sure that he will be very glad to see you. If the conversation turns serious you can hint that it's still not too late to get out of Poland. If you have money you can get out whenever you please. I doubt if he will heed the advice. His opposition to Zionism is even stronger than his fear. During my last visit, when the business about Danzig had already made the headlines, he tried to convince me that I could still give up my youthful follies—Zionism, Palestine, scout games, training camps, and other foolishness—to settle down at a decent Polish university and become a mentsh.

By the way, the whole business about his illness was nothing more than a pretext to get me back from Aretz. He is no sicker than you or I. At first I resented it a bit. In '37 I left Poland. In '39 I was on my way back to visit my family. They don't like that in the kibbutz. They especially don't like it when you combine a trip to the Congress with a personal visit, even though you save money by doing it that way. And I don't want to be considered one of the privileged few, one of those who can afford things that are out of the reach of ordinary kibbutz members. In any case, if his wife had not written that he was deathly ill I would never have come. I hope my comrades never find out that he put one over on me. At any rate, now I'm not sorry about the trip. If he hadn't sounded the alarm we might never have met. If we had never met you might never have thought of coming to the Congress. If you hadn't come to the Congress I might have thought "happiness" meant a dull, routine existence, undisturbed by either highs or lows.

I anticipate the meeting between you and Papa with some trepidation. I have made a few strong statements here, but don't misunderstand. We seldom see eye to eye, but that does not mean a break has occurred. I am devoted to him, and from the day that Mama died he has been both father and mother to me. We go our separate ways, but a father is a father. I want him to love you. That love would close a circle. The moment his knowing eyes took in your beauty he would give me a father's blessing. I find a special magic in the thought of such a meeting, for nothing would be said, yet everything would be understood. It would be enough for you to tell him that I had asked you to visit; he would understand the rest.

There is only one thing that should be avoided. Don't tell him your father's name. The way he has of fawning before the very rich always saddens me. But this may be unavoidable. You won't be able to stand up under the barrage of his polite cross-examination.

Perhaps I am making too much of this meeting, as if there were something in it that could secretly bind you to the family. As I said before, the deeds of lovers are charged with symbols. And the link between the *signans* and the *signatus* is not always clear. But when the Messiah comes what difference will it make if there is a link or not?

So much for that. Tomorrow I shall write you about the Congress: what is being said, what has been decided, what is going on, and so forth. Now I must hurry to the post office. Maybe if I send it by airmail the letter will arrive before you.

Yours (even the most hackneyed cliché suddenly acquires the dignity of a simple truth),

Jerzy

The same day close to midnight

I am holding the letter in my lap as I write from the Congress hall. Rabbi Nurock is speaking and I cannot hear a word. But anyone who sees me must think I am taking notes. These are fateful days, and every word counts. I am keeping my promise and writing you a blow-by-blow description of events.

Well. The morning began on a disappointing note. You can see for yourself. The letter was not sent. Monsieur Perrier saw me with the letter in my hand and advised me not to send it. He had been listening to the radio and heard something about a breakdown in mail and telegraphic communications. In a few days, when the situation stabilizes, postal service will return to normal. I did not want to take his advice, but when I went to the bank I discovered that he was right. The teller refused to accept Polish money. He said that no rate of exchange had been established for the zloty this morning. I realized that it made no sense even to go to the post office. Europe is waiting to see what happens. But, just to make sure, I dropped by anyway. I was told that the telegraph was not working, that letters had gone out but not by airmail. I stood by the mailbox for a while trying to make up my mind. In the end I decided not to send it. I did not want my letter to get lost in some pile of forgotten mail. Just then I got an idea: Froyka was flying to Warsaw. I would ask him to take the letter along.

On the way to the Congress I stopped in at the office. Everything was as it had been: the portrait of Herzl, the maps of Eretz Yisrael, the picture of the *Galila*, and the plaque with "If I forget thee, O Jerusalem" behind your desk. The sight of your empty chair took my breath away. I asked Olga something, and from the way she replied I could tell that she knew everything. She spoke about you with great warmth. She said you were a conscientious worker even though you sometimes disappeared for hours on end. But what can you expect of volunteers? We should be glad that they come at all. She complained that this year she missed all those young people who, on their way through Europe, used to drop in for a look at the leaders of world Jewry and at the same time lend a hand with the clerical work. As she spoke, Olga's eyes subjected me to a stiff cross-examination, as if trying to determine what effect the mention of your name would have on me.

The other offices were empty. It is only at the office of the Congress bulletin that business goes on as usual. Every word is taken down and printed. History stands up for her rights and demands that both the sublime and the ridiculous appear in the record.

The general atmosphere here is one of fear and confusion. Many of the delegates hang around the travel agencies to make sure of their reservations. Shameful things have occurred. Our people, at least, are not implicated. The Labor faction has been above reproach. Instead of every man looking out for himself, our people put their trust in the preparations committee. Now Rabbi S. Goldman from the United States is speaking. Good Yiddish but with a hint of an American accent. I am just able to make out a few sentences. The reassuring, conciliatory words of a person who will go home to safety when this is all over. Even he will have to surrender his claim to my attention. I pick up the paper and notice that my writing has gone through to the other side and defaced a beautiful picture in the Geneva album that serves as my desk. A few words are chiseled into the mountains and others have fallen into the lake. I don't know whether to attribute it to your going or to the world situation, but since this morning I am in a state of torpor. All the questions before the Congress seem meaningless and unimportant. When I think of my comrades who scrimped from their own table money to buy the Zionist shekel something rebels inside of me. A nation of paupers, with its head on the block, has made a party for its finance committee. What a crying waste of time and money! People put on top hats, take leave of their real lives, run to Switzerland, stay at luxury hotels, eat in expensive restaurants, and then have a go at parliamentary fun and games, which have only the slightest bearing on what we do in Eretz Yisrael. Nor are we innocent, either. We, too, have donned strange garb, and with it a sense of our own importance. We deliver the speeches of a loyal opposition, and make proposals that haven't the slightest chance of passage. If only you could see the smugness with which a certain one of our boys shows his delegate's pass. As for me, I don't think I'll ever really feel comfortable with the little privileges we take for granted as representatives of the people. Even though I am here as a voting delegate, I cannot see myself as part of that self-righteous bunch who come to congresses thinking the whole world hangs on their words. They quarrel over chickens that haven't even hatched.

I shared some of these heretical notions with Victor. They weren't at all to his liking. He spoke with great confidence about the effect of the Congress on members of the movement. Its representatives are taking their rightful place in the Jewish world. In other words, we have graduated from scout games to a full-fledged political struggle. And this, of course, has special appeal for our younger members. If they don't find it with us they will go over to the Communists. The Communists have a better theoretical grounding and more advanced techniques. What's more, even minority proposals have a certain propaganda value. In a word, he let me understand that I was nothing but an unsophisticated clod. Later, even I was ashamed of myself, for there definitely is an element of self-deception here. I seem to be trying to enjoy a vacation in Switzerland and to confront absolute truth at one and the same time. This is like the attitude of an aesthete who sprinkles on a few drops of cologne when he really needs a bath.

Maybe this, too, is a symptom of that malignant disease we have caught. You fall in love with a woman, but at the same time are bitten with a passion for the truth. We feel a powerful desire to know ourselves, to bare everything, to abandon forever any sort of lie or deceit. It is like purification before being allowed to serve at the shrine of a particularly demanding goddess.

Isn't it strange that I feel this way? For nine days we strained, you and I, to hide our relationship from our comrades. All that time we were playing undercover agent. We pretended to have met by accident. We hid. We covered our footprints. We disowned one another publicly. Was there a single trick we skipped in trying to deceive our comrades?

And yet, we feel this overwhelming need for honesty. It is a contradiction that we must live with whether we like it or not. I long for the day when we can tear off our masks and walk together with our heads held high. Not like thieves in the night . . .

I promised to write about the Congress, and here I am writing about myself again.

Well, the morning session began late. All sorts of rumors were flying. Somebody said that Mrs. Dugdale said that war would break out within two days. And, after all, she should know. She comes from England. Many people insisted that the Congress be adjourned today. We learned that Italy and France have closed their borders, and people are starting to worry. How will we get home? They phoned Lloyd-Triestino and learned that the *Galila* would sail behind schedule, if at all. It has been apparent for some time that this Congress will end on a note of defeat. Decisions will be adopted, and there will be a closing session, but it won't be the real thing. People's minds are elsewhere. Mine, too. I try not to think about the war. My imagination takes over, and I see horrible things. At times I envy people who lack imagination. Nothing exists for them until it has happened. But even if war does not materialize, if there is only tension and the borders are closed, what will become of us? Maybe it isn't nice to think about ourselves all the time, but I promised you that I would write everything and with complete honesty. If a training group doesn't leave for Eretz Yisrael this year the aliyah of your group will be postponed as well. The White Paper still puts a quota on immigration. True, we have adopted clear-cut decisions to fight the White Paper, but how strong are we? And if your aliyah is postponed by a year or two—my imagination cannot even encompass such a length of time. It seems like an abyss opening up. Is it possible that we shall not see one another until three years have elapsed? The thought makes me despondent. Three years is an immeasurable span of time. Even you said that we were made for one another. But will you still think so in three years? And I? What am I to do in the meantime? I'd rather not think about it. I am afraid that I could never go to Poland again, even if my father really did take ill. The kibbutz wouldn't like it. And could I ever stand up at a meeting of the kibbutz and say that I'm in love with a girl in Warsaw and that I can't think about anything else?

I'm ready to fall all over anyone who proclaims himself an expert in international affairs and who insists that there will be no war. Take Alper, for instance. He says that Hitler is no fool. Witness the pact with Russia. (Alper is careful to say the Soviet Union.) If the Germans can get what they want without war why should they start killing? From his mouth to God's ears.

Back to the Congress. The morning session proceeded in the light of all these things. First of all we were told that the General Zionist Alliance had decided to return to the sessions of the Congress and to participate in its deliberations. This is all to the good. It is absolutely ridiculous to think that only a few days ago they were arguing themselves hoarse about irregularities in the elections! Now one of their people adorns the dais along with the others. "But thine eyes shall see thy Teacher" (Isa. 30:20). Then came a memorial service. The list of names was a long one. Then three more people got up and added some more names that had been left out. And Ussishkin promised that still more names would be added in the published version. Then the presidency passed to Sprinzak and we heard the committee reports. Do you want the truth? I wasn't paying attention. Frequently I didn't even know who was speaking. But I was always sure of the speaker's political leanings. Sitting next to me was a serious-looking man with a pencil behind his ear. From the carnation in his lapel I could tell he was from Mapai. Whenever the speaker made him angry he would take the pencil and jot something down furiously, as if condemning the man on paper to life imprisonment. Whenever I saw a smile of satisfaction cross his face I knew that the speaker was one of our people. They spoke about the shekel and about the budget and about the special status of Eretz Yisrael. And it was decided to cancel this special status, as well as the privileges of the smaller countries.

Had lunch with Froyka. We went to a small teetotaler restaurant opposite the Congress hall. You and I once ate cheese pancakes there. It's the restaurant Sonia calls "WIZO." We ate very little, since we are trying to watch the budget. It's impossible to say how long we'll have to wait for a ship. Also, they are trying to put aside money for those people from Palestine who are going on to organize in their countries of origin. We gossiped about this and that and all the while I was wondering whether or not to give him the letter. What could I tell him? Of all the kids I had once worked with in the movement in Warsaw why should I suddenly have to rush off an urgent letter to you, especially when you were with us here only yesterday?

Froyka really astounds me with his knowledge about every single thing under the sun. Did you know, for example, that about a hundred years ago Mickiewicz wanted to be a professor of literature at Geneva. Well, for your information, Celina got sick and he had to go back to Paris. Froyka also knows how many planes Germany has, as well as Britain and France. Later on Froyka became a bit sentimental. He spoke of his return to Warsaw as if he were brave Perseus going off to save fair Andromeda from the Gorgon (which took place at Jaffa, by the way). And he obviously expected me to admire the deed. This I did, according to all the rules of proper etiquette. He could never have known how much I envied him. At any rate, the impassioned speech about his mission made it difficult for me to turn him into a letter carrier. Less still, a bearer of love letters. Least of all, the courier of a forbidden love. Meanwhile, it was time to go back to the Congress hall. We had to be on time. The afternoon session opened with the recommendations of the subcommittee for youth and propaganda. These were accepted in record time. There were no minority recommendations. Meanwhile, Froyka ran into someone he knew from Poland and disappeared. He left during the discussion on finance and the budget and never came back. I was a little angry. When I missed a session Alper wouldn't let me live it down. He made it clear that I was there at the expense of others. But for Froyka it's okay. After all, he's going to Warsaw . . .

In the afternoon there were also discussions on agricultural settlement. Hot air. Any kid who backpacks it up to the Galilee is worth more than a dozen of these Congress delegates. But I may be exaggerating. Without the Jewish Agency allotments you couldn't even plant a tree today. One family contributed 10,000 pounds to name a settlement after their grandfather. With one string attached: it had to be a settlement for middle-class immigrants from Central Europe. And what about us? Actually, what about me? You're a member of the upper class. Sorry about splitting hairs, but a fact is a fact.

With your permission, I won't bother writing about Commerce and Industry or even about the Committee on Labor, the Merchant Marine, and Social Action. I looked for Froyka. Then I learned that he had gone to pack. He takes off tomorrow morning. Now I certainly can't go to his room on the other side of the lake to hand him a letter. That would give the letter special importance and would only serve to emphasize what we have tried so hard to cover up. Meanwhile, I found out that the delegates from Poland leave for home tomorrow by way of Hungary. I thought of something new. I'll give the letter to Kleinbaum. I'll put it into an envelope addressed to Papa. Papa was Kleinbaum's teacher at the University and Kleinbaum will do it gladly. Papa will call you, and you'll come over to pick up the letter. That way I'd be hitting two birds with one stone. My long arm reaches out to you from Geneva. Even if you hadn't intended to visit my father, now you won't be able to get away with a mere telephone call . . . I haven't altogether forgotten how to get things done.

It's now ten after one. Ussishkin is launching into the final speech. On the whole, the evening session hasn't been as gloomy as the other sessions. It began very late. It was nearly ten. Weizmann spoke first, since he has to leave before the end of the Congress. There are all kinds of rumors. Some say he's going to ask the Americans for a battleship to get the delegates home. Others say he's leaving to say good-bye to his son who is joining the British army. In any case, he spoke with great emotion, and a few people were actually crying. His parting words were cordial, but also a little frightening. He was not sure, he said, if we would ever, all of us, meet together again. At the next Congress, whenever that is, if there is one at all, many will be absent.

When he took leave of the delegates from Poland I thought

of you. There were sustained applause and great excitement. Even I secretly wiped away a tear. Only Alper, sitting at the end of the row, saw, and he wore a peculiar smile, the smile of someone who is determined not to be shaken. Well, to each his own. He didn't even get excited when Weizmann shouted, "Our people is eternal and our land is eternal," even though it was obvious that the words came from his heart and were much more than just a slogan.

When Weizmann said, "The saving remnant will go on working, fighting, living until we see a better day," a shiver ran through me. To speak of a saving remnant when we're not even sure there will be a war is something of a shocker.

The political discussion somewhat weakened the impact of Weizmann's speech. There was the old divisiveness, all over again. The Jewish State party made its own proposal. Then we raised objections. Then the standing committee made its recommendations. And, just as our people had predicted, there were no changes whatsoever in the composition of the Zionist Executive. Two members were added to the Actions Committee. Eight honorary members were elected, with Ussishkin at their head. Next, there was a little argument about guidelines for the composition of the Actions Committee, there were elections for the Congress tribunal, and it was decided to charge the Zionist Actions Committee with the job of setting up an auditing body and appointing its chief. Business as usual. If during Weizmann's speech there were moments when I felt, "This is it. We're at war," the ensuing discussions had a tranquilizing effect. Because if people really thought that war was at hand they would hardly be arguing about the number of members on the Actions Committee.

2:40 A.M. The session ended about an hour ago. We're back at the hotel. Alper is asleep. All the way home he ranted about the coalition with the Right, but no sooner did his head hit the pillow than he was asleep. Now I can sit at the desk and write a few more words. The last few pages seem dry and don't really express my feelings.

Last night I must have had about three hours' sleep. Nevertheless, now I'm wide awake and even if I tried to I couldn't fall asleep. I go over and over the experiences of the last few days, and there's a terrible churning deep down inside me. Details and fragments of details poke their heads up with alarming urgency. Just a moment ago I felt a draft from the window and there we were at Chamonix, a pair of runaways. Your face is radiant from the snow, your scarf flaps about, and your eyes sparkle. From the direction of the Cornavin comes the whistle of a locomotive and I taste your lips.

There is no doubt about it. This was not love at first sight, but, rather, something hidden that took its time, like a seed pressed deep into the earth biding its time. Now I know that I loved you even then, in '34. I remember how you stood beneath the picture of Bet-Alfa and recited Tchernichovski's poem. Your beautiful face shone in the torchlight and suddenly I was happy. As if the power of the movement had suddenly been revealed to me, because pretty girls like you could prefer it to the pleasures of glittering Warsaw. But then I didn't dare to call that feeling love. After all, there was a yawning chasm between me and you. You were only fourteen and I was twenty-two. Inexperienced as I was I could still respond to your burgeoning femininity. Even then you had the intelligent smile of a woman who knows that every word directed to her speaks both for itself and for something deeper, more turbulent. But I couldn't even hint to you about what I saw. You were a kid in the movement and I was a representative from Eretz Yisrael. And don't we demand of people in the youth movement restraint, self-control, sublimation? Even at the training farms members are supposed to avoid intimate relationships. I had to deny my feelings and even be a little hard on you. If I had allowed myself to show favoritism great harm would have been done from an educational point of view. I remember how, in '37, at the farewell assembly, you stood next to me. The flag waved over us like a red marriage canopy. I saw something symbolic in that. And, afterward, I was proud of myself for not having spoken a single word to you. I noticed that you seemed put out. After all, during the previous months you had helped me a great deal in correcting the proofs for the *Leader's Manual*. And still you showed up the following day to see me off at the railroad station. And I only waved from the train window in the most general fashion, like Mussolini from his balcony . . . as if I wanted to avoid insulting, by singling you out, thirty thousand graduates of the movement in whom I personally had instilled self-discipline and love of homeland.

Now you won't be able to accuse me of being stingy with my words. I realize that I have written another page, and yet another. From the street one already hears the rattle of wagons on their way down to the station to meet the arriving passengers. In vain. There won't be any trains from Italy or France today. I had better try to get a couple of hours' sleep now. I must wake up in time to catch Kleinbaum before he leaves.

I tremble to think that in just a few days, maybe even the day after tomorrow, your delicate fingers will touch these sheets.

Geneva, Friday, August 25

What a crazy day! I got up early in order to catch Kleinbaum. It took a whole hour to get to the Beau Rivage (12 francs for a room with breakfast). But they told me he wasn't staying there. I had been sent on a wild-goose chase. I phoned the offices of the Congress. Nobody answered. I went there. Olga was polite and found out where he was staying. At the other end of town. Geneva is nothing but a small town, smaller even than Tel Aviv, but at that moment it seemed enormous. And the tram stopped every two seconds. It seemed as if the good people of Geneva had it in for me. The time it takes them to get onto the tram and then to pay their fare. Everything in slow motion, as if they have forever. By the time I got to the hotel he was gone. No one knew where. I was somewhat relieved that his things were still there. In other words, he hadn't really left yet.

For two hours I looked for the other movement people. It seemed as if the earth had swallowed them up. I went back to my room. Alper had gone (when I left he wasn't up yet) without leaving a message. Madame Garni forced me to eat the breakfast she had prepared two hours earlier. She said I looked awful, like someone home from the wars. Without realizing it everybody has begun to use military language. It was not until noon that I managed to track our people down. They were having a meeting at Shraga's hotel. I couldn't even get angry at Alper. He had probably said something about it when I wasn't paying attention. They kept me for a long time, and I couldn't leave. This was an important consultation on the White Paper. We had to formulate our reply to Ben-Gurion's proposals. Yitzhak made a long admonitory speech. Even in a group of eight he makes speeches. In times of emergency he is at his best. His words were powerful and convincing. But I was sitting on tenterhooks. The consultation was over at three. They went to eat and I ran to see Kleinbaum. I jumped into a cab—3 francs, the price of two meals—and got there more dead than alive. Kleinbaum had left an hour before. Furious and at my wits' end I went back to the post office. Again they told me that I could put a stamp on the letter and drop it into the box, but they couldn't guarantee that the mail would go out before Monday. If at all. I went away with the letter burning a hole in my pocket. I stopped off at the British consulate. I remembered seeing a notice at the Congress offices about having to register. A clerk flipped through my passport and eyed me suspiciously. What had I been doing in Germany? I explained that I had traveled through Germany on my way from Poland. What was I doing in Poland? Visiting a sick relative. He looked at me as if he had never heard such a miserable excuse in all his life. But perhaps I'm imagining things. Maybe his is just the standard look of a well-trained bureaucrat. In any case, he took down my name and returned the passport without further ado. For a moment I entertained a wild hope. If they confiscated my passport I would be deported to Poland . . . In the waiting room I heard hair-raising tales of espionage. The editor of *Le Figaro* was arrested as a spy for Germany.

Meanwhile, all sorts of rumors continue to circulate. Everybody speaks about the war as if he alone has firsthand information. Krugeliak from the Tel Aviv workers' council heard it from Ben-Gurion, who heard it from Weizmann, who heard it from God. Anyway, one thing is certain: the borders are closed and there is no telling how we will get out of here or when. What a letdown! If you hadn't been in such a hurry to leave we would both have been trapped here. And I, fool that I am, encouraged you to go. The movement before all else! Is our crumb of happiness something to be ashamed of? A wave of giddiness washes over me when I contemplate the following possibility: we are both here for an unspecified duration. While everybody else is down in the dumps you and I provide an example of Olympian serenity. As befits movement people whose spirits never flag . . . Even when your heart is breaking, laugh, clown, laugh. I can seek some consolation in telling myself that it was only to be worthy of your love that I resisted trying to stop you from going. To avoid disappointing you I played the bitter role that sealed my doom. Because actually you would have gone anyway, but then you would have regretted wasting your love on such a schlemiel.

I try to believe that there will be no war. Levelheaded people are saying that the hysteria we are witness to now is being provoked deliberately. Tension is being created so that when the Germans march into Danzig the world will breathe a sigh of relief. The hell with Danzig! I would rather not think of the horror stories they told about the last war. I was only a child, but I remember well the fear in Mama's eyes as she spoke about the war. I already feel the urge to treat the war the way a religious Jew treats the name of God. Not to mention it and by so doing not to look for trouble. Meanwhile, I blot out of my mind anything that has to do with war.

This letter is as confused as the entire day has been and as my emotions. And yet this is a letter that is being written under decent conditions. I am in the room. Alper has gone to the French consulate. We may be able to get transit visas. Then we would take the whole caboodle and descend upon Marseille. It's now seven-thirty in the evening. A soft twilight is settling over this beautiful city. A pink blush is reflected off the snowy peaks. The chestnut tree in the yard rustles its leafy petticoat. "The Death of Summer" was the name of the composition I wrote for Balaban on my matrics. The radio is playing sweet, quiet music. Madame Garni is dozing in her room. Monsieur Perrier put on his striped jacket, waxed the ends of his mustache, and has gone off to see what he can dredge up. I am eternally grateful to the French consul for detaining Alper and enabling me to write in peace. But now of all times my letter comes out confused and incoherent. I am not even able to observe the simplest rules of syntax. Halperin's red pencil would have a field day with this last page.

Again I had to pretend that I was asleep. It wasn't until I was absolutely certain of Alper's snoring that I could afford to slip out of bed. I lit one of the weird lamps in Madame

Garni's parlor, and that is where I am writing. I can barely see what I am doing. You'll have to excuse the handwriting.

In the evening Yitzhak called me to an important meeting of the Labor faction. He wanted me to take part. I couldn't figure out why it had to be me of all people. Maybe because of the course for auxiliary policemen I attended. I could tell that Alper was insulted at not being asked. After all, he is used to being included at the top. I would gladly have bowed out in his favor, but Yitzhak's face was so grim that there was no way I could get out of it.

For obvious reasons I shall spare the details. One never knows who else may read our letters, especially in times like these. At any rate, it was the continuation of an earlier discussion in which I had not taken part. I didn't understand everything. The overall mood was serious, even gloomy. It reminded me of the riots. One night we learned that an attack was expected, and a man from district headquarters came to check up on our defense plans. You can imagine the rest! At any rate, this meeting was absolutely businesslike. For once they stopped beating around the bush and got down to business. The meeting was conducted in Hebrew. B-G has high hopes. He says that we can mobilize twenty thousand men from the Yishuv. The old feud between Ahdut Ha-Avoda and Ha-Poel Ha-Tzair has yet to be laid to rest. There are some who think that if the English are forced to spill Jewish blood in Eretz Yisrael the whole civilized world will tremble. Yitzhak did not mince words. Nobody will lift a finger if the English decide to shoot down Jews in the name of law and order. And certainly not in time of war. I was somewhat shaken by the thought that a number of the people who have been at the course have lost their sense of proportion. They really think we can afford to get tough. Shraga was right when he said that we can't behave like the Arabs. They can afford to destroy everything. If what is ours is destroyed together with what is theirs they will be able to start again from scratch. But not us. We need quiet now in order to build.

A few of the speakers reminded me of Yeruham. You remember. He's that relative of mine I told you about the night they gave out the leaflets with the quotations from William Tell. There is a reward of PL200 on his head. To Alper he is a fascist. To me his is only a case of extreme parochialism. In his settlement the Jews are on top and the Arabs are the underdogs. He touches a piece of metal and it gives him a childish sense of his own strength. But Yeruham is a mixed-up kid. And these are mature individuals. Maybe it's their disillusionment with Britain that causes them to take leave of their senses.

I hope we're not at a real impasse. In any case, there were no hard and fast conclusions. It was only a discussion of approaches. The practical decisions will have to be made elsewhere, of course. And we shall not be there.

Afterward we went to Shraga's hotel and were joined by Eliahu and Shlomo and two representatives working in the youth movement who can't get back to the countries where they are supposed to be. We spoke about the situation in the movement. From Poland of all places there has been some encouraging news. There are many new opportunities for work at the local level. Of late a more sympathetic climate has developed in the Jewish community. The contributions of the Jews to the defense fund have far outstripped those of the gentiles. Anti-Semitism appears to be on the decline. The student patrols have disappeared from outside Jewish shops. The people from NARA no longer prowl the streets on the lookout for victims. The movement is flourishing. Even former adversaries, who used to love to joke about our leather jackets, now ask the movement to take their sons and daughters under its wing, to keep them off the streets. The rabbis of Kamieniec lifted the ban from the man who rented a meeting room to the local branch. Even the Molotov-Ribbentrop Pact has its positive side. The Communists will no longer wield as much influence over our younger members. They have lost the right to speak for internationalism, or, as they would like to think, the days of the Messiah.

These are the miserable joys of beggars. And I rejoiced with them. Rejoiced for you. For if there is no war it will make your job easier. As if, by participating in a discussion on the future of the movement in Europe I could somehow be of assistance to you.

On our way out we met Sonia and Victor. She told us how shocked she was to learn that two people from the Congress had gone to the Café Lyrique and left without paying. Eliahu laughed at her. The things that make her wince! I kind of like the story. All the backbreaking labor paving the roads and loading ships at Haifa port has not managed to cure her of certain bourgeois notions . . .

When I got back to the room Alper subjected me to a thorough cross-examination. Like a real prosecuting attorney. I didn't know whether I was at liberty to tell him everything, and he sensed that I was holding back. I told him I wanted to sleep and he got into his bed in a huff. I waited half an hour until he fell asleep. I could barely hold out.

By the way, even he remarked that I am not looking well. He stared at me as if he knew the reason. "There are difficult days ahead," he said, "and a person must steel himself for whatever comes." I laughed to myself. He thinks I'm worried because we don't know when we'll get home. He pretends to be impassive. That is the mask he has decided will get him through these difficult days. Anyway, I decided to be a little careful. My moods have become too obvious. I must learn to play down my emotions.

I still don't know how this letter will get to you. If we go by way of France, as we hope to do, it will be sent from there. Mail between France and Poland is still getting through. Poland and France are allies, after all. Meanwhile the letter has put on weight and is reaching unwieldy proportions. I hope the handwriting is legible. I have tried to fit as much as possible on one sheet so that I could send it by airmail. (We have just heard that another Lot plane took off for Poland today.) Whether or not it's true, somehow the letter will finally reach you. And then, even if you have forgotten me, you will be forced to live with my memory for a long while . . .

Geneva, Saturday, August 26

These lines are being written in a small café near the railroad station. The platform is abuzz with our people, but I see only your face in the window. In a little while we leave for Marseille. This paper comes from Shraga's hotel. My writing things are packed in my valise.

Well, here's how things turned out. In the morning Victor showed up and grabbed Alper and me for an urgent job. The French had let it be known that we could get transit visas if we crossed the border by Sunday. At first this was seen as some kind of trick. After all, the consulate is closed on Saturday and Sunday. But it seemed that they were willing to send an official with the necessary rubber stamps to our offices to complete the formalities. So there I was, once again in the Bâtiment Électoral, in your very room. (The wind had ripped the *Galila* off the wall and it was lying on the floor. Why would it want to hang on the wall with you not there, anyway?) Alper sat in your chair, in some sort of grotesque exhibition and said, "I'm Perla now." Victor replied: "Only you haven't got her looks." You can imagine how I felt.

We worked like dogs, under the official's watchful eye. Little by little we got all the passports together and copied the details onto the questionnaires. There were snags. The French had agreed to issue visas only to those who held

British passports. We had to phone Paris for permission to grant them to the Czechs and Germans as well. Sometimes it positively frightens me to see the influence that Jewish Agency people can wield with the authorities. The official said, "Absolutely not." Dr. Cohen, without getting excited, simply picked up the telephone and asked for Paris. He said a few words in his quiet, musical voice and handed over the receiver to the official. The official literally turned white when he realized whom he was talking to. He nodded respectfully a few times, gazed at Dr. Cohen with a sort of idiotic admiration, and sat down to work on the foreign passports.

It was afternoon when we finished. We sent Sonia and Victor ahead on the first train. They may be able to find someplace for our people to sleep. It is said that Marseille is flooded with refugees, and there are more than two hundred of us. Those who have money may be able to arrange something. But our kitty is almost completely empty. Still, we won't mind sleeping on a park bench, as long as it brings us closer to Aretz.

I said, "We." The farther south I go the more distant I shall be from you.

I didn't do a thing all afternoon. I read the papers. I took a walk in order to have a last look at our old haunts. I came back and sat on our bench in the League of Nations Park. I could actually smell your fragrance. It was hard to get rid of Alper.

At the students' cafeteria I met some German refugees. It was depressing. Not because of the stories they told, but because they're studying English! Only a few of them think about Eretz Yisrael. Most speak about America. They intend to take advantage of Swiss hospitality until visas for America come through. It's hard to argue with them. They look at you weary eyed and ask why they should go to Eretz Yisrael. Only to run away from there in a few more years? You speak in abstractions, and they reply with personal experience. They remember how their parents emigrated from Poland and were positive that in Germany they had found a haven. Only a large country with a mixture of races can absorb the Jewish element, they say. Kibbutz makes them laugh. To sacrifice higher education for the life of a simple peasant? Maybe rich kids from England or France can afford a Levantine adventure for two or three years. They have homes to go back to. German Jews must plan for the future. They have no more time to waste. It's depressing, really depressing.

Then I took to the streets again. I was feeling terribly low. When I had had enough of that I stopped into the museum. Old works of art have a tranquilizing effect on me. It's a pity we didn't know about it sooner, but there's an exhibit of art treasures from Madrid. During the Civil War they removed the pictures from the Prado, and now they're about to return them. Meanwhile, the exhibit will be shown in a few cities. It's an opportunity not to be missed.

I stayed there quite a while. It was a soothing intermezzo. For a short time I was able to forget everything. Everything, that is, except the one thing that is thrown into relief at such moments. The pictures seemed to have lost some of their magic because you were not there. Of my four eyes only two were really looking, and I seemed to be missing a certain dimension. No words are adequate to describe art. All I could think was: a man comes along, takes a brush, seizes a moment, and makes it live for a long, long time. The prospect dazzles me. I am full of such moments, moments that I would like to seize and transfix, and never let go of.

In the El Greco room I had a peculiar experience. Apart from me there were two girls. Suddenly they began to speak in Yiddish. One said to the other: "Come here, Perla. Look at how beautiful this is." It gave me gooseflesh! And the most amazing thing about it is that the girl actually looked like you. Only a little chubbier. I had to move away, because the other girl sensed something and motioned to her friend.

My emotions are written all over my face. I would never pick me for a secret agent.

By the way, if you ever come across an album of El Greco reproductions, take a careful look at the portrait of the Dominican friar. You will discover a slight resemblance to Alper: the same serious, thoughtful mien, with just a twist of slyness. "I wisdom dwell with slyness, and get knowledge of devices" (Prov. 8:12). And also a kind of stubbornness that does not always bring credit to its author.

Maybe because we shared a room, I'm beginning to see shades of Alper everywhere. In any event, when I looked at the picture I had the strange impression that this monk must be of Marrano descent. The profound sadness in his face is so Jewish.

Something parenthetical apropos of Spain. When I finished my work on the movement Executive I wanted to volunteer for the International Brigade in Spain. The movement saw this as an irresponsible whim and wouldn't let me go. When I got to Aretz I applied for permission again, but this time there was someone else—ever hear of Nusia Orbuch?—who wanted to go. The executive committee said that if they agreed to let us go, tomorrow the whole kibbutz would pick up and disappear. The general meeting decided against our going. I accepted the decision, but Nusia went anyhow. Later he returned to a hero's welcome. My conclusion: being an idealist is not enough. You have to have chutzpa, too. I'm not crying over spilled milk. In the end I should probably have been bitterly disappointed, as Nusia was. But he never admitted it. He may have had a few adventures, but when all is said and done, I got the impression that he never really understood what was going on around him. Most of what he knew he learned from the newspapers after he got back.

When we went to say good-bye to Madame Garni she took out a bottle of French cognac. She said that Monsieur Perrier would never forgive himself for missing us. She wanted to hear from our mouths whether there would be war or not. Since we had been taking part in a political convention she was certain we had inside information. And Alper played along. He reassured her that there would be no war.

The alcohol had its effect on me. I grew very sad and then talked a little too much. Alper had had nothing to drink. I could tell that to him I must have seemed weak. I just couldn't refuse the good woman who offered us this expensive brandy as an expression of her deepest feelings. I still feel a certain heaviness in my movements and a slight dizziness.

By the way, in the middle of our conversation Madame Garni surprised me with an unexpected remark. She asked why I had never brought home "that lovely girl." A naughty smile spread across her face. I think she wanted to show that although she is a devout Catholic, she's no archconservative. She let on that she had seen us by the lake. Geneva is a small town. I'm beginning to think that maybe we weren't careful enough. Monsieur Perrier saw us in the rue de la Confédération, Rabinowitz at Slatkine's shop, and now Madame Garni!

It's our luck that Alper was concentrating on his newspaper at just that moment and wasn't paying attention. When he left the room for a moment I mentioned that you had left for Poland. Madame Garni got all upset: how could I have let you do such a thing! I told her, "Look, didn't Alper just say that there would be no war?" She laughed good-naturedly: "Who was talking about war? It's just that it's foolishness to let such a pretty girl get away." I told her Jews are used to waiting. She said, "That's what you think! Jews or no Jews, out of sight, out of mind."

There has been a delay. The train won't leave for another half hour. For some reason, this silly delay has suddenly made real for me the threat of war. Timetables all fouled up. Masses huddling in the railway stations.

Those with means managed to get out of here last night. They didn't wait for the general arrangements to be completed. They just beat it on the sly. Everybody is furious with them. As if they had just found out that money lets you get away with anything. Funny, how the whole business leaves me without animosity. Only hope. I am trying to believe that your father will know what to do. If havoc breaks loose and work in the movement becomes impossible, don't hesitate. Go with him. Leave Poland for a neutral country. Don't wait for a certificate from Palestine. Communications may be interrupted, and if you wait for a letter from Aretz it may be too late.

I tremble just to reread the words I have written here. Crazy thoughts occur to me. I am imagining all sorts of extreme possibilities.

Zimmerman from Ha-Poel Ha-Tzair just sat down next to me. He asked if he was disturbing me and, of course, I couldn't tell him that he was. He wasted twenty minutes of my time. He is all I needed. He said he was positive that war would break out. "England and France won't lift a finger over Danzig. The Poles will fight for their honor and will go down to a glorious defeat. The Germans will bite off huge chunks of Poland and Lithuania. And the Poles will have something to dream about for the next twenty years." *Wiatr od Morza* by Zeromski was required reading at school. In Gdynia they'll sing "The Sea Is Bread Too" in the underground.

Zimmerman hates the Poles with all his heart. I could never find such hatred within me. It is true that some elements of the population have behaved despicably and certainly deserve no sympathy. But when I think about Poland today all I can feel is pity. Fate has not been kind to her. She has only been independent for a short time. She was always crushed between two giants. I cannot say as Zimmerman does that Poland deserves to be punished. It is true enough that the government's conduct over Czechoslovakia was ugly, but if Poland is beaten it will be very bad for the Jews.

Zimmerman says that history exacts a high toll for mistakes. High and mighty talk!

He finally left. He found himself a sympathetic ear at another table. But there isn't much for me to add. I see people beginning to move in the direction of the train. In Marseille I'll add these pages to my letter. If Alper wins out over Zimmerman I shall be able to send the whole thing by airmail.

Marseille, Sunday, August 28

A cheap hotel. Filthy, smelly, but the view from the window is delightful: a square, a port with fishing boats, and the sea. And the fish market at a safe distance—the color without the odor.

The blue of the sea is charged with memories of another place. At will, I turn it into Lac Léman. I conjure up your thin body in its navy blue bathing suit, your foot touching the water and drawing back, the warmth in your eyes, my tanned skin, full of Eretz Yisrael, the whiteness of your arms upon my shoulders. Droplets of water sparkle in your hair. And if I try I can see the "Gold Coast" near Hadera. "Singing, we climb . . ."

It is noontime. It looks as if today once again we shall have to forget about having a real meal. I spent my last remaining money traveling from place to place. A light vapor rises off the sea and blurs the distances. Haze comes up off the sea like a harbinger of violence. Once again I have to share a room with Alper. Nobody asked if he wanted it this way. It is an accepted fact that we are friends, and so we are inflicted upon one another. Well, we are friends, but a certain tension that you, intuitively, have probably been able to detect has crept into our relationship (for a moment I forgot that I never even sent off the first pages). What I seek now is to be alone with your presence. Alper was hurt when I told him that I didn't feel like taking a walk with him.

"You're all hung up on one thing," he told me, not without resentment. "We may never get to see this town again."

He didn't say what I was hung up on. I'd like to believe that he meant the business about the war. But I can't be sure. I have my suspicions.

Last night, after we had boarded the train and I was standing, looking out of the window, he came and stood alongside of me. For a while he just stood there looking quietly as the buildings of Geneva faded into the distance. Then, suddenly, he turned to me and said, "It's hard to say good-bye, isn't it? You spend a few days in a strange town, and a certain attachment is formed." I nodded my assent. I must have looked awfully sad, because he shot me an inquisitive glance. "Especially if you're not sure you'll ever see it again," he added. And immediately afterward he began talking about you, as if the two subjects created their own association. His expression was penetrating and secretive, as if he were trying to hint at something.

When I think it over again I realize that we may have been too naive. We thought that nobody saw and nobody knew. Was that, in fact, the case? Monsieur Perrier saw us in a small café at the edge of town and probably realized that we were hiding. Madame Garni must have known. She, after all, insisted on seeing my passport when she rented the room and saw that I was married. And now Alper, too. Do you think we made him look foolish? I am beginning to think that he could take the facts in stride but would never forgive us for believing we could pull the wool over his eyes.

Once, when I missed a session of the subcommittee for

youth affairs, he asked where I had been. I told him the most extraordinary things. He must easily have seen that I was making them all up. I was a fool for not preparing better excuses. It was as if I were taking unfair advantage of his good manners. Because he is a courteous person and would never call a friend a liar, he ends up looking like a gullible fool. And that is just the sort of thing Alper could not bear.

I might never have noticed this under different circumstances. Alper is both a very discreet person and one who is indifferent to matters of less than earthshaking significance. Normally he is not a gossip. But lately, because of the very tension I have alluded to earlier, I am beginning to have my doubts about him. He won't gossip, but he will put two and two together and pass judgment.

In order not to be vague let me clarify: we have never quarreled, heaven forbid, about tidying up the room or putting out the lights. We have never experienced any of the friction that is almost to be expected between two men living at close quarters. Alper is the sort of fellow who bends over backward for the sake of friendship. Little things roll right off him. But the Molotov-Ribbentrop pact became a bone of contention between us. The pact, as you know, really caught me off guard. That is something I cannot conceal, nor do I see why I should try to. And, of course, I never did try to hide my confusion from Alper. But he was thoroughly shocked. Not just because of the pact. It was that he didn't think me capable of such "political illiteracy." As if to say that all my Marxist education had been for naught. Alper is a happy man. The pact hasn't shaken him a bit. On the contrary. If ever he entertained the slightest doubt about the Soviet Union's ability to go it alone in a hostile world he is now absolutely certain that Stalin is a strategical genius. To Alper everything is really very simple: the capitalist states tried to isolate Russia, and Stalin has frustrated their plans. Did I ever imagine that the talks held by second-rate military experts in Moscow were more than a ploy? If Britain had honestly wanted an accord with Moscow wouldn't she have sent a senior official? And other illuminating arguments of the same ilk, which, in Alper's view, just cry out to Heaven. On the face of it everything he says can be substantiated and makes sense. And yet, the emotions refuse to accept the facts. It is true that one must not forget the Western powers' efforts to abort the Revolution. And yet. This pact was something I couldn't swallow. "Politically, you're a babe in the woods," said Alper. Conducting the affairs of a revolutionary movement is too important a business to be left to confused people, he suggested. He went no further. I can't say that we actually quarreled. But I have the feeling that my esteem has somehow fallen in Alper's eyes—to the extent that he has permitted himself to gossip with me, a thing he would never do with a person he really respected.

In retrospect I am beginning to think that many saw and realized. We were the only ones who thought we had put one over on people. When I recall the farewell scene with your parents I think that even your mother saw. I remember the way she looked at you when you picked up your knapsack. It was a movement that brought out both your femininity and your stubbornness. Hers was the knowing look of a mother who is certain that she can do a better job of finding you a husband but who realizes, at the same time, how futile it is. Then she turned her gaze to me, begging mercy with the resignation of a dumb beast. She wanted me at least to understand what was at stake. And I put on an air of the utmost gravity, which to her must just have looked plain silly.

I'm not sure that you ought to tell her everything. At any rate not before we are absolutely sure of ourselves. If I am not mistaken I had your mother sized up from the beginning. She is an enlightened woman, not entirely without a sense of adventure—as far as she alone is concerned, but not for her daughter. I know that she has liberal friends, some of whom are real bohemians, like Hubermann and Tuwim. People like that would take our *petite histoire* in stride without batting an eyelash. But those are all parlor games for her. When it comes to your happiness, everything frivolous is forgotten.

Your father is the one who is bound to raise objections. Serious ones. His are the ways of a typical magnate. His shrewdness only impresses those who are after his favors. Such people always think if you're rich you must be smart. I cannot be mistaken about him. He is conservative and hates anything that smacks of change. Religious piety is only his way of gaining respectability for his accomplishments. The knowledge that his daughter has been "fooling around" with an unsuitable male will arouse all his latent powers. He will fight with everything he has got.

Alper, by the way, spoke about you with great affection. For just a few minutes he let his hair down. He said that he liked to go into the Bâtiment Electoral because you always had such a welcoming smile and treated everybody on an equal footing. He was surprised that I hadn't noticed how all the older delegates paced the corridor outside your office try-ing to think up excuses to go in. He also spoke about your work in the movement and said how wise they were to pick you for the national Executive, because you never can tell if the boys will be able to do the job. What is more, your Aryan features may make it easier for you to travel among the local branches if, perish the thought, war does break out. At the same time he declared that war never would break out, but he wasn't taking any chances! Chances of what, I wondered. Would it be worth endangering your life just to make sure that banned program materials got delivered to the various branches? I wanted to get away from him, but he actually had me cornered by the window and spoke into my ear with a weird sort of compulsion, as if there were a fixed quota of things I had to hear before he would let me go. He tormented me with gloomy descriptions of what Poland will be like-the movement, the institutions of the Jewish community—if war breaks out. The boys will be drafted into the Polish army, and for a while our educational work will go completely to pieces. But at the same time he had a "consolation" for me. He said that you were an intelligent girl, who would know what to do even if regular communications with Aretz were disrupted. He kept on talking in a similar vein and every now and then said something extravagantly nice about you, all the while probing deeper and deeper with his eyes.

For about an hour he left me alone, but then came back and started talking about you again, as if it were the most obvious thing in the world that third-person feminine singular could only be you. He launched into an analysis of your character and qualities and expressed regret, as if positive that this was exactly the way things would work out, that in the end, despite your loyalty to the youth movement, you would never make a *kibbutznik*. The dirty work, the crowding, the living conditions, the food, the lack of decent cultural facilities, and all the other shortcomings, real and imagined, of life in kibbutz, all these would, in the end, break your resolve. He permitted himself to speak of you as if he really knew you inside out and even suggested that your behavior at one particular summer camp, where he had had the chance to "watch you from up close," gave proof of a Jewish-princess strain that you would never be able to conquer. I disagreed with him about that, but he evoked his educational experience and bragged that he could piece together your future out of all sorts of minor reactions, like your attitude to dirt, flies, and shouting, just as the failure of some to appreciate ceremonies and symbols and other things of no intrinsic value can serve as a barometer of their loyalty to the movement. That's what I was forced to listen to when all I wanted was to be left alone and to remember.

The trip lasted all night. The atmosphere in the car was depressing, with an undercurrent of tension everywhere. Only a few people were able to get any sleep. Two representatives of the State party were off and away in a bitter argument over the White Paper. And I was thinking that maybe it doesn't pay to make elaborate plans, because you never know what tomorrow will bring.

The minute we crossed the border into France the war became a concrete thing. All the towns and villages along the way were completely blacked out. Stations loomed up out of nowhere and disappeared just as suddenly. Here and there you could make out a blue lantern with a group of people immobile but ready for action in the mysterious light. Even the sea seemed up to no good in the moonlight. And the conductors did their work with utter disdain, barely able to keep their grumbling under control. In one station there was a drunk singing at the top of his lungs, and for a few minutes a different mood swept through the train. We reached Marseille at dawn. To our disappointment we learned that no hotel rooms had been found for us yet. The cheap hotels are full to bursting, and it is only the luxury establishments that still have some vacancies, at appropriately inflated prices. We sat on our valises and waited. A few went to try their luck with a local Jew who had once belonged to the movement in Romania. I asked Alper to keep an eye on my bag and went off in search of a post office. On the way I changed a few Swiss francs for less than they were worth. A bitter disappointment awaited me at the post office. Mail for Poland won't be leaving today or tomorrow. And there won't be any planes, either. I went back to the station utterly crestfallen, and Sonia tried to cheer me up. But not without a gentle scolding. We're all in trouble, but only I am taking it this way. What could I say to her? I smiled. That mollified her, of course. Now she must think that one little smile from her is enough to make me happy. Well, that's something too. Afterward they all went to get something to eat, and I volunteered to watch the baggage. Alone on the platform, I let my imagination run wild. Again we were alone for a while, you, I, and the trains. I saw your feet lifting off the platform and mounting the high steps, the slight dimple in your knee as your foot rested on the topmost step. And your face in the window. And your white palm fluttering at the window like a bird.

Then they gave me a little money and directed me to a small restaurant near the station. But I only had a cup of coffee in order to save the rest for stamps. I am still hoping that communications will be restored. In all likelihood we shall still be here tomorrow. Very few ships are leaving for Aretz and they're all full. At noon they found a hotel for us and we moved in.

A hotel for us. That, of course, is a joke. It's a hotel for our pocketbooks. My olfactory glands are in revolt. The hotel resembles a whorehouse more than a place for people to stay. When the desk clerk and the doorman speak to one another it seems more like a string of obscenities than normal conversation. They treat us like refugees, with suspicion and contempt. Even in this stinking hotel they demanded their money in advance. As if we had somewhere else to run.

Finances are becoming a bit of a problem. We don't yet know if we'll be getting additional funds. We pool our resources to buy food. Lunch is eaten in Sonia's room. The pocket money is minimal, and I save mine for stamps. The letter has become a bundle and airmail is expensive.

This is the place to apologize for that silly quarrel in Geneva. It's funny to think that the only difference we had was over money. I didn't want to hurt your feelings, but I couldn't let you pay for me. I wouldn't have felt right if our trip to the mountains had been at your father's expense. Since I cut corners on food I was able to pay my way. I didn't want to enjoy a higher standard of living than my comrades. If my comrades wanted to take side trips they had no other source of income than their daily allowances.

[41]

And I was one of those in favor of not giving our delegates the full allowance provided by the Congress. You must know that we put some of that money to other movement uses. I appreciated your sense of humor when you said, "Let's burn this tainted money together." But, even so, I couldn't do it. You yourself used to tell me how the starched sheets at your parents' seemed to sear your flesh after you had visited the training farm and seen the conditions there.

It doesn't pay to talk about this too much. Maybe I should add just one more thing. I weigh something ten times before I say it, because I am even more scared of self-righteousness than I am of snakebite. (When you get to Aretz you'll see just how much substance this picturesque expression has!) Well! It's easy enough to walk the straight and narrow in a place where all you get to eat is half a hard-boiled egg and all you have to drink is tea with watery jam and dead flies floating in it. But it's quite another thing to deny yourself luxuries in Geneva. Here nobody expects you to make sacrifices because you come from a poor kibbutz, any more than they would make you sleep under a net here because there are mosquitoes in the Hule Valley. But I cannot forget the comrades back home. Not even for a moment. The feeling that has come over me very often, that the Congress is nothing but a bunch of hot air, has really gotten me down. There is important work to be done at home, and I run around Geneva trying to look important. It's strange, but only in your company did I lose the feeling that I was taking advantage of my comrades. As if emotional sincerity made everything we did all right. But if we went overboard in our enjoyment of material things I have felt a burden of guilt. I may be too sensitive. Or, the life of a functionary may not be for me. My movement education goes very, very deep. It has become part of my breathing, of my circulation. I shall always feel a step lower than those who live the Zionist ideal in terms of lentil soup and malaria rather than congresses in Switzerland or such applause as I received. When they applauded me at the plenary session I was ashamed. I don't like being praised for ideas that do not originate with me and that my comrades carry out in their everyday lives with a degree of humility I lack.

So much for that. I can hear Alper's voice in the hall. I don't want him to catch me writing. Last time I told him I was making an outline for an article, and he eyed me with suspicion. If this many pages are the outline how long will the article itself be?

In Sonia's room we had lunch and supper all rolled into one. She is staying at another hotel, cleaner, but in a bad neighborhood. She is sharing her room with a girl from Kibbutz Banir who is on her way to join her husband in England. It's funny to meet someone fresh from Aretz reading the minutes of the Congress in *Hege*. (*Davar* was closed down in consequence of its reaction to the arrest of the immigrants of the *Colorado*.) Sonia and her friend managed to create tasty food out of nothing. Only fruit was plentiful. The mood was convivial. Young people have the knack of forgetting everything when they are together. For a short time worries melted away. The threat of war was staved off, as if by force. They even told jokes. It was like a get-together of counselors at summer camp after the kids have gone to bed. Alper surprised us all with his dirty stories.

I tried as hard as I could not to seem down in the dumps, but I took no part in the general hilarity, either. There was only one joke, told by the girl, that I liked. It was an Arab joke of all things.

A young peasant comes back from the big city. He goes up to his father, who is fiddling away at one string, and says, "Know what I saw in the big city? A man playing a fiddle with four strings. His fingers ran back and forth and up and down over the strings with the speed of lightning, and beautiful sounds came out." The father keeps fiddling away at his one and only tune on his one and only string and says calmly to his son, "That man is still searching for his sound. I've already found mine."

When I shut my eyes I can hear your voice.

Tonight we meet for a briefing at Shraga's. Tomorrow is Monday. I hope the post office will be open. Victor bought a newspaper and was none the wiser as a result. On the contrary. If beforehand he had had a "clear picture" of where things stood, afterward everything seemed muddled.

I raise my spirits by toying with the hope that when I get to Aretz there will be a letter waiting at my uncle's house. It is hard, very hard, not knowing what goes on with you.

Marseille, Monday, August 28

Maybe I'm too finicky. At least I console myself with the thought that Alper didn't shut his eyes all night either. It is true that my tent at Mishmar Hagalil is no Grand Hôtel. The flap is torn and when it rains the legs of my bed sink into the mud; nor are my work clothes the cleanest. But all that is clean dirt, even pure, by comparison with the filth of the Hôtel de France. Here the whorehouses come labeled with the names of all the countries in the world. If we ever have a state of our own I will come up with a bill to ban using the name Eretz Yisrael for commercial purposes. (I write, "I will come up with a bill," as if my participation in the Congress guarantees me a seat in the legislature.) Anyway, I can say of the filth here that it inhabits the room like a third presence. As if every passerby dropped off his stink and forgot to take it with him when he left. Tonight I finally managed to get to the bottom of my mother's fear of communicable diseases.

Just imagine: a city completely blacked out, army in the streets, a searchlight turning in the harbor, a mood of war, and Alper and I sitting on our beds telling each other jokes about bedbugs. Tonight I learned that there are little torments that don't allow your mind to wander for even a minute. Accursed creatures! Why else were they created except to show us how lowly we are that we have to keep company with creatures even smaller and more contemptible? Alper surprised me this time with his high spirits in the face of adversity. Some grumble and curse. Alper tells jokes. He is an absolute walking dictionary of Jewish humor. As long as I knew only his movement-activist side he seemed dry, goody-goody, orthodox in the ways of revolutionary theory, and unwilling to depart from the script by so much as a jot or a tittle. In the Hôtel de France I have discovered other facets of his character. A platform of bedbugs has drawn us closer. No party congress could possibly bring us to such a plumbing of common depths as that scratch-in: two merry old Jobs on an insomniac high. The hysterical, idiotic laughter, which became neither of us, succeeded in tearing down all barriers between us. By early morning Alper was telling me the story of his life. Childhood in Lwów, orphaned early, brought up by a strict uncle, an opponent of Hasidism but very religious, the scheming of anti-Semitic teachers at the Warsaw Technological Institute, encounter with the movement, first love, with the girl in charge of the oldest group. The typical story of your typical member of the movement. I, too, told him a little about myself. My father's house, movement experiences, and unsuccessful attempts to gain admission to the University. I think I disappointed him a bit. He told me a few intimate details and expected me to do as much. But I held back. I'm not sure I can trust him. I didn't allow myself to be drawn into speaking about you even when he mentioned your name, as if by chance.

I could like him except for his obvious awareness of his own cleverness, as if there were no room for dialogue with him until you acknowledged his superior wit. I wonder why he always has to be such a smart aleck. His very glance says,

"You're trying to put one over on me, but I won't let you."
Sometimes I feel sorry for him. He has a head full of proverbs
and aphorisms that he tries to store up in order to impress
his listeners. He wants people to like him and to be a little
afraid of him, both at the same time. But his orneriness
doesn't win him much sympathy. By the way, he reads an
enormous amount of fiction. Poetry, too. But he is extremely
hard on the poets. His remarks are intelligent, but he sounds
as if he had caught the poets with their pants down. Let's
leave Alper. I know you admire his power of analysis. And
you are right. Perhaps I could admire him, too, if we were
not forced to live in the same room.

A few words about Marseille. A total disappointment.
Each of us treasures his own private France. A France of history and of calendar art. Even though I have never been to
Paris I can call it up in my mind, street by street, and meet
all the heroes of the novels I have loved. But Marseille is a
real Levantine town. The very Orient that we had longed
to meet on our arrival in Eretz Yisrael—and failed to meet,
because Haifa was like so many other Mediterranean coastal
cities and Tel Aviv was like nothing at all—we have found
here in Marseille, in all the colors of the rainbow. Life with
all its noise and squalor. The sounds and smells of an Arab
marketplace. Even the food is similar. The Moroccans,
Tunisians, and Algerians in their traditional costumes make
a contribution of their own to creating the feel of an oriental
bazaar. The cars have a hard time plowing through the dense
throng, who prefer the gutter to the sidewalk. The streets of
the port are full of dark-skinned peroxide blondes. Near the
movies and restaurants one finds ragged beggars who are
obviously not at home in French.

The city is full of refugees. Some live in hope of obtaining
American visas, and some are so expressionless that you don't
even find despair in their faces. The French despise foreign-
ers, as if all France were a small town, its ways to be pro-

tected from deviants. At the newsstands conversations are carried on by strangers in a babble of tongues. There are some who are almost drunk on this war that has not yet broken out. They snatch up each newspaper expecting the worst and then curse the government for seeking a peaceful solution. They clamor for the public hanging of spies and traitors. A peculiar kind of lust has taken hold of them. In a little while there will be war, and then all the stops will be pulled. They look at you, the foreigner, with animal hate and you shudder to think what might happen if such people were allowed to purge the streets of traitors. On the other hand, there are those who hate war and fear it, like Bernard in the bistro where I drank my first aperitif—but even these people hate the refugees, as if they were responsible for the threat of war instead of being its victims. Some of the Congress delegates, who just a few days ago were honored guests of the Swiss government, cannot bear the decline in their status. Here they are just refugees like all the others and are greeted with hostility and contempt.

The war atmosphere is more pronounced than in other places. Many soldiers wander about the streets. Trucks with searchlights have been stationed at the entrance to the port. Once in a while a staff car passes with drawn shades. It flies through the bustling streets at a dangerous speed, as if war had just been declared and as if getting its faceless riders somewhere or other were the most important thing on earth. The trams and buses are full. It looks as if people are traveling from place to place just for the heck of it. Maybe somewhere else someone knows something that they don't know here. Many gather outside the offices of the travel agents, especially Lloyd-Oriental. When it became known that the *Champollion* would not sail, a few wept. Noisy arguments go on in the bars. A man in work clothes who defended the Soviet position was beaten up and thrown out of Chez Bernard before our very eyes. Alper wanted to come to his aid and I had a hard time stopping him. The tellers at the banks don't even bother to look up when you bring them European bank notes to change. The postal workers are nervous and impatient. The mailboxes are full of undelivered letters. As night descends the streets seem to fill with hate and fury. The shaded automobile headlights disclose vague, shadowy figures. Policemen with barely discernible faces stop pedestrians on the street and angrily demand to see their papers.

A shameful thing happened today. I wasn't there myself, so I can't say if it really happened the way I heard it. A few ships sailed for Egypt today, but there was no room for us on any of them. Each country was looking out for its own citizens, and, of course, nobody was looking out for us. If we had taken steps early enough to set up a Jewish fleet—if you listened to the speeches on Israel Maritime Day in the passengers' lounge of the *Général Dufour*—we, too, would have been able to sail in ships of our own. Anyway, after the British consul intervened, the captain of an Egyptian ship of the Khedive Line agreed to take two hundred Palestinian residents, including a few of the Congress delegates. Mostly older people, but also a few athletes returning from international competitions, started to board. All of a sudden, just as they were about to sail, some Egyptian scouts appeared on deck. They spoke with open hostility about the Zionist Congress, which, according to them, had adopted a decision to seize control of Arab lands, and demanded that all residents of Palestine leave the ship. Anyone who refused was forcibly removed. The intervention of the British consul and the captain were of no avail. Not even the efforts of the Egyptian athletes on behalf of their colleagues had any effect. In utter humiliation, everyone was forced to get off the ship, to the jeers of the Egyptian scouts. The incident caused great agitation, and some of the more infuriated delegates wanted to take drastic steps against these hooligans. But, of course, that was nothing but empty talk. The ship was already on its way, and, anyway, nobody knew exactly what steps to take. It would be nice to think that none of this would have happened if we had been there. That's what Victor says. But it's our luck that we weren't there. We would have been removed like the others, only with bloody noses and wounded pride.

I have mentioned bars and bistro and aperitif and one might think ʾve were carrying on like sailors on shore leave. That's not it at all. We don't go in for pub crawling. The aperitif mentioned earlier—a kind of *rite de passage* for movement types who neither drink nor smoke—is the cheapest drink you can get around here. And the bistro is where you feel the pulse of time. I can't whip myself into a flurry of activity the way Victor and Alper do, and, therefore, I have a lot of time on my hands. I know that all their running around will change nothing for us. If room is found for us on a ship it will be thanks to the effectiveness of Jewish Agency employees, who keep a low profile. All the bargaining with travel agents is useless, but there may be something therapeutic about it. When a person runs from one travel agent to another at least he feels that he is doing what he can to bring himself closer to Eretz Yisrael. But I am of two minds. Part of me wants to go home and part does not. Sometimes it seems that if shipping were halted and we were forced to remain in Europe I would manage somehow to make my way to Warsaw. And then . . . dreams, just dreams . . .

I wander the streets a bit, absorb what I can, and help Sonia a little with the cooking. And when nobody is looking I shut myself up at the hotel and melt into the letter, which, by the way, I still do not know how I will send or when. It has become an internal dialogue, a testimony that, when it reaches your hands will provide a key to the state of my soul in the days after our parting. The heart lapses into believing that such a testimonial is unnecessary. You have but to look into your own heart to know what I feel . . .

My coming back to the hotel at all hours has given one of
the chambermaids strange ideas. She has begun to suspect
that it may be on her account. What else could a man want
in this stinking hole? All my comrades leave in the morning
and are not seen around here at all during the day. Sometimes she comes into the room on a flimsy excuse and hangs
around until I have to say something to break the silence. I
struck up a conversation with her in my broken French and
she spoke gaily and animatedly and let it be understood that
she would have nothing against making a few centimes on
the side with a young, clean-cut fellow. There was a touching
naiveté about the polite way she offered herself and at the
same time asked for money. I couldn't be too explicit about
letting her know that her services were not required. I allowed myself to be drawn into a long conversation in which
I heard the story of her life. When I told her I was a tiller
of the soil she was terribly impressed. Perhaps because of the
apparent contradiction between my occupation and my manners she made it quite plain that, in view of my financial
straits, she would be willing to dispense with the payment.
I played dumb, and she left with an embarrassed but disappointed smile. She wasn't the youngest creature or the
prettiest, but she had an earthy sensuality and natural
exuberance and such simple goodness that for a moment I
wavered. I would not have known how to reply if she had
been more outspoken. There! You see, I'm telling you everything, even things that never happened. And I try not to
conceal from you even the finest nuances of feeling. That,
after all, is what you meant when you asked me to write
whatever is on my mind, because the proceedings of the
Congress and details of the trip are things that you will be
able to read about elsewhere. A sizable group of newspaper-
men are tagging along this time and they will certainly do a
better job than I of describing the Day-of-Judgment atmosphere that prevailed on the closing night of the Congress

and even of describing this Marseille, whose smells are more numerous than the words that exist to describe smell. They will surely know how to put a literary gloss on all this.

I spent the early evening hours in Shraga's company. The others got themselves invited to the home of a local businessman, who had belonged to the movement in Romania. They went there to get a decent meal. Shraga didn't want to go along. He has too much self-respect and doesn't want to be the guest of a man who got stuck in France on the way to Aretz. And perhaps he really was tired and a little sick, as he claimed. He asked me to stay with him, and I was happy to comply. It has been many days since I last spent time with him. I still don't know why he asked me in particular. Maybe he was just bored and tired of looking at newspapers, and perhaps he was overcome by the loneliness of being in a strange city. Without the support of the movement and people rushing to him for advice and disputes with political rivals his life has grown empty. At any rate, he sounded as if he wanted to ask me about something, but in the end, he didn't ask anything at all. For a minute I got the feeling that he wanted to size me up and that began to look unbearable, but since he was doing most of the talking and I the listening, the whole thing passed and no harm was done.

He is nice to talk to. His manner of speech is like a talmudic scholar's. Even though he is engaged in a struggle to the death with religion and firmly believes that it is the opiate of the masses, his talk is studded with rabbinic expressions. He is wary of the excessively high hopes entertained by certain leaders, who believe that no disaster is too great to permit of recovery. But, even though all the signs are present, he is not yet convinced that the messianic era has dawned. He stated that the freeing of the "illegals" on the *Colorado* does not in any way imply that England is ready to reexamine the White Paper. On the contrary, he believes that the English will be harder on us than ever, because in time of war they will not wish to have a hostile Arab population at their backs. And oil and all that. He has had some news from Poland, too. He said that in Warsaw trenches are being dug and he hoped that the Jews were doing their share. The last time he spoke with Froyka, before Froyka left, he gave instructions for the movement people to mobilize for work on the fortifications. He also spoke about Germany and her aims and about the Soviet wager. He sees no way of avoiding a confrontation between Germany and Russia. I got the impression that the pact was very unsettling for him, and he was trying to prove to us, the younger generation, that his political outlook was broad enough to encompass the most devious turns. He is afraid that if he lets his own confusion become apparent those whose views have truly been shaken up will throw out the baby with the bathwater.

After that he asked about my family. He remembered Sarah. About ten years ago when he visited an isolated branch of the movement in Reissen, he told me, she asked "wise and courageous" questions. He has an amazing memory and he stores up images of people he has not laid eyes upon more than once. Once they have stood before him or by his side he will never forget them again. It surprised me somewhat that he had so much to say about Sarah, since he hardly knows her. He also tried to draw me out on that subject, but I hardly felt like speaking about her when it is my concern for you that absorbs me day and night. I would have been deluding both him and myself. Then he said something about close family ties. He told me that in the early days when "some of the boys ran around with all sorts of crazy ideas," those same "boys" tended to see the family as an "atavistic remnant" standing in the way of social progress. He dismissed "that school" with a smile and said that the family unit is the cornerstone on which the kibbutz will be built. He said that people will always manage to dig up theories out of the romantic ragbag to justify their urge to cast off responsibility. I timidly tried to make a case for life's complexity, but he tore my argument to shreds. The flight from responsibility tries to disguise itself as philosophical profundity. For the sake of some imagined profundity of their own the followers of "that school" allow themselves to play havoc with other people's emotions. As if they were all exaltation and profundity and the others nothing but sheer superficiality. At first I thought he was trying to call me to order and remind me of my obligations but I later saw that this was not the case. Shraga could not know anything. He doesn't even see what is happening under his own nose. All in all he was just sounding out the main points for an article on social themes. Someone said that he is so absorbed with politics that he has completely forgotten that the kibbutz is also a place where people live, and this has made him furious. Now he plans to surprise people by proving that he has something to say in this area as well. I do not mean to say these things disrespectfully. That's not it at all. At the end of our talk he said he was glad that I shared his view. "Son of a gun," he said to me. "You were playing the devil's advocate in order to get me to use up all my ammunition. . . ." Anyway, he said with a sympathetic smile that my articles in the movement paper amply demonstrate that my head is in the right place and free of learned nonsense and vain theories.

I was completely exhausted when I left him, partly because of the effort—a talk with Shraga is hard work—but also because of cumulated fatigue. A sleepless night and a wasted day. Nothing is more exhausting than total inactivity. It was only during the moments that I was helping Sonia prepare lunch that I forgot my tiredness. By the way, Shraga ordered me some tea and stale cake, and that way I was able to save my supper money. Tomorrow three musicians from Germany are giving a concert here, and if it's in the cards for us still to be here tomorrow, I'll buy myself a ticket. I'll sit awhile in an upholstered chair and listen to music. Whatever they play, I'll be listening to my own melody, the one I picked up on the train from Warsaw to Berlin.

I nearly didn't manage to hide the papers from Alper, who came back early. Now he has gone to the bathroom—that in itself is an experience—and I am hurrying to write a few last lines. Tomorrow I'll make another attempt to mail the letter from here. If that doesn't work I'll take it along with me. I may be able to send it from a neutral port on the way. If not, I'll send it from Aretz. Somebody here said that planes from Poland are making it to Aretz as usual.

Alper peeked into the room, scowled at me, not wholly in earnest, and said: "You've been keeping to yourself. We must get to the bottom of it. There must be reasons . . ." And he ran to the toilet, which was vacated at just that moment. I can't tell if he had anything in mind, or if it was only a joke.

I am so tired that I may just be able to ignore the bedbugs.

In order not to conclude the daily installment with these wretched creatures I recall the little beetle that climbed onto your shoe when we sat in the League of Nations Park. And you took it up in your hand and set it down away from the path so that it wouldn't get trampled. Your hair was swept up and I noticed that you have a dimple at the back of your neck, too. And for a moment I was elated, as if something had been revealed that I should never have known if that small beetle had not crept onto your foot.

Marseille, Tuesday, August 29

Everything is packed and down at the port. We sail to-night on the *Cairo City*, a Greek ship sailing under the British flag. I am in the lobby of the Hôtel de Berry. That explains the letterhead. I came in a cab to take Shraga down to the port. He is not well and cannot take the tram. While he was packing and I was waiting I discovered this beautiful letter paper and imprinted envelopes. Shraga asked, "What's the urgency? Have you had a brainstorm?" I told him I was writing a letter. He was surprised, "We'll get there before the letter."

We bought food and deck chairs with the last of our money. They say that the food on board is awful. A few cabins and eighty places on deck have been promised to the Labor faction. The cabins are expensive. We will probably book just one berth for Shraga, who cannot sleep on deck.

Last night we managed to get a little sleep. In the morning I felt as if I had a hangover. During the day we were running all over town. Knowing there was room for us on board a ship did something to make us stand a little taller. We were tourists once more, and not refugees. We sat in a café and spoke Hebrew out loud. It is still hard to shake off the impression of the proper Frenchmen with their dirty looks. Our irreverence infuriates them. Tomorrow may bring war, and there won't be enough bread and coal to go around. And here we are. Instead of behaving like poor relations who know their place, we make ourselves loud. After the disgrace of the Egyptian ship we enjoyed their ill temper. Such are the delights of beggars.

S/S Cairo City, Wednesday, August 30

The sea is calm and yellow-green in color. A gray haze covers the sky. Anxious expectancy hangs in the air. The surface of the water glistens in the sunlight as if oil had been poured over it. If not for the golden wake of the ship and the slow movement of the prow one might think we were standing still. Even the sun seems stuck in the sky, not brilliant but with a muted light, visible through the dense mist. You can stare back at it without suffering its ire.

On the deck there is perpetual tumult. We are packed together very tightly here. Bundles, deck chairs, blankets, ropes, and tarpaulins are all jumbled together. I had a hard time finding a small spot under one of the lifeboats. My left elbow is resting on a pile of rags and my right one is writing. But even in this out of the way corner someone managed to come and peek over my shoulder. "The fifteenth of Elul," he reproved me. His face was somber. I had disappointed him. Didn't I realize that the gravity of the present situation demands that we stick to the use of Hebrew dates? I nodded as if to say I would correct the oversight. He was a member of the Labor faction. Such poker-faced people never allow themselves a single moment of fun, as if any joke represented a compromise with an imaginary enemy. Last night we stood on deck a long time, until the lights of Marseille blended into a glow on the horizon. After that there was total darkness and only occasionally did we see a light twinkling in the distance, and then we couldn't tell if it was a ship or a village on the Spanish coast.

We are hugging the coast out of fear of Italian submarines. I was completely oblivious to this fear until an engineer from Tel Aviv sat down alongside of me and explained in detail the technical side of submarine warfare. If truth be told, even now when I look over the rail at the still surface of the water the whole business about the submarines seems unreal to me. People who are constantly in the grip of their fears never cease to amaze me.

At night we arranged ourselves on the deck each according to his preference. For the first time I slept without Alper. I didn't miss him. I was amazed to find Dr. Ruppin nearby. He could easily have afforded a cabin but preferred not to set himself apart. I imagine his gesture annoyed some of the labor leaders, who were staying in first- and second-class cabins. And, after all, he is older than they. It was a pleasure to sleep out in the fresh air, and the fact that I was lying on wooden boards in no way prevented me from sleeping soundly. In the morning a massive reorganization got under way. Everyone wants to be near his friends, and even we have gone back to being a single bloc. Alper lost no time in setting his bundle down next to my "bed." So much for independence. From the morning on we turned out to be a perfectly organized social unit. We set up an improvised workers' kitchen and discovered that we could buy hot water from the ship's galley. At dawn we had boiling-hot tea, and our initiative was warmly received by the people from Hakibbutz Hameuhad, who were invited to join us. Sonia has the knack of turning the poorest beggar's repast into a banquet, and even the tea drinking became a minor celebration. And drink, as you well know, any drink, even tea, opens the Russians' hearts. These people know how to derive joy from the most ordinary thing. It would do us no harm to take a lesson from their hearty enthusiasm. All we have to do is laugh at one of their jokes for them to say, "Look, we're so close in custom and outlook, why can't we join forces?"

Life on board is complete idleness and prolonged expectation. You cast your lot with time and time carries you forward, on toward your destination. But still there is tension. We don't yet know our route or where we will anchor. The mists we see off to the south—are they the Algerian coast or a mirage? At any rate it's obvious that we're headed south and approaching the coast of North Africa.

Despite the total inactivity—apart from the preparation of meals and cleaning up—I haven't been in the least bit bored. I read a story by Brenner, I talked to people, I followed, not without amusement, the progress of a lady on the upper deck who, befuddled by the salt sea air, was trying to catch the captain's eye, I took walks on deck, and I imagined I was in Warsaw, in Geneva, and not by myself . . . We even had our little moment of drama. Wherever Alper goes there is drama.

While I was reading from Brenner's book along came A. (You don't know him so that there's no point in using his name. You'll see why right away. Anyway, he's a prominent person. He has a position in the Department of Education and does a great deal of lecturing to youthful audiences, who are always eager to listen. Unlike his colleagues, who are clumsy and pretentious, his talks are interesting and to the point. Since he is sympathetic to us, he is often invited to speak in our kibbutzim as well.) He noticed what I was reading and struck up a conversation. He related a few episodes out of Brenner's life, whom he knew in the days when he taught Hebrew in the Labor battalion. Later he asked about the movement. He expressed sorrow over our stubborn adherence to revolutionary doctrine.

A little while later Alper came over to me. "Is he a friend of yours?" he asked. His voice betrayed some inner turbulence. His eyes darted to and fro as if we were being eavesdropped upon. He took my arm and led me to the stern. There, as if disclosing a deep dark secret, he told me a story that he was sure would shock me. When he had gone shopping for food with Victor in the market in Marseille he saw the man coming out of a street known for its shady establishments. He looked as if he was trying to avoid being seen. At the corner he stopped for a moment, looked around, and walked away in a hurry.

My reaction was not what Alper had anticipated. "You and Victor were there, too," I laughed. That laugh brought his anger down upon me. He absolutely refused to let it pass without a scene. "We were there together, and he went there alone," he argued heatedly. "Maybe he went casually, just to have a look, just to broaden his horizons, and committed no sin against God or man," I said.

It was a mistake to egg Alper on. At least not where a question of morals was concerned. He was furious. "For some reason you feel the need to stick up for him," he said to me in his rage, and his face took on the mysterious expression of someone who knows a thing or two more than he is willing to tell.

I would not devote any space to this incident if not for the fact that deep down I felt that I had refused to share Alper's indignation for the wrong reasons. As if I had no right to judge because I myself had sinned. I was angry at myself for that. Did I really sin? When I examine myself thoroughly, being as cruelly honest as I can be, I feel no need to castigate myself.

True, I am twenty-seven and you are nineteen. But when I covered your naked breasts with my two hands I felt that I was obeying the movement's commandment of sexual purity.

My first emotions are distilled in the memory of that moment. Your trembling flesh. Your warm, moist lips. Today I am no longer certain that the restraint that followed was really an act of heroism on our part. But I was trying so hard to prove to you the seriousness of my intentions.

I had better stop here. These things lose their innocence when they are set down on paper.

At the hours of the news broadcasts we crowd into the first-class bar. At first the crew tried to throw us out. But when they discovered how close the ties were between the deck passengers and the first-class passengers they backed down. We are too numerous for them to make us feel ashamed of our poverty. The democratic ways of our leaders irritate the ship's brass, as if too much fraternizing might give the sailors ideas.

Some of the news was encouraging, so that even the engineer from Tel Aviv stopped being afraid of submarines. Ribbentrop has promised Stalin to settle the business of the Polish Corridor peacefully. Russian officers have left for the

United States on a study tour. A French diplomat believes that the conflict can be resolved by political means.

The general mood has improved considerably. I was able to devote myself to my own private misery. The sea supported me in this. It wore a pale yellow fog, a gray sky, and a lifeless sun. The water moved slowly, pensively, sadly.

S/S Cairo City, *Thursday, August* 31

At night we cruised along the Tunisian coast. The illuminated towns threw off a halo of light. We were able to imagine their tranquil, unperturbed life and to envy them. At dawn we passed very close to Sicily, and this was reflected in people's conduct. "Ours" were perfectly calm or at least felt constrained to behave themselves. As for me, I'm not at all sure that it is courage that guides my actions. I am simply elsewhere. If there is danger in being here it does not apply to me. I feel the need to sharpen my memory for detail: words, looks, gestures. My private time flows backward, like the foamy wake of the ship.

We are now headed southward toward the Gulf of Gabès, To our left is a large island, Pantelleria. The sight of a lone island has a tranquilizing effect on us for some reason, though this must not be the case for the people who live there. The sea is now blue and deep and the sky is clear. A few gulls are following us and make their sharp cries heard. These are like dismal prophesies that crop up every once in a while.

Eight days have now passed since the pact, and still there is no war. Italian ships again set sail for the Middle East. Everybody laughed when one woman, on seeing a large fish, cried, "Submarine!" Maybe Alper is right and all the artificial tension over Danzig is just another clever capitalist ploy.

You can see for yourself. The paper from the Hôtel de Berry is used up. I dug up the old pad from the bottom of my valise. Even the blank paper remembers. The trembling hand that writes "My dear Perla" seems to be tracing the outline of your face. Then I still believed that my letter would leave by airmail that same day for Warsaw. I even imagined this charming scene: you get off the train at the Central Station, go home by cab, and after you have greeted the old doorman, your heart suddenly flutters with joy. The white of my letter, waiting for you, can be seen sticking out of the mailbox. You open it and read with subdued excitement. And perhaps you even whisper my name.

This morning Yitzhak surprised me with an interesting proposition. He thinks I should take on the coordination of the youth movement in Aretz. He said that Shraga likes the idea, too. When we get back to Aretz he will raise the suggestion in the councils of the movement. That means that a committee will then come to the kibbutz and demand that I be released for the job.

I objected, but not vehemently enough. The idea entices me, but I have many doubts.

I said to him, "My kibbutz has been in Aretz for seven years, three of them encamped outside a village and four settled at its permanent site. Before that the kibbutz spent two years at a training farm in Poland. For nine years now my comrades have been engaged in every sort of hard labor. And what of me? I was only at the training farm for four months. And nobody knows as well as I how hard they were for me. The rest of the time I was assigned to the regional executive. At the village I spent only a year and a half. You could almost count the number of days I worked in the orange groves on the fingers of your hands. Part of the time I was unemployed, and for the rest I was on the workers' council. I put out a bulletin and did all sorts of other, similar jobs. When the kibbutz moved to its permanent site I was in Poland. I came back from there only two years ago. I have no trade and I don't belong to any of the production units. For two months I was down with malaria. For three months

I was away on a police course. And then they put me into feed crops. I had barely gotten over the farewells when I had to leave on a family visit. And to the Congress. Of course everything was done by the book, but many comrades are left with a bad taste. They get up for work every morning without giving it a second thought. Some members were just not meant to be workers, they say to themselves. They say it to themselves, but not out loud, and that's even worse. And I can't even stand up for myself. That's not the kind of person I am. I want to work. I have no great personal ambitions. And yet.

Yitzhak looked at me, and that intriguing smile of his never left his face. When I was through his expression was grave. "I am surprised at you," he grumbled. "That's a new theory you've come up with: working in the youth movement doesn't count. Well," he said, "if that's how you feel about it there's not much to say. And I thought that a person who takes the children of merchants and shopkeepers and turns them into tillers of the soil was doing more than just goofing off. That's what I thought, but if you think otherwise that's your privilege. Take me, for example, what do I do? The very thing I'm proposing to you. Am I just wasting my time?"

I agreed that movement work is important. But you cannot open the eyes of sophisticated young people to the beauty of manual labor if you yourself do not engage in it. He spoke about the division of labor and about mutual responsibility. "You can't expect each person to put in nine hours of work and then devote a tenth hour to the movement. Therefore, one person works ten hours growing fodder and another works twelve hours in the youth movement." I mentioned the names of two or three people who could do the job, but he rejected them out of hand. He doesn't think such a job ought to be given to an unmarried person. "You need a married man, whose family life is in order," he said, and I smiled to myself. All the same, he put me on my guard. He has a certain puritanical streak that frightens me a little. What he might excuse in others he would never forgive people in leadership positions. Of them he requires a kind of ethical perfection, as if we were some sort of religious order or sect.

Afterward, he mentioned half a dozen other reasons. I have educational experience. I have some acquaintance with matters of defense. I am a moderate, levelheaded person who knows how to instill enthusiasm in others. I am trusted. My Hebrew is good. I will be able to supervise the editing of the paper, which is in the hands of a bunch of clever kids who like to play around with words. "This youth is eager for knowledge," he said, "but acts rashly, even aggressively, and lacks good manners altogether. The idea of kibbutz is something that these young people have accepted with enthusiasm, but the people of the kibbutz disappoint them. Adult needs are perceived as a betrayal of values. Essential compromises are dismissed as the Polish mentality." If it's dirty work I'm looking for, this is where I'll find it. It will be no bed of roses.

I suppose he's right. There is a kid from the movement in Aretz here on board, a boy of about seventeen. His father is an architect, his mother a dentist. They're on their way back from a visit with relatives in England. He's not altogether rude, yet he never misses a chance to show that he's a sabra. He speaks at the top of his lungs. He interrupts the adults' conversations with little put-downs. Spouts Marxist formulas like an old pro. But none of that bothers me. What really frightens me is his attitude to war. He doesn't give a damn. As if war were something that can only happen to other people in other places. Deep down he knows it's bound to come. It would probably make life more interesting and the newsreels less dull. When I mentioned that war could seriously hurt the Jewish communities of Europe, he scarcely understood what I was getting at. Hadn't we discussed negation of the Diaspora? The Diaspora is bound to be eliminated one way or another . . .

At lunchtime I had an interesting chat. I don't know if you're ever heard of Kuperberg from *Davar*. He, too, lived in Warsaw for a while. He edited some literary magazine there.

He sleeps on deck not far from us. This morning they lent him a deck chair near the workers' kitchen. We invited him to eat with us, but he declined. He would only have some tea. He hardly eats a thing. Only crackers. He probably keeps kosher. Or maybe he's ill. He drank his tea with us but said very little. Shraga tried to strike up a conversation with him. Kuperberg shot back a withering glance. Kuperberg struck me as the kind of man who opens up only to those he judges to be on his own level. But after lunch, when I had taken out my pad and set down a couple of sentences, I suddenly heard his voice from behind, "Do you write too?"

At first I was embarrassed. I thought he suspected me of being a literary man too. I mumbled something. His eyes shone with amazement. "Take a look around," he said. "Everybody here writes."

And sure enough it was a strange sight to behold. At different points on the deck people were sitting and writing. It looked as if the ship were a traveling seminar with the rest period after lunch set aside for homework. One fellow even wrote leaning on the ship's rail and had to struggle to keep his paper from blowing away.

As Kuperberg took in the scene his look betrayed just a hint of condescension. "History cannot fail to get her due," he said with a smile. "But she is not especially selective. Every piece of paper on which these good people preserve their impressions is a document in her eyes."

I tried to fathom the mood beneath the words. Sarcasm? Peevishness? But I could detect neither. Only a quiet sort of wonder. "It's just a pity that these episodes in our history are being written in such poor Hebrew," he said. And I recalled an article of his I had read in *Davar*. Proper thought requires unambiguous language. Deficient language hinders the thought process.

"I'm writing a letter," I said, as if to reassure him. One fewer competitor. "That's good," he said. "In other words, you're writing something that is needed. At least by one human being." And immediately afterward he added—as if sharing his secret with me after I had unwittingly revealed mine to him—"One day I, too, shall write a story for one human being. But I suppose that I would have it printed after all. Print is easier to read."

In these last words I detect a veiled reproof. A person of his refined tastes might well be offended by my scrawl. "Don't you want people to read what you're writing? Or is it supposed to be some kind of riddle?" And that is how we embarked on a long conversation. He asked about my father's home, about Warsaw, my impressions of the Congress, and whether I had the strength to read after a day of back-breaking labor in the fields.

For the first few minutes I felt uncomfortable. I remembered the eloquence of his writing, his pithy phrasing, and it seemed as if he were laughing up his sleeve at me. Like a Polish nobleman having a chat with the village priest in order to pick up a few new folk expressions. But later I observed that his language was straightforward and plain. As if he were deliberately holding back the wicked epigrams, the verbal fireworks, in order not to test the sharpness of his partner's wit. It was only later that he permitted himself a few flashes, probably when he had decided that a hint would do for me. It's hard for me to set down the entire conversation here. And it's a pity. You probably would have appreciated it. A man whose manners become more and more elegant the more he disagrees with you. When he spoke about scientific socialism, which, as far as he is concerned, is the source of all contamination, his efforts to avoid hurting my feeings were positively touching. You would like him. He is a handsome man, with a thin, emaciated face, but whose eyes sparkle with life. Like a heretic priest. Sometimes he formulates his thoughts very slowly, as if writing them out, and then his eyes narrow for an instant. His hands dart about swiftly at eye level. As if it were their job to pluck the words out of the air as they flew by. One butterfly in a hundred.

We talked for two and a half hours. Until my throat was dry.

S/S Cairo City, *Friday, September 1*

We are following the Libyan coast at some distance from shore. This morning we were approached by a British man-of-war. For a while it cruised alongside of us. There was a moment of panic. Someone said that if Italy goes to war all British subjects will be arrested and put into a concentration camp on Rhodes.

The ship is sailing toward the Gulf of Sidra. Later it will turn northeastward. On Saturday we anchor at Piraeus. It is said that we will be allowed to go ashore. Greece is an old dream, but for some reason I feel none of the excitement I would have expected.

Maybe the time has come to say something about what is really bothering me.

We have taken great care to avoid the question of the pain we may be causing others. Not even this sentence dares to call things by their proper names. "Others," in order not to say simply, "Sarah."

You said you didn't want to profit at her expense, and I kept my mouth shut. I knew you expected me to say something, like, "It was all finished before you came along. The breakup had nothing to do with you." But I couldn't say that. I could not lie.

Perhaps if you knew her you might understand. But I

didn't even have a picture of her, and you couldn't get over that. "We're not sentimentalists," I boasted. But in Geneva I saw to it that we took a group portrait so that I'd have a picture of you to keep.

I don't know if I can manage to describe her. She is tall, thin, and strong. When she smiles her eyes are beautiful. Her voice is halting and a little tired, but her movements are deliberate and efficient. That is the description, but actually I haven't said a thing. When my father asked me to tell him about life in the kibbutz, and he specifically wanted me to talk about her, I didn't know what to say.

For a minute I wish you could meet my father. I'm sure it would be love at first sight. When he saw you he would say to himself: "This is the girl I would have picked for my son." He would even forget to pay lip service to the darker side, neglecting to say things like, "Divorce is the verdict of fate, a sort of curse passed down through generations." He would take one look at you and give his blessing to the match. And not because you look like his second wife. You don't look like her. You look like the woman he would have wanted as his one and only wife.

You would look at him, and you, too, would learn something: what our lives would have been like if we had not been born into this turbulent age. I am sure you would like the sensitivity he radiates. And the fine irony. And the natural courtesy.

Sarah has never met my father. She doesn't want to, either. This is the place to tell you about it. Father sent two tickets but Sarah refused to use hers. She would have none of his honey and none of his sting. When we began to live together in one tent she sent him a letter, in bad Polish. He sent her back a chilly reply. He wrote me something, as well, couched in the form of an allusion lest she read my letter. The picture I had sent, he wrote, was out of focus. I got the point at once. He didn't mean the picture. He meant the person in the picture. Sarah had disappointed him. He had expected a lovely creature, ethereal, gay, graceful, ready for an adventure in the marshes. Instead he saw a child of hard times. Grim. His instincts did not deceive him—an enemy.

I didn't push her into going. Even though I knew she would welcome the chance to visit her own parents. I was afraid of the meeting. I didn't want to see them hating each other from the first glance. Sarah felt slighted that I had not urged her to go, but she said nothing. That's the way she is. She doesn't express her annoyance in words. Only a fine wrinkle in the corner of her eye. You have to know her well to detect it. Words are kept for matters of consequence. The family is too important for her to allow our conjugal life to be turned into an unending discussion of petty insults. She has nothing but contempt for people addicted to such nit-picking pleasures as straightening out relationships tied up in knots by foolish talk or trying idiotically to analyze Freudian slips.

Something else. Before we left for the Congress I visited her parents in Reissen. Two days there and two days back. A village. You will not find it on a general map of Poland. Ten hours by express train from Warsaw and ten hours by wagon over rutted dirt roads. A long, long way through white fields of buckwheat and thin stands of birch, red-necked peasants and their buxom, wanton women. The village itself belongs to another world. An island of Jewish life. A dirt-poor village, straight out of Mendele. But you sense a certain wholesomeness that Warsaw cannot boast.

In my youth I had been there a few times on movement business. By a clear brook separating forest from meadow I would teach a bit of anthropology. It was as if I had enabled this depressed youth to discover Man and the joy of living. Once I was asked to speak before the parents. The talk took place in the synagogue. To avoid giving offense I put on a yarmulke, and two of my kids left the movement and joined the Communists. The parents listened to me politely. They peered into my eyes, as if they had their own way of discerning if there was God in my heart. The science part didn't excite them. They, too, had read some secular books. Some essential point was missing for them. Since I preferred spiritual treasure to material wealth, they forgave me the error of my ways. The movement, as far as they were concerned, was better than Sabbatian heretics and false Messiahs. It, at least, did not take the name of the Lord in vain. My claim to speak in the name of science must have amused them, but their politeness kept them from showing it. In this village—a Jewish island deep in the marshes—there are two libraries, Hebrew and Yiddish. Thousands of books. And half a dozen associations: Ha-Shahar, Pirhe-Zion, Lovers of the Hebrew Language, Sons of the Maccabees, and more. And I sought to brighten their eyes with learning and to bring tidings of a new day. My host, a local merchant who supplied seed and tools to the peasants, spoke six languages and read eight.

Sarah's father was a Hebrew teacher. Wretchedly poor. But despite his poverty he was like the village squire. Because his Hebrew was better than the others'.

I thought: I shall never be able to get Sarah's parents together with my father. Not because he wouldn't treat them with respect. He is an enlightened person with progressive ideas. But because he would surely find amusing the aristocratic airs of a man with nothing to show for himself but his knowledge of Hebrew. I wouldn't want him to snicker at my father-in-law. Not even in his heart of hearts. In Warsaw there is a sharp separation between movement and home. Not in Reissen. When a young person joins the movement his parents join with him. At night parents and children sit together and in Hebrew words try to emulate the juiciness of Yiddish.

In that village I discovered how different we are from one another, my wife and I. You and I are cut from the same cloth. Sarah belongs to another culture. When we make aliyah to Palestine we experience moral uplift. We give ourselves a pat on the back for forsaking the fleshpots and going out to the desert in search of our god. When Sarah decided to pick up and do the very same thing she was taking a great moral risk. She knew that by saving herself she was abandoning two old people to their fate. In a few more years they will have no means of support. The rough wool blanket whose odor disgusts me makes it easier for her to bear the torment of her conscience. There I was able to appreciate the resentment that the village youth feel toward the conceited children of Warsaw, who pride themselves on their education, their broad-mindedness, and their rich European cultural background. A resentment that nobody is willing to acknowledge, but that splits our kibbutz right down the center. For a moment I was ashamed that in my own shallowness I had taken that resentment to be the hatred the masses feel toward the intellectual elite. It would be closer to the truth to say, "They don't like the fact that our link with Jewishness stems from wounded pride."

You must be wondering: if all this is so, why the decision to live together?

There is not much I can say. There are parts that I don't know. There is a spark that is ignited for no apparent reason. If we wanted to be hard on ourselves it would be better to put it like this: the restraints imposed by the movement are appropriate to the turmoil of adolescence. And they probably serve to sensitize the emotional response of those born sensitive, appreciative of subtlety and aware of others. But at the same time they cause hidden suffering. And one grows tired of the need always to be restrained and balanced and cautious. And then you rush into the forbidden that has suddenly become permissible.

Let me take a deep breath and say one more thing. It is difficult to speak about the experiences of the body in words that do not hark back to some individual recollection. The body cannot offer anything that does not exist in our imaginations. It has not in itself a single particle of happiness. One should not exaggerate the importance of this matter. One does not fall into the abyss or hear the angels sing. One satisfies a hunger and is grateful. And you learn to appreciate the person who shares bread with you when you are hungry. Many ascribe to this release virtues that are not proper to it. The act does not take place in the holy of holies. The golden fleece is inside our heads.

And that will have to do. I cannot put it more plainly.

Love is probably much rejoicing about nothing. When we were walking along Koszykowska Street an old man came out of the Main Library holding tightly on to a golden-haired little girl who wanted to pull away and run across the street. A vehicle passed. And suddenly you grabbed my arm, afraid that the girl might get away from the old man. At the point where your hand touched my arm there was love.

Sometimes I think about the moment of my return. What will I say? How will I say it? Will I be able to say to Sarah, "Such and such has happened to me, and that's that"? Perhaps I shall speak rationally: "There are no children. Our marriage is an experiment that has not worked out. This is the proof." I am afraid that I'll have to keep it short. Speeches on this kind of topic tend to become maudlin. Tired words falling on ears deafened by pain.

I may not have to say a thing. Sarah won't come to meet the boat. That isn't done. It would be a pity to lose a day's work. If the ship gets in in the morning I may be able to catch the truck from the cooperative. First there will be hours of talk about old times as we drive along. The driver will barrage me with questions, and I won't have time to think about my own problems. Once I get home I'll barely have the chance to say, "Shalom." In the shower house they'll keep me sidetracked for a long time. I'll be asked to tell it all from beginning to end. After supper the members of the kibbutz will probably gather round, and I'll have to start all over again. At night when we get to the tent we'll be all tired out.

If the ship arrives in the afternoon I'll stay over at my uncle's in Haifa. And not until the following morning will I take the only bus that reaches our kibbutz. My chief concern will be this letter. I'll go to the post office and have it weighed. My uncle will lend me the money to send it by airmail.

It may well be that for the first day or two nothing will be said, and by the third day there will be no need to say anything.

Today I spent some time with Kuperberg again. I told him about my visit to Reissen, and he wanted to hear all about it, down to the minutest detail. "That's where you'll find real Jews," he said. "Russian Jews can't always be taken at face value. Warsaw is nothing but a station along the way. There you have not only a simple, horse-and-wagon Jewry but also a Jewry that uses cologne to cover up the onions and garlic of the others. Inside an ornate synagogue a world-famous tenor woos God in pure bel canto. German Jews have been dragging out an affair with Destiny, which has suddenly turned up in the guise of a sadistic sign painter. For two hundred years they waited for a Jewish Bach to come along and write a cantata based on the Torah cantillation. Since no such thing has happened, they're beginning to wonder whether, perhaps, God might not be Jewish after all."

The Arab riots brought us closer, too. Sarah and I, I mean.

She was afraid of the dark, and at those moments she was soft and feminine. But when shots were fired and one of our people was wounded, she knew what to do. And I was ashamed of the fake toughness I had tried to put on. She is not able to speak convincingly about duty and responsibility. I know that. But she doesn't need to. To her they are simple and completely obvious things. We subscribe to standards of behavior. She simply behaves. So much for that.

Later Kuperberg spoke about the Congress. He was not at all impressed with certain speeches that I had found deeply moving. He said that Zionism tries to be like manna. It gives the Western Jew a taste of Yiddishkeit, while to the Eastern Jew it holds forth a promise of Europe.

He said that he could not see a Jewish bureaucrat without throwing up his hands. In the Zionist movement, at least, you had a gathering of the merciful ones. The Jewish commissar was a more cruel specimen. I pointed out that even among us instances of human frailty had come to light. For example, the obsession with standing on ceremony. What petty quarrels had broken out in the planning committee! And here he was, elderly and in poor health, and, nevertheless, he was on deck while they occupied the cabins. Kuperberg smiled. There is nothing wrong with his health. He just doesn't carry about any more flesh than is strictly necessary to house his soul. "The less the merrier." And as for the preoccupation with first-class berths, that is nothing but an extension of the Congress. Here we have all the political persuasions on one ship, and each has to look out for its own prerogatives. I said, "In one drop of seawater you have everything that swims in the ocean." "Except sharks," he said. "There is no need to judge people, unless the judgment is in their favor," he said. "On the contrary, they are to be pitied. They are not able to break loose from themselves, not for a second. When they get up in the middle of the night they remember that they belong to the Executive Committee. And then they rouse their wives and ask to be admired. They are ruining their marriages that way. Women, you know, tend to judge men on their performance." We both laughed at the double meaning as we hurled our darts at those self-important little men. VIPs! Visibility Is Precious! If they surrendered one iota of the respect due them they would be condemned to eternal damnation. "If an internal revenue functionary had to stay in second class while a functionary of the pension plan was put in first the world would revert to chaos. People would forget where the money comes from." Kuperberg joked about one high Jewish Agency official who is also something of a writer. If he sleeps on deck, word will get around that he's a good writer but an unimportant official. Since he's in first class everyone knows who he is and what he is. Finally Kuperberg said that he himself, at any rate, has nothing against these people who have exchanged freedom for power. Even the private lives of these public servants is public property. Only the person who has elected himself is completely free. But, of course, if these people were a bit more modest he would like it better. In the end he looked at me shrewdly and his eyes twinkled with affection. "Even halutzim," he said, "would be well advised to forgo some of the applause."

Evening is coming on. Not long ago we saw Benghazi from the distance. We are sailing in the direction of Crete. The sky is cloudy but the sea is calm. The slow lapping of the waves has a soporific effect. But life on deck is too charged with interest. In the afternoon there was a lecture on the Mediterranean. They even took up a collection for the Jewish National Fund. They managed to take in ten Palestine pounds. Even we gave something, although our finances are approaching an all-time low. When we go ashore at Athens and at Alexandria we'll have to keep expenditures to a strict minimum.

All of Eretz Yisrael is on the *Cairo City*. In the late afternoon I suddenly noticed a fellow on deck who looked familiar. At first I couldn't place him. He recognized me too and for a while he looked at me in a puzzled way. Then all of a sudden he turned pale and walked away in a hurry. And then I remembered where we had met: at my Uncle

Yeruham's. I put one and one together and realized that he was one of the young men who had been giving out Irgun leaflets in Geneva, those leaflets with Schiller's lines from *William Tell*: "Vengeance has been exacted, and that is the end." It's strange that he should run away from me. What could I do to him? Would I tell on him? To whom? After all, we're all in the same boat.

There's a violinist of sorts, too, who interrupted her studies in Paris because of the war scare. She played in the first-class bar, and we crowded in, too. Afterward we overheard a sad argument between her and her father. She accused him of wrecking her career. There was no need to run away from an imaginary danger. Today nobody speaks of war any more. He replied that Russian Jews have learned to smell danger from afar. Funny reasoning. I interrupted. I told her about the Palestine Philharmonic. She dismissed my remarks with contempt. That's just philanthropy. That's no orchestra. She's very sure of herself, that girl.

Saturday, September 2

This morning we got word of the bombing of Warsaw. I wish I could believe in the power of prayer.

All day we crowd around the radio and listen to the news. In several languages. Reception is very bad. The announcements are contradictory. The German radio announces that this is not war. Germany is only interested in border adjustments. Hitler has promised Roosevelt that the Luftwaffe will not bomb open cities unless the Poles start first. Then why did they bomb Warsaw? Idiotic discussions rage here. Someone said that the Poles have only themselves to blame. Warsaw is full of military objectives. They laughed at him. Every railway station, power station, bridge, is a military objective. Someone else dug up a map of Warsaw and they are trying to figure out where the bombs have landed. I looked for Godecka on the map and was relieved to learn that it's far away from both you and from my father. My eyes suddenly filled with tears when I noticed Aleje Jerozolimskie. I had to go out on deck to hide my tears.

All night the sea raged and driving rain pummeled the deck. We found shelter in the corridors and the lower lounges. It was a wretched feeling. All night I threw up until I was too weak to climb the stairs. And once I vomited on the floor, and I was really ashamed of myself. There were moments when I didn't think I could bear it any longer. I wished I could fall asleep and not wake up until it was all over. The truth is that I wished I would die, if only to stop the nausea. But now that the storm has subsided a bit and the rain has stopped and I can lie on deck and breathe the fresh air and I have even managed to write a few words, this expression seems overblown and unreal.

When word of the bombing reached us we welcomed the storm. The heart has a way of fooling itself. As if we could somehow partake in your suffering.

All night long we puked our guts up. We were like rags, putrid blobs of worn-out flesh, without souls. But the war seems to have brought us to. One evil blots out another. At noon we passed Crete and now we're approaching the Greek islands.

The storm abated all at once, and all the suffering and loathing and revulsion passed, and only Warsaw was left.

It's difficult to live with the realization that one is so far away, so incapable of doing anything, except for constant arguing and interpreting. Rumors run wild here, as if everyone had his own private source of information. Some of the leaders got together in one of the cabins for a consultation. What did they have to say? They emerged and said that we must keep calm. "Let everyone do his bit conscientiously. That is our answer." Ridiculous! But really what can we do? I had something to eat out of a sense of duty to my body. My face was greenish yellow, and I looked like a walking ghost. Nor did others look much different. And they ate too. Well, at least we saved a few Jewish lives, the moral equivalent of saving a whole world. But cynicism doesn't bring relief either. When there's nothing you can do you look for someone to be angry at. At any rate, our leaders sounded absolutely ridiculous when they came out with that old bromide. They have one panacea for all ills. All we have to do is to step up our pioneering efforts. Let the plowmen plow and the sowers sow and the builders build and the speculators speculate and the Arabs work in the orange groves of Nes-Tziyona and the kindergartners go to kindergarten. And do everything more intensely. That's how we reply to the enemy. At such moments as these I can understand men who want to take up arms and perform acts of desperation.

R. and S., their faces beaming with a sense of their own importance, stood up before a disappointed assemblage and said things that didn't seem to matter much one way or the other. "Ben-Gurion went to London," they said. "When he gets back we'll know where things stand." It's as if they said, "We've done everything in our power." When they were gone a member of the Committee on Immigration told how he had once gone to London with the members of the Executive. That was in the days of Hope-Simpson. They had gone in order to find out what the government's true intentions were. There was a question of whether there had been a change in policy or whether the administration in Aretz had simply been ineffectual. He had embarked with great excitement on this, his first visit to London. Here he was, in the company of top-echelon people going to speak with ministers and rulers. He imagined a round table covered in green baize, with distinguished gentlemen sitting around it engaging in weighty deliberations. He believed that his eloquence, which had earned him quite a reputation in Aretz, would make the desired impression here. But nothing of the kind happened. They got off the train at the crowded station with nobody there to meet them. They went to a small, dirty restaurant where they had tea. One of the group phoned an influential Jew who pulled what strings he could and arranged for them to meet a junior civil servant who spouted a lot of diplomatic nonsense. Later, all sorts of ridiculous commentaries appeared in Aretz: "England has not yet made up her mind."

The best we can hope for is a friend at court. Like beggars at the door. Nobody will be bothered about the Jews. At Warsaw the fate of the Jewish people will be sealed. Bitter remarks of that kind are what you hear on board. They can drive you out of your mind. On terra firma you can do something. And not just "step up our pioneering efforts." And here we are condemned to bob about in a floating ark for who knows how long. The ship is taking various detours to stay out of the way of submarines. Nor does anyone know yet how long we'll stay at Athens and Alexandria.

But impatient remarks don't help either.

People talk about enlisting in the British army. The Mapai people say that we have to stand up for our rights. Shraga is not happy about having our young people serve under a foreign flag. As if there were any possibility of serving under our own flag. I am seriously thinking about enlisting. I know what I shall be told. Everyone has to do his duty. And each one should try to do the thing he does best. But I hope that military service is the sort of thing I'll be capable of. At the course for guardsmen I was far from the worst.

An insane idea: perhaps we'll reach Warsaw ...

As a child I was scared to death of the army. I pleaded with my mother to hide me in the cellar till I was past draft age.

I try not to meet people. They only make life harder for one another with their depressing forecasts. The real pessimists drive me out of my mind. Alper still swears that there will be no war. The bombings are only meant to intimidate. Poland can't stand up to the German war machine. England

and France are unprepared. In a few days it will all be over. If only I could see historical necessity in everything as he does! I am even fed up with his dialectic fatalism by now.

Even a conversation with Kuperberg made me angry. I am no dogmatic Marxist, but there was no way I could accept his view that the politicoeconomic factor is only a pretext. As if wars were caused by the fact that man's motives are intrinsically evil. "Man is bloodthirsty by nature," says Kuperberg. "Only a small minority have refined their instincts sufficiently to care about humanity as a whole. And within that minority Jews are a majority." And so on with other, similar, views. I told him as tactfully as I could that these are general observations and cannot explain why war broke out precisely on September first, nineteen hundred and thirty-nine. He looked at me affectionately, as at a star pupil who has given a shrewd answer and added, as is his way, in evidence, as it were, an item that appeared in the papers recently. The executioner at Sing Sing suffered a nervous breakdown. The prison authorities advertised the vacancy. Three hundred candidates turned up, among whom five were young women.

Afterward he went on to say that even boredom is a factor. I couldn't take that. Men going to war because of boredom! I was really vexed at his need to express himself in paradoxes. But Kuperberg meant what he said. What experts call the death wish is nothing but the fear of boredom. A man who can't stand his own company for even a short time sees life as an endless desert. Putting a heroic end to this aimless existence is the essence of fascism. I tried not to show my anger. I said, "That's an angle, too." He got my point but wasn't offended. "Young man," he said to me, "if there were only one point of view we would never have advanced beyond the caves . . . "

In a newspaper a few days old it says that the German people are not eager for war and that the disclosure that

Nazi leaders had smuggled their money abroad aroused great anger in Berlin.

The tendency here is to describe the Germans as monsters. I spoke with one Jew from Germany. He said you have to distinguish between Nazis and Germans. Ninety percent of the Catholics are revolted by anti-Semitism. The SS men are young boys crazy for power. A few of them are actually deranged.

For me, Germany is that sweet little lady at the newsstand in the station in Berlin. Fragile, transparent, with tired, very light blue eyes, arms thin as birch twigs with the veins showing. She sells all their filth, yet remains untouched by it. I pictured her as a clean, modest widow with a hand-wound gramophone at home on which she listens to classical music.

Perhaps I remember her because of the smile that spread across her face when we came up to her. Hurried travelers spoke to her brusquely and she lowered her eyes in humiliation. When she lifted her eyes and saw us she smiled. It was the gentle smile of a sad woman who doesn't begrudge others their happiness.

I wouldn't dare to say such things here, today. I, too, have been ensnared by the pervading hysteria. Feelings are mixed. I would like to believe that Germany is incapable of the atrocities attributed to her by the Czechs. But if the accounts prove to be true I would like to fight. With gun in hand.

I wonder whether I'd be capable of killing another human being with my own two hands. I have no answer.

I am very vulnerable now and quick to anger. Somebody here has seen fit to settle accounts with the rich Jews of Warsaw. Eight hundred Jewish refugees from Germany withstood the disgrace of starvation at Zbąszyń, and the local Jewish nabob, who had contributed fifty million zlotys to the defense of Warsaw, couldn't find it in his heart to cough up anything for these fellow Jews. Victor and Sonia looked at me with consternation when I spoke up, albeit ever so tentatively, in the rich man's defense. I was thinking of your father. But is this the time to bring that story to mind? German bombs don't distinguish between rich and poor.

In the late afternoon, facing a magnificent view of smaller and larger islands, with the sun setting over the hills of Sparta, I borrowed the map of Warsaw and "took a walk through the streets."

I remembered the last day in Warsaw. We were happy and carefree in each other's company. We had not yet found a name for this simple, natural happiness that had taken hold of us. I remembered the elegant ladies of Marszalkowska who were literally begging for their new dresses, cut after the latest Parisian fashions, to be noticed. And the Chekhovian damsel with the unnecessary parasol dragging a spoiled pup behind her, and a few Tarzanic youths. And your father at the café, with his blue coat and gold-topped walking stick, chatting familiarly with the bank president. And our way of joking and the embarrassed silences. How peaceful all that was. The matter of Danzig was no cause for concern. Hitler was just a clown. England and France were strong. And Poland had confidence in her own might. How badly we wanted to believe all that.

My eye wanders over the map. Bielańska, Długa, Ogrodowa. You can only pause a moment, then you have to go on. The arms depot, the barracks. Near my father's house I stop with a sudden twinge. And then Leszno. A street charged with memories. My childhood, my youth. Lag ba'Omer. A parade with waving flags and bugles. Head held high, heart beating fast.

What naiveté! Our walking together where everybody knows us . . .

Suddenly there was a gust of wind that disheveled your hair. And that moment had some great importance. I don't know why. There are moments like that. They are hardly past that you look back and long for them. And tremble, lest they never return.

Kuperberg came over to me. He asked if he might take a peek. He likes maps. They serve as a kind of guide for the imagination. He stood beside me for a few minutes. Then he asked tactfully if I had any family there. He bowed his head humbly as he awaited my reply. As if he were unworthy of entering my private world. He only has friends in Warsaw. Again we exchanged a few words about the war. But this time he didn't try to startle me with paradoxes. In a house of mourning these have no place. He said that everyone prophesied that the war was imminent, but nobody believed it. They just wrote and warned. Every second-rate news-paperman was a prophet of doom. If they had truly believed that war was imminent they couldn't have spewed forth so much rubbish. Sensitive people don't talk about things that are beyond their grasp. Like death, love, war. Just as a Jew never mentions the Ineffable Name. He tried to console me. He spoke of the power of survival of the Jewish people. But there was nothing consoling about it, because all the while I was thinking of one person in particular. Of two. My father, as well.

He told me about his visit to Italy. In a park he saw an old man and an old woman. The old man was peeling an apple for his wife and cut his finger. A marvelous smile lit up both their faces. A story of the Garden of Eden in reverse. And without the peel. But this time there is no snake messing things up between them. Here the happiness is complete. These two old people are just as much Italy as Il Duce is. And perhaps they are even a bit more Italian than he. They have no need of Roman pomp. All they need is a little happiness, a little sadness, and a little red wine. Such people do not kill others. It seems he was trying to say that

Italy will not enter the war. Or at any rate, that the alliance between Germany and Italy cannot endure. I must have looked sad and depressed, and this was his way of trying to cheer me up.

Piraeus, Sunday, September 3

The ship is flooded with light and there is a curiously festive air throughout the city, where life goes on as if nothing has happened. Some of the delegates to the Congress are caught up in the carefree mood. Here we are, only one day after the bombing of Warsaw, and somebody speaks of the end of Nazism as if victory were in sight. Only those who hail from Poland are mournful. Among the Russians there is talk of the positive results that the war is likely to produce: every war brings about radical revisions, new states, new borders, a new order. I am unable to share their enthusiasm.

And the whole time we were in Athens I saw nothing but the vision of a bombed-out city.

"The power of the imagination is a cruel gift," says Kuperberg. "It fosters pity, but also fear."

I won't bother describing Athens. In Marseille I still believed that there would be no war, so that I could afford to try my hand at describing the scene. Now I see no point in it.

All day we wandered about the city. Together. For financial reasons. They split hairs over nonsense. We ate what the treasurer felt like eating. We visited the sites that interested Alper. But we do not seem to have missed anything. Whatever has to be seen we saw.

Meanwhile we learned that women and children had been evacuated from Warsaw, so that at least I was able to enjoy what I saw.

I always wanted to visit Greece. Actually I have wanted to visit almost every spot on earth.

Along the way there were minor skirmishes over who was to be in charge. Alper decided that he was first among equals. Eliyahu decided that that distinction was his. He holds the money. Alper prevailed, because he knew what he wanted to see. And he wanted it with all his might. I have just this to add: Athens imposes a mood of its own. But all the same, Warsaw won out. Streets full of Greeks looked to me like Niska, Krochmalna, Genichowski.

Alper made a nasty crack about my mood. As if I were the only one concerned with Warsaw. I got angry and answered back. Later I was sorry.

It's not too wise to walk around in a dismal mood all day. It doesn't help anybody, either.

We returned toward evening, all worn out. After several days of idleness on board ship it's hard to keep walking for so long. There were still a few hours left until sailing time. We went to the first-class bar to listen to the news.

Today I told Kuperberg, without using names, of course, about a Histadrut official who let his passions get the upper hand. Kuperberg's reaction was surprising. His face lit up. "That's wonderful," he said. "That fellow still has a spark of humanity left." He said that even more than he fears people who are unable to sin thoroughly, he is afraid of those who chastise themselves in order to be able to torment others.

A clash between me and Alper was apparently inevitable. It all started with an argument over the war. One of the Hechalutz people was critical of the Soviet Union. He said it was the pact that had emboldened Germany. Without the Soviet Union's acquiescence Germany would never have embarked on the war. Alper stood up for Russia. He repeated things he had said before. Stalin was paying back the West as the West had conspired to pay him. A few more people gathered round. The discussion became heated and shouts were heard. Afterward Alper turned on me for having kept quiet. I told him I didn't know if he was right. These matters are beyond me. I have no inside information, so that I haven't the slightest idea what goes on inside Stalin's mind or what the leaders of the West were conspiring to do. He shot back that politically I am a babe in the woods, and that one cannot live "outside of history" and so forth. I realized that I had hurt him deeply, but there was nothing I could do. I truly believe that one cannot justify the Soviet course even if it was taken in order to protect the land of the workers and peasants.

Actually he was accusing me of cowardice.

It may be wrong of me to write you these things. Alper was your leader in the movement, and you are right to admire him. But his way of suggesting that my being on the Executive was due to my being a sort of errand boy really hurt me. These were very insulting words, especially since I never laid claim to any of the privileges of leadership. Practical work suits me fine. And working the soil is something that I actually like. My reply really ought to have been more forceful. But I am always afraid that harshness will wound him too deeply.

Today I no longer suspect him of knowing all about us. He may have a vague intimation, nothing more.

I look at him and I can tell what he is thinking. His contempt for me comes from the bottom of his heart. My kibbutz is desperate for each man-hour and I go off on a family visit. I am chosen as a delegate to the Congress because "I'm in Europe anyway." During the Congress I behave with utter disregard for the proceedings. I absent myself from the deliberations of the Congress in order to go traipsing about with a girl. I deceive my comrades and make up all sorts of excuses. And worst of all, I'm fooling around with a girl who has an important job waiting for her in the movement. At a time when all human resources are needed for matters of paramount concern, I entertain myself with a minor flirtation.

I won't try to defend myself. I'm not going to start talking to him about love.

Today we learned that England has declared war on Germany, and that has lifted our spirits somewhat.

Monday, September 4

At sea once more. There is some kind of unspoken fear of Crete, a storm center. This time we will pass to the east of the island, in the hope that the sea will not be rough. I remember the last storm with revulsion, the way I was lying in the corridor like a bundle of rags! Powerless, without any will of my own . . . and that was the day the war broke out! The thought that a person, through lack of strength, can reach such a spiritual low, such a subhuman state, troubles me. It calls forth the most profound loathing. As the psalmist says, "A vile person is despised in his eyes."

Breakfast as usual. Tea and fresh vegetables that we bought in Greece. Once again the friendly spirit of the first days. The comradely instinct grows with the isolation and the feeling of being cut off. The oneness of our destiny is what Yitzhak calls it. I am trying to put my quarrel with Alper out of my mind. He made a civil reply to my good morning, but what coldness! I may come to prefer the rough ways of the youth in Eretz Yisrael to such cold civility. The people from Hakibbutz Hameuhad have joined us again. We discuss literature. Kuperberg gets dragged in against his will. Why doesn't he write about positive people, working people, without twisting things! He withdraws and becomes evasive. Perhaps beautiful people ought to be photographed rather than drawn. The artist's hand may tremble and a line may be thrown off. Then there are complaints. Alper, as usual, speaks in the name of history. One must discuss general trends, not unimportant details. Anyone can talk about disease. How to heal is the question. The discussion has left Kuperberg drained. Of all the words our forefathers used for the visionary, the madman of the spirit, he prefers "seer." Neither "prophet" nor "prophet's disciple" will do.

Czestochowa has fallen. Well, the war is real. Once I quarreled with my grandfather over Jasna Gora. On a hike with the kids in the movement we had stopped off there. Grandpa spat. Into *their* house of worship! His eyes flashed lightning. I tried to say something in favor of autonomous aesthetic values. "Even their music was made to kill Jews," said Grandpa.

The bombing of Warsaw continues. There is some profound contradiction between the calm of the sea and the news on the radio. But suddenly an English torpedo boat approaches and signals that there are German submarines in the vicinity. And again an ugly sort of excitement takes hold of the passengers.

Meanwhile it was learned that a German submarine sank a passenger vessel in the Atlantic Ocean and that the English have caught "Berman." These bits of information transformed the war into something much more concrete. In the second-class lounge there is one lady who sits and trembles all the time. Her husband is unable to calm her. In contrast, the bravado of two fellows from Rishon le-Tziyon, on their way back from a vacation in Paris, is positively infuriating. They strut back and forth on the top deck like a couple of peacocks. They are satisfied with "the way things are going." They also have a surefire way of getting America into the war. All you have to do is sink an American passenger ship and put the blame on the Germans. Such things have been known to happen. They have other ideas of that kind. The Arabs are strengthening their ties with the Germans. We are in a position to help this along. Then we volunteer en masse to serve in the British army. And when the war is over we are rewarded with a Jewish state. The dawn of redemption . . .

I hope the kids in the movement are not like that. Such arrogance makes me very sad.

Meanwhile we have heard a little story, entertaining in its own way. People's desire to ascribe human failings to the Gestapo is touching. In Prague they confiscated the gavel used at the Congress, which they found in a drawer of Dr. Kahan's desk. They were positive they had uncovered a secret group of Freemasons.

That is why, Kuperberg said, the gavel used for the last Congress had a different ring.

I saw the storm approaching.

This one was not so long or so severe as the previous one. There was no rain. And I was able to say up on deck. And close my eyes in order not to see the mast in its drunken reeling and swaying. Whatever I had eaten the sea got to eat. But there were no really revolting scenes. Kant describes the Sublime as a turbulent sea. That's all right if you happen to be on dry land.

Now the sea is calm. But the blue color is deep and menacing. There are light ripples that break into little islands of foam. Each wave has a short life. It is barely born and it has white hair and then it is no more.

Now that we are coming closer to home, time seems to crawl. Suddenly we have too much of it on our hands. The fear of submarines also contributes to this impression. The ship doesn't seem to be moving at all. Some people know how to use this spare time. The "Germans" read English newspapers with a dictionary. The flirts flirt. They seem to believe that at sea the captain is held accountable for everyone else's deeds. He is even responsible for their morals. One woman has taken a fancy to Yitzhak and doesn't seem to mind that everyone can see her trying to entice him, whenever she gets the chance, with her ample bosom. In Haifa her husband is probably waiting, and she will rush into his open arms. But who am I to cast the first stone? The gossips have plenty of free time and many captive ears. Kuperberg says that people who do not respect the time of others probably are not much concerned for the lives of others, either. Only yesterday he said that the Italians are so likable because they always have time. And the Germans are dangerous. Because they have no time, and they're ready to kill whoever gets in their way. And ordinary people who haven't a minute to spare are destructive. But when one of the bores comes over to him his eyelids begin to flutter with impatience.

People talk with anyone about anything. There are even discussions about God. Just like in the youth movement. It is difficult to explain to someone from Ha-Poel Ha-Mizrahi that our secularism is the result of a moral judgment. For we do not say that there is no truth or honesty or moral imperative. We dare to seek these things within the rotten bundle of impulses under our own skin.

Sometimes it seems that I am being too hard on myself. As if I had been unfaithful to your memory. In one of the cabins "peace talks" are under way. Representing our side are Shraga and Yitzhak. The other side is represented mostly by Ha-Poel Ha-Tzair people. With kid gloves. They are talking about amalgamation as the command of the hour. Here on board ship the things that keep us apart and the reasons for the separation are not all that clear. Especially since the pact.

The people from Mapai tend to dismiss us as spoiled children. We want the best of all possible worlds served up on a silver platter. As if we had all been brought up expecting a gentile maid to bring us breakfast in bed. They only bother with us because of our hold over the youth. Youth likes ideas to be clear-cut, consistent, revolutionary.

Had a short talk with Kuperberg. It seems that he overheard the last argument between me and Alper. It's crowded here and easy to hear things you aren't meant to. He said we're lucky to be Zionists, thoroughly compassionate. If we were in Russia we might shoot it out. He hates the Soviet Union with all his heart. Like a disappointed lover. Once he believed in the revolution, as did every restless young person. Until he saw it from up close.

In the afternoon there were rumors that Italy had entered the war. There was nothing to that effect on the news. One of the "Germans" said that didn't mean a thing. The days for gentlemanly declarations are past. Today deeds come before words. The world is reverting to chaos. He had a brick factory in Munich. Some uniformed men walked in with sealed orders, and in a matter of minutes he was out on the street. His brother committed suicide, and his wife had a nervous breakdown.

"And I came to Palestine to be footloose and fancy-free."

Alper is deliberately avoiding me. Well, so be it. I have no intention of running after him. Yitzhak has noticed. He seems preoccupied with his own affairs but never fails to take in what is happening around him. "Has a black cat passed between you?" he asked. Without wanting to I told him what had happened. He wasn't very happy with Alper's outspoken position. He was afraid that it might be bad for the movement. "It's no good rushing to conclusions, this way or that." But he got in a gentle dig at me, too. "It's sad, very sad," he said. "But there are those who criticize out of a sense of real hurt, and there are those who do it out of spite."

Then he went over to have a talk with Alper. They stood together a long time, and Alper gesticulated excitedly. Once Yitzhak turned around and looked at me.

But maybe it only seemed that way.

Toward evening I was jumpy and nervous. Kuperberg seemed worried as he looked at me, from close up, from far away. In a little while it will be dark. Completely dark. And the ship will make its way like a black mass concealing the light within.

Everyone says that I'm keeping a diary, but I deny it. I was asked if I'd let them publish excerpts in the movement paper.

Port Alexandria, Tuesday, September 5

Before us is Alexandria.

We've been here since this morning. They are loading and unloading. The ship is tied up at the wharf, but they're not letting us off. The official reason is that it's the queen's birthday. But there may be another reason. Egypt has declared war on Germany. But we, too, are the enemy.

People are sitting on deck and watching. A teeming port has a certain rough and ready charm. Longshoremen run this way and that. Waving arms circle our heads. Officials get on and off. Even a few peddlers got permission to come on board. They spread out their colorful merchandise with obsequious smiles, but their eyes flash hatred. The most impressive sight of all is the British fleet anchored here. It is a mighty force made up of thousands of tons of armor-plated steel and is vastly reassuring. One suddenly understands the placid, bored expressions of the British soldiers as they go about their tasks amid the nervous uproar. A potbellied port official makes apologies. The celebrating mob is dangerous. It is better that we not get off. The police cannot guarantee our safety.

But even from here you can see masses of people streaming every which way. There may be a parade passing somewhere out there. Perhaps Farouk is there, in all his glory. It is marvelous to see so many men, all in white robes, and to think that each has a house, a wife, a bellyache, all his own.

The official is a mini-Farouk. The same belly, the same mustache, the same sly, malicious smile. Not even the sunglasses have been omitted.

Gradually it became clear that the smile was more than just a sign of good humor. It meant something. Those born in Palestine got the message. They paid and were permitted ashore.

My cousin's friend is holding a handkerchief over his face. British soldiers have come on board and seem to be looking for someone. If I were in their shoes it would be obvious to me who that person was. Nobody else made any attempt to hide. When they were gone I went over and stood by him. Now he's not afraid of me. After all, I didn't turn him over to his enemies. He looked at the massive steel shapes and his spirits suddenly fell. One battleship let off a deafening blast. When it was over he spoke to me. "When we have a Jewish state, we, too, shall have a fleet like that," he reassured me.

"The righteous shall live by his faith."

It's odd to sit in a deck chair doing nothing in the midst of life's hustle and bustle. Like an Arab foreman. The landscape is somewhat reminiscent of Eretz Yisrael, a bit of Jaffa, a bit of Gaza, but with some mansions the likes of which you only see in Jerusalem. From afar, along the coast, you can see a mosque painted in pink and white zebra stripes, an obelisk, a neat army camp, golf courses, the royal summer palace.

Along one of the inlets across the harbor you can make out sun umbrellas and tiny figures in the water. It's the same all over the world, in Aretz, too, probably. People go to the beach, they sunbathe, they get to look good, and are happy. The war is so far away. How many of these people running about in the marketplace have any idea of the location of that city whose name fills the airwaves?

A smell of fish and of tar comes up from the harbor. And some other stench that's hard to make out. The streets down by the port are narrow, but the coffeehouses sprawl all over the sidewalks. The gramophones try to outscreech one another. Buggies wait at the gateway to the port. Their turbaned drivers look at us in disappointment. As if we were responsible for not being allowed off. They've missed another chance to fleece the dumb tourists. Few women are to be seen in the nearby streets. This is a city of men. The few women go about in pairs, in black or white veils, Turkish style. Even a black limousine has driven up. We had some bigwig on board without even knowing it.

Alexandria is a bare city. One scarcely sees any trees. A few palms tower over the houses; cypresses, poincianas enclose a shadowy road; purple bougainvilleas grow on the terraces. On a distant hill a grove of fruit trees bears its late fruit, figs or citrus.

The landscape of Eretz Yisrael.

But for some reason lines from Mickiewicz come to my mind, provocative lines. An attempt to pit himself in a humorous vein against the eternal longing for the sun-drenched south. I don't remember it by heart. I remember only that the cypress is compared to a German watchman, guarding a nobleman's door, the very embodiment of reaction, while even the citrus trees have been stripped of their glory. A roly-poly female dwarf who loves to show off her gold is supposed to represent . . .

I never thought all this would lead me back to being homesick for the Polish countryside. The thin, upright birch, the linden, the fir fraught with Jewish fears, the willow bending over a river, which flows into a marsh. And little waterfalls, and endless forests, and "the crab-apple tree whose trunk is wreathed with hops . . ." I don't know why that of all lines sticks in my mind.

In Egypt, on the Mediterranean coast, to the smell of rotting fish, my eye is suddenly filled with Polish images.

But you're never alone for long on the *Cairo City*. Whosoever wishes may peek over your shoulder and register amazement at the amount you have written. There must even be a few who wonder whether they have earned a place in the "diary." Perhaps many years hence it will be an historic document. After all, any scrap of paper clever enough to lie low in a forgotten drawer is eventually transformed into a primary source.

A young prostitute, hardly more than a girl, is walking up and down the pier. A thin garment covers her flowing limbs. She lifts her eyes toward us with what she must take to be a come-hither glance. Her face wears a dumb, technicolor smile. But she succeeds in projecting a keen sexuality. Her breasts are almost completely bare and when she walks she sways her hips almost as if she were dancing. Maybe that's the custom here. Someone is giving the customs officer a bribe and bringing her on board. She doesn't stand a chance with us. People look at her with contempt, pity, revulsion, with concealed lust. A person looks at an unaccustomed spectacle and gives himself away.

I am sitting near Kuperberg. He dispatches an apologetic glance in my direction and writes a few lines on a long sheet of newsprint. As if writing were my privilege, and he is trespassing. Somebody comes over to us and looks at the prostitute. "Disgusting!" he says after a few minutes. Kuperberg remarks, "Taking pride in a sage's prayer shawl doesn't make you a sage."

Then a strange conversation ensued. Without looking at me he suddenly asked, "What is a person like you doing at congresses?" I got the message. He was speaking out of friendly concern. The revolution had soured on him. But from his revolutionary period he preserved a deep-seated objection to authority. All authority: big shots, VIPs, leaders of any kind. As if he wanted to protect me from a fate that I do not deserve. "A person who sets out on that obstacle course," said he, "is round and whole. But like a ship on a stormy sea he must toss all excess baggage overboard. In the end, there's nothing left of him but his curl, his pipe, one fake smile, and the imprint of his fingers on your shoulder."

He related a typical incident. One big shot invited him to have coffee in first class. He sat for a long time and talked about himself. He spoke about how important he is, how indispensable, and what a sacrifice his position of leadership demands. Actually he is a poet, but is forced to renounce his poetry. Yet he still has a soft spot for poets. A Greek waiter approached. Not just any old waiter, but a first-class waiter, a waiter who knows how to grovel in four languages and is an expert in all the fine points of protocol. Well, the big shot was not going to pass up this chance to play at being high and mighty. He ridiculed Kuperberg in order to ingratiate himself with the waiter. Kuperberg had forgotten to take his spoon out of the cup before drinking the coffee. The waiter smiled. The big shot was in seventh heaven. He had received his first-class stamp of approval as man of the world. And in the end he let Kuperberg pay for both cups of coffee. Nothing high and mighty about that.

I laughed. I agreed with him that the man in question was not a nice person. In Geneva I once had occasion to use the toilet after him. I saw a few drops on the toilet seat. It got me all upset. He preaches solidarity and can't be bothered with lifting the seat.

A few minutes later he said to me, "You're not made of that hard stuff. You ought to learn a trade. There is no happier man than one who can build something with his own two hands." And he immediately added, "Perhaps if I knew how to build sturdy tables I would never have become a writer."

I told him a little about the movement and its ways. Maybe it was my Hebrew that got me involved with congresses. Administrative ability too, but mostly my Hebrew. Fluency excites admiration among our people.

It all goes back to my mother. She wanted to get even with my father. Since he had enrolled me in a Polish high school, she put me into a Hebrew high school.

This is where I allowed myself to be led into talking about you. I don't know why I did it. Maybe I just couldn't keep it in any longer. All this time I have been guarding a secret that fills my entire being. And I have nobody to share it with. It was easy for me to speak to a complete stranger. And I have no fear that he will talk.

I don't enjoy making confessions. As a youngster I once got burnt. I had told some of my adolescent problems to a leading educator, whose abilities Korczak admired. Several weeks later I found my remarks in an article this person had written. The name was changed, of course, but I was hurt, nonetheless.

I felt that I could trust Kuperberg. But he wasn't happy about the whole thing. As if he had set a limit on intimacy that he didn't want me to pass.

"In matters of this kind a person can't even give himself advice," he said. But I never asked for advice. I only needed to get the thing off my chest.

Perhaps what he wanted to say was, "In this your isolation is complete."

The latest news from Warsaw is not encouraging. Smigly-Rydz and Moscicki won't lead the nation into war. If the Germans conquer parts of Poland the anti-Semites will rear their heads.

In one of the cabins talks are being held among the leaders of the Labor factions. In a spirit of magnanimity and with anxiety over subsequent developments. There is talk of consolidation. But there is fear that back in Aretz, on terra firma, the old differences will flare up. And the old suspicions.

S/S Cairo City, *September 6*

We set sail toward nightfall. The sea was calm. There was subdued excitement: our last night. Some hurried to pack. As if there wouldn't be ample time later on, what with all the formalities in Haifa port.

Now it's morning. Everyone is standing at the rail. It looks like the *Tashlikh* rite. They are emerging from their seafaring state and preparing to become terrestrial creatures once more. The woman who was running after the captain is wearing a high-necked dress. The first-class waiters have made it clear that we are not welcome there. We listened to the news for the last time. Australia and New Zealand have declared war on Germany. Italy, Bulgaria, and Romania are neutral.

I couldn't sleep all night. It was hot. And I was itching with impatience.

I am returning to Aretz with mixed feelings. For many of the people, coming back to Aretz is like being immigrants all over again. They were afraid of being stuck in Europe for the duration of the war. And I want to go back to Poland. At times I think I would be more useful there than in Aretz.

I am returning to my home with the feeling of a man setting foot in a new land for the first time. Whatever happens will be unexpected. I don't know where I will be or what I will do. The business about the youth movement is uncertain. My gut feeling is that the whole thing is off. Yitzhak avoids the issue as if he had never raised it or sought a reply. Of course, I haven't mentioned it. It wouldn't do to be pushy.

The whole thing irritates me. I won't deny it.

I never had high ambitions. If they put me in charge of a team of mules I could be happy. But I can't stand being in favor one day and out of favor the next.

And the annoying thing about it is that I'll never know why. Nobody will ever tell me the reason.

Is it really because of you?

Alper says hello to me again. As if something was set straight and now he can speak.

Maybe it really is impossible to live "outside of history."

The bombs that fell on Warsaw fell between you and me. If ever we meet again, many years from now, you will not be you and I shall not be me.

Even now I feel that I am not the person I was. I'm suspicious, nervous, careful about what I say, sarcastic. I don't venture opinions. I shut myself off from my friends. I see enemies everywhere. People look at me, and I imagine they are hiding something they know from me.

A secret verdict has been passed against me, and I can't defend myself. My private life is not the movement's affair. But I know what Alper thinks: whoever has treason in his blood may commit an act of betrayal at any time.

The coast has come into sight now. The Carmel, the hills of Galilee. Purple. The distant mountains seem detached from their base. In the Golan the sky is turning red. It looks as if a city were going up in flames.

People are milling about on deck, excited. They are crowding toward the prow. Every man for himself, with his own feelings. Even Kuperberg has emerged from his customary serenity. "Come on," he said. "The words can wait. The picture will never repeat itself." I promised that I would come right away and stayed where I was.

A few words about the day that is upon us.

In a few hours I'll be home. Comrades will surround me with questions, and I will answer gladly. Even a little proudly. As if I had escaped from some real danger. Later we'll talk about the war. And I'll tell about how normal Warsaw seemed, when all the while a great danger hovered over her. And we'll all nod our heads. And we'll be glad that Italy is neutral. Afterward the comrades will leave and the tent flaps will come down.

I don't know if I'll have the strength. Has one the right to destroy when one cannot build? Has one the right to knock down a tent when the city is being laid waste? Will I be able to come to a tired woman and tell her I have been transfixed by a vision? Presence is a truth unto itself.

The war will teach us to be happy just to be alive.

Now we can see Haifa from up close.

In the cruel light of summer's end.

Here are the tugboats, the huge cranes.

And the market waking up to a life without dreams. On the wharf stands one lone man, waving his hat at a large ship. And in a little while we'll be getting off, each to go his separate way. Glad to be going home and not ashamed of being glad. And only I shall bear in my heart, like a searing wound, the agony of Warsaw. Because Warsaw is you.

A final blast. The clanking of chains. And time stands still. We have arrived. And now?

THE OTHER SIDE OF THE WALL

CHAPTER ONE

[1]

After supper she usually goes to the reading room. Occasionally, she returns to her own room. It's nice in the reading room. The Lux lantern spreads a soft white light. The chairs are comfortable and there is no noise. The members sit in silence and read. Few permit themselves to speak out loud. But even these are silenced by the dirty looks. Nobody scolds and nobody shushes. It's the sort of thing she likes.

This used to be the dining room. Now that the kibbutz is large and still growing, a new, more spacious bungalow has been put up. During the day it is a kitchen and dining room and in the evening it is a social hall. That is where the radio is, and many members get together there to listen to the news and to analyze the situation as reflected in the various war dispatches. In the reading room the books and periodicals and the record player are kept. But there is music only once a month. On all other days silence reigns.

The walls are covered with light wood panels and hanging on them are pictures by Masereel, Kaethe Kollwitz, Murillo, and Ephraim Moshinson, a member who committed suicide during the second year after the kibbutz settled its land.

All of eight years ago. Time flies.

She likes to read. Mainly belles lettres: poems, stories, and even plays. But these she reads in her own room. In the reading room she reads newspapers and looks through the movement monthly, which comes out about once every three months. Sometimes she takes a peek at *Window on the World* or *Our Way* or *Cooperative Farming*. She knows that if she tries to read movement literature in her room she'll fall asleep. The flickering light of the kerosene lamp makes her drowsy, and the pillow, too, is a great temptation.

Those who remain in the reading room until late do permit themselves to break the silence. Somebody says something in a whisper, and his neighbor answers just to be polite. Little by little a conversation evolves. Sometimes she joins in too.

She loves these nighttime discussions. But none ever ends in her room. She doesn't dare to invite anyone in. The person in question may not be serious enough. Once she became deeply engrossed in a conversation with one young man and, without realizing it, walked him back to his room. The minute the door was shut he started getting smart. Since then she's been careful.

When the talk turns to books she has a lot to say.

The members who stay latest in the reading room are the

ones who are closest to her. They are glad enough to talk with her in the reading room. But when they meet in the farmyard, coming from opposite directions along a narrow path, they rarely even stop to exchange greetings.

Her father says, "Books are our best friends. They give freely and ask little in return."

When she is last to leave the reading room she locks it and leaves the key in the customary place.

Sometimes Kuti, a member of the Palmah, is there to keep her company. He looks at books that he has brought along and takes notes in a thick high-school composition book. Kuti is preparing for the entrance exams to the Technion, even though he doesn't know when he'll be able to go to school, whether next year or ten years from now. At any rate not before the Allies beat the Germans. Although Kuti volunteered for the Palmah, he still intends to join the British army. He wants to fight the Germans in hand-to-hand combat. He told her that one night and then swore her to secrecy.

Sometimes she fancies that Kuti is secretly in love with her. But Kuti is an eighteen-year-old kid, and she is a woman of twenty-four. He only talks about mathematics and politics, and these are not of much interest to her. His father is a typesetter at the Ha-Poel Ha-Tzair Press and knows all the authors and poets personally. But the only things he can say about them is who drinks and who is paranoid, and that's boring, too.

She loves the reading room as if it were her own room. When she turns out the light at night there is a twinge in her heart. For a few hours she was sitting there, yet she read no more than a few pages. What did she learn? What kind of knowledge did she acquire? The days stand still; the years rush by.

She spends hour after hour in the reading room, but that does not mean that she dislikes her own room. On the contrary. She loves it with all her heart, even though it is cold in the winter and sweltering in the summer and the roof leaks and the walls are cracked and the partition between one room and the next is a thin wood panel and one faucet serves her and her neighbors and the basin is broken and the stairs are rickety and there's nowhere to hang work clothes outside. One mustn't complain. Not even a year has passed since she joined the kibbutz and already she has a room to herself. The men live two by two.

In her room she has everything she needs: a bed, a chair, a wardrobe closet, a bookcase, and a table. But not all of these are actually worthy of their names. Her bed is a folding army cot and the mattress is filled with straw and gets all out of shape whenever she turns over at night. The chair is an oil can and the wardrobe closet is made of three Tnuva Export orange crates joined by a thin strip of wood. The bookcase is an unplaned board resting on two cinder blocks. But the table is a real table. True, it's a little wobbly and whenever she writes the flame dances in the lantern, but her needs are simple, or so she would like them to be. "This is how I am: still like the waters of a lake, loving the tranquillity of the everyday, the eyes of babes . . ." Who is Francis Jammes? Nonessential possessions, after all, make slaves of their owners. Even books. There is a library, and there you can get all the books you want. In her room all she needs are a few favorite books of poetry and some novels that she likes to go back to from time to time. *The Enchanted Soul, Ingeborg, By the Road,* and others. It doesn't bother her a bit that she has a poor, dreary room. Whatever there is of beauty in it she has made with her own hands: the tablecloth, the checkered pillow on the chair, the pretty patchwork coverings on the bed and the wardrobe, and the humorous appliqués on the dull burlap curtain.

If she had been endowed with a talent for self-expression she might have written an ode to possessions. Beloved possessions as well as despised ones. She will never have the nerve to write a poem in the startling, flashy rhymes that are so much in vogue nowadays. If it were still possible to write simple, melancholy poems like Rachel used to write, then she might write a poem. If. For herself, her diary is enough. One of the first pages is devoted to her room. I am surrounded by grateful furniture, it says there. Before I gathered them into my room, these were just unwanted, cast-off objects. Now they form a cozy home.

Her parents' home is mentioned, too. A house full of self-important furniture. Somber objects implying grave prohibitions, an accusing finger.

Her mother would say, "We didn't just find them on the market. We paid top price for them. An arm and a leg." She hates the words "an arm and a leg." She hates dramatic gestures. Arms and legs are for more important matters than joyless furniture, heavy with foreboding. It is the cruel symbol of bitter victories won in a frantic struggle for survival, she wrote, but she wasn't certain she hadn't copied it from something she had once learned by heart.

I want to work out of a sense of joy and not to accumulate anything, it says further. "Thine am I, forbearing, wholesome poverty!"

[2]

The diary is a thick leather-bound notebook, embossed with fleurs-de-lis. The paper is stiff and smooth and the pen makes deep furrows in it, like a delicate Chinese drawing. The writing is a secret passion. Nobody knows about it. Not even a close friend.

There is no close friend. Only the friends she makes at work, and they change from day to day. These rarely come to her room. It is an arrangement not without its advantages. Nobody will just drop in on her to discover that she is keeping a diary.

Around here they don't like emotional, dreamy, hypersensitive girls who carry on dialogues with themselves in writing. Just the opposite. Admiration goes to those girls who can work on a tractor or in the machine shop, who can listen to a dirty joke and respond with boisterous laughter. Love is reserved for those bosomy girls who are ready to take on all comers. And for the pretty ones, of course. Like everywhere else. Many girls smoke cigarettes, speak with a shrill voice, and spit the words out with a sort of haughtiness. But one must not be finicky, it says in her diary. Wherever I go I carry with me my parents' house, which I left as the result of a deliberate decision.

Sometimes she quarrels with her parents in the diary. It is easy to argue with her father, because he expresses opinions you can disagree with. It is harder to take issue with her mother's painful barbs. What kind of answer can you give to a person who says, "Only a pretty girl can afford to dress so carelessly"?

Every night before she goes to sleep she gets the diary out from under the straw mattress and looks at it. She hasn't always something to write. Things that were important during the day suddenly become unimportant in the profound silence, in the light of the dancing flame. Sometimes she regrets what she has written the previous night. Petty insults that deserve to be forgotten assume gigantic proportions when they are written down, black on white, in a leatherbound diary deeply embossed with dark fleurs-de-lis. But she never erases anything. The day's pain slowly ripens in the diary at night. Insulting jokes, bits of nonsense, a painful lack of attention, the glassy-eyed stares that wipe out her existence. They are all there. On the lines and in between the lines. Later on she will read and realize how vulnerable and petty she has allowed herself to be.

I am constructing a girl that I can love and admire, and finally I will become she, it says on page three in rounded, undulating letters, written slowly and carefully.

When there is nothing to write she draws straight, even letters: Sunday . . . th day of Elul, 5702—nothing to report.

And then she copies onto the empty pages verses of a poem that was printed in the literary supplement, like:

And your poor hovel so dark in the night,
The sadness there too deep to plumb.

Her father says that modern poetry is nothing but an empty game. He admires Bialik, Shneour, and Tchernichowsky. He says, "I do not understand the meaning of 'My life, undone before it reached your sight,/Delivered to the outer reaches and the drum.' "What is 'drum' doing there? Is it there just because it rhymes with 'plumb'?"

Before getting into bed she likes to stand in the window and look at the tall shadows of the cypress trees at the edge of the orange grove. Dull black on silvery black. The curtain, fluttering in the breeze, caresses her arm and her shoulder. Deep silence envelops her and the orange grove opposite. Only the wind can be heard in the trees and the distant pulsating of the generator. At this time of night it seems to be asking for something in vain. Sometimes, when the wind is particularly strong, you can hear a sort of rumbling or surging of waves. This is the sound of the British army trucks making their way south on the road at the other end of the orange grove. And then she prays that the battle for the western desert may end in victory. A lecture by one of the Haganah commanders caused her some concern. Can it really be that they will hide on the Carmel? And what will happen to her parents? Where will they go? Afterward, she blows out the thin flame of the kerosene lamp and stands for a moment in the absolute darkness, which fills with voices becoming clear and fading away, and then she pushes herself under the itchy blanket and waits for sleep. Two sheets per person are a luxury in the opinion of the woman in charge of the clothing supply stores, but she is not going to complain about such trivialities, which purify the soul anyway. The delicate shadow of a casuarina tree flutters across the curtain just as she shuts her eyes.

Sometimes painful verses of poems that she likes stick in her mind.

This is the hour for my door to shut,
And it will not open before the morrow.

Or something even more wrenching:

To fix in the darkness imploring eyes,
To spread the hands of yearning out into space,
To tilt an ear to the sound of rustling leaves,
And pray for a miracle, and hope for a sign—

She shoves them out of her mind and tries to think about something else, but they return with even greater intensity. She tries to direct her attention to current matters and in silence plans her activities for the following day, but the verses keep coming back. Tomorrow will be like today, she knows. Urgent activity imposes its own pace, its own value on time. And in every humdrum affair lies the expectancy of the unexpected, which probably won't materialize tomorrow either. Isn't this the best of all possible lives? People who are content with their lot want tomorrow to be just like today. They want no changes in the routine upon which their happiness is based. And she? Could it be that she seeks the unattainable?

Here is all the goodness of the Earth,
And only you can fail to see its worth.

Tomorrow she will work in the kitchen. Or the truck garden. Or the laundry. Everything will be simple and clear. She is needed, and her work is vital. Pity the person who lives in idle expectation of tidings, good or bad.

At times her thoughts turn to her parents. Their house, isolated at the edge of the village, its blinds always drawn, seems even emptier at this time of night. Maybe her parents are talking about her. Worried. Is she happy? Is she sure that she has made the right choice?

If she had let life take its course she wouldn't have had to resort to manual labor for her living. She could have learned a respectable profession or even have been a lady of leisure. Along the well-trodden path. But her character is her destiny. The means at her disposal would have determined the sphere of activity. And also the cold, sober reckoning of a wise mother doing her job, who is completely unruffled when charged with the sin of selling out to petit bourgeois values.

She is able to fling at her mother the very same words that, spoken at a blazing campfire of the kibbutz, take off like flying missiles. Her mother brushes them aside like pesky flies. Her sharp eyes, which love her with open hostility, give away their shameful secret: big words, but with bitter melancholy covering them over like a dark veil.

She used to be proud of the fact that she came to the kibbutz through the strength of her own decision and nothing else. Without the youth movement, without the training camp, without close friends. A fascinating stranger, that's how she wanted to be. A strange girl, unfamiliar with the others' way of life, which is a sort of continuation of the youth movement style. But before much time had elapsed she learned to conceal her pride and even to be ashamed of it. And has she any right to feel superior to the others just because her choice of a life of labor involved giving up more? If all the trappings of life that she is teaching herself to do without constitute a loss, then what spiritual gain has she achieved by being here? And if she is not here for spiritual gain what is she doing here?

In childhood she pictured herself strutting across an elevated stage in silks and laces with the upswept hairdo of a princess. Today she is teaching herself to be happy when the kitchen is clean, and there is somebody to see and acknowledge the fact.

[3]

Whoever takes the trouble to come up really close can feel her warmth. She is neither fanatic nor ascetic. All she lacks is friendship.

She recalls with affection a friend of her youth, a broad-bottomed girl with a strong and beautiful face. In the past—she can now say ten years ago and remember a girl she parted from in childhood—she would share wild ideas with her, fierce, uncompromising opinions, and the kind of friendship that involves painful revelations, cruel honesty, and absolute fidelity. Both despised their lot in life; both were better off than their comrades and chose to become proletarians. The word enchanted them with its menacing foreignness and a universality that smacked of far-off metropolises. They would listen to music in the bachelor quarters of an educated laborer, many years their senior, who walked around day and night in whitewash-spattered work clothes. One day they found out he was a paid organizer for the Communist party. When he tried to set them up as the center of a cell, whose purpose was not at all clear to them, they cut off all contact with him. Her friend got married to an Englishman and left the country, and she went back to her old love—kibbutz people, who were not really proletarians, but who used to come in white shirts to the cultural evenings arranged by the Workers' Council and could listen to a lecture on a literary topic after a day of back-breaking labor in her father's orange grove.

And now she is here. Lectures on literary topics are few and far between, and friendship isn't what it used to be. As long as she was the class enemy they courted her. Now that she is here, and they do not have to win her over, they no longer spread their tail feathers. On the contrary, they seem to take pride in a sort of bleak hardheadedness, a cold honesty devoid of even the basic courtesies. As if to say that once a person stands with both feet in our camp there is no more room for that sense of "mission." There seems to be a kind of masquerade. If you speak without thinking you are above suspicion of false piety; if you fail to notice your neighbor's distress you are certainly without ulterior motives.

The old-timers are friends among themselves. There is in their friendship something of a striving to preserve their uniqueness. Pioneers, forerunners, trailblazers. They founded a movement, said we put deeds before words, and did put their deeds before their words. The others are nothing but followers. And whoever comes along singly has to make the best of things. Let him not think too highly of himself until he has reached the position of those worn out with fatigue.

That doesn't mean that they have become alienated from one another. Perish the thought. There is the collegiality of those who practice the same trade, and the friendship for a person who shares a tough job with you and is reliable, and the closeness of parents who all come to put their children to sleep at the same time in the same place and who sing with one another at holidays and birthdays in the kindergarten. And relations between neighbors. But not even being a neighbor is permanent.

During her first days she lived in a tent, and the tent

dwellers were her neighbors and friends. And one stormy
night, when the tempest knocked down the tents with the
people inside, for a few moments they truly shared a bond.
Now that she lives in a bungalow, the bungalow dwellers
are supposed to become her friends. But it's just her luck
that she lives in a bungalow with very few neighbors. The
room to the south is the infirmary for the Palmah people,
who live in tents, but they go home when they are ill. The
only people ever to be found in that room are those stricken
with something really serious who are on the way to the
hospital. And these aren't people to talk to. In the next room
lives Meir Avrahami, who works at movement headquarters.
In the fourth room, to the north of hers, live Raheli and Big
Yitzhak. Big Yitzhak got that title because there is another
Yitzhak, smaller than he, who is not part of the original
group, all of whom have their own particular place and
designation. But Big Yitzhak is also away a great deal. A few
months ago he enlisted in the British army. His leaves are
few and far between and even these are for purposes that are
not disclosed.

Big Yitzhak's absences don't bother her a bit. Just the
opposite. But it isn't nice to be glad that Raheli her neighbor, who not long ago got married to Big Yitzhak in a
modest but impressive ceremony at the foot of Mount
Masada, sleeps alone. She does not begrudge her friend her
happiness. It is just that whatever Big Yitzhak does he does
out loud. And when he is home he has no consideration for
her feelings.

A thin plywood partition separates one room from the
next. And anybody with a sense of modesty realizes that there
is no alternative but to live life in a whisper, even though
there are some sounds that cannot be held back. But Big
Yitzhak's delicacy wouldn't even cover the head of a pin. All
his carryings-on with his dearly beloved are broadcast loud

and clear. The blanket she puts over her head in order not to hear is permeated with the odor of dust. But not even the fits of coughing that this provokes are sufficient to arouse in Big Yitzhak a sense of decency.

At these moments she hates her room. Her modest room fills up with wild guesses and indecent lovemaking. Sometimes this state of affairs suits her until it hurts. Everything is temporary. The Palmah is a provisory thing. In half a year, they say, everyone will go home. Meir Avrahami will work in the movement until the time comes for him to be replaced. Not even Big Yitzhak's military service is for very long, and the same applies to Raheli's status as a grass widow. She may even hope that her own loneliness is only transitory. A life of makeshift permits you to skirt the deeper questions. Once the war is over they will be able to put things into permanent shape. After the war it may not be necessary to keep such a stiff upper lip. Maybe then her sensitivity, her generosity, the great power to love welling up inside her will be noticed. Almost every morning she meets Raheli her neighbor on the steps of the bungalow, while they both put on their work shoes. On rare occasions they speak to one another. Raheli likes company, but only in the midst of great commotion. In her room she prefers to remain alone.

They hardly ever drop into one another's rooms. To borrow something, occasionally. But not even then do they actually go inside. They just stand at the door apologizing for having put the other to so much trouble. This kind of delicacy suits her, but there are times when she regrets it. Sometimes she feels like gabbing, but Raheli is not talkative. She only knows how to laugh, out loud, a little coarsely. Once, when she explained a rather obscure poem printed in the literary supplement of *Davar* to Raheli, Raheli nearly died laughing. "Where do you get all of that from?" But she did not take offense. There wasn't the slightest hint of malice in Raheli's laughter. On the contrary, her eyes betrayed a certain cautious respect.

She would like to tear down the invisible wall between herself and Raheli, for she respects in Raheli her ability to bear life's bumps with equanimity, a quality she would love to be able to adopt as her own. Her spouse comes and goes, and she never has a word of complaint. Perhaps because the things that take Big Yitzhak from her are more important to her than her own ennui and perhaps because she knows better than to bemoan her loneliness to someone who has nobody at all to wait for through the long winter nights. Raheli just doesn't seem to need anybody to pour out her heart to. Maybe it is because all the others are ready to unburden themselves to her that she is relieved of the need for a close friend. How many secrets are guarded by a beautiful woman! Hot coals that burn anyone else are like icy gems in Raheli's care, undisturbed by the human hand. How many desperate confessions were spilled out before her, without even having a beneficial effect on Raheli's limited vocabulary.

She is so beautiful, Raheli, that you can't really be jealous of her. Three days of sunshine and she is tanned the color of a ripe date, encased as it were in a clinging garment that caresses the round breasts, the narrow hips, the long, slender legs. The repertoire of local folklore places her in a tale about a poet who was much taken with her appearance. "I know that girl from somewhere," said the man, who had a reputation for his bons mots that he liked to live up to. "Oh yes," he said, as if suddenly reminded, "from the Song of Songs."

An amused, bewildered smile regularly hovers about Raheli's face when she speaks to the young men, as if she knows that somebody is about to say something stupid that her silence cannot forestall. Sometimes she reveals the kind of acute perception that is unusual in a person who does not require such finely calibrated tools for survival. She keeps a special smile for Meir Avrahami, who greets her with the angry mien of a man possessed, as if her open blouse and shorts might cause him to deviate from the party line. But nothing is said. Communication takes place in a flash of recognition through a corner of the eye. Raheli seems to accept the unwanted proximity imposed on them by the common wall, in itself a temporary thing, and to let it go at that. And, actually, nothing more is needed. For everything ripens in the silence of the deep. Nothing can be forced. Not even friendship. What does not happen by itself is not worthy. Still, she is sorry that she cannot knock on Raheli's door, cannot go in without waiting for an answer, and without beating about the bush cannot launch into a story about something that has happened to her. Until something does happen and the barrier falls. Like something that has collapsed. Not like something that has been torn down deliberately.

[4]

One morning, as they sit next to one another, their heads bent over their shoes, she notices a question forming at the end of a tentative glance from Raheli. She peers into her neighbor's face, who turns her eyes away. If she knew what Raheli was asking she might be able to answer. But there is no point in trying to find out. For Raheli wouldn't share so much as a fraction of a penny's worth of her thoughts with a stranger. She goes over last night's events and is unable to discover anything. Things went on as they do every other evening. Although it did surprise her that Big Yitzhak, who only last night returned to camp after an extended leave, was already back for a quick "after duty." It also seemed strange to her that he wasn't loud as he usually is, but that he took off his shoes before going into the room, as if he were suddenly afraid of waking her. And one more thing. Even though it isn't nice to spell it out. He was away from home for one day and already had the appetite of a man who is breaking a long fast.

As she recalls Big Yitzhak's good manners of the night before she smiles. But Raheli does not return the smile. Raheli's face is pale and tense, and only her eyes flash a kind of obscure apprehension. She is offended. She doesn't deserve to have a door slammed in her face as if she had tried to burrow into her neighbor's affairs. But after mulling it over all day—four-eighths of a day in the laundry and four-eighths in the kitchen—she concludes that she must have made the whole thing up. Raheli wasn't tense and wasn't pale and certainly hadn't tried to put her in her place. Raheli hadn't smiled because she was just too tired to smile. Many people need time before they are fully awake.

But that very evening she has to put another interpretation onto what happened. After supper she stays on in the dining hall and listens to the news and to Meir Avrahami's analysis near a map of the Middle East, which hangs next to the work schedule.

Tobruk has fallen to the Germans, and everybody is discussing this heatedly. The gloomy predictions of the Haganah man are coming true and who knows what will happen from one day to the next? It may really become necessary to leave everything and hide out in the woods on Mount Carmel. Of its own accord an unscheduled town meeting is forming, and the secretary is saying that the kibbutz ought to put itself on an emergency footing as these troubled times require. But when he is asked to be more specific it all boils down to more patient compliance with the work schedule, canceling leaves, and strengthening the security committee. In the end they decide to wait for Big Yitzhak to hear what he has to say. "A pity," she says to whoever is sitting near her, "only yesterday Big Yitzhak was home." But her neighbor replies, "Not yesterday, the day before," and she doesn't bother to correct him, because she doesn't like to argue. She knows he is wrong. But it bothers her. Later on she lingers at the dining-hall entrance and listens to the story of one member who just got back from Egypt a few days ago. He speaks of the panic that befell the British and of the consultations that the Jewish soldiers held among themselves. By the time she gets to her room it is very late. She is confused, for time and time again she has resolved to enlist in the British women's army corps and then relented at the last minute. It is a hundred and fifty paces from the dining hall to her bungalow, yet that stretch of road is enough for some thorough soul-searching. First, they won't let her enlist, because there is a quota and she is not that firmly rooted in the life of the kibbutz that they would let her serve as their representative; and second, she would be of no use, since she would never have the nerve to drive a car or to go about all alone in a foreign city where she doesn't speak the language.

All at once she starts and feels gooseflesh at her neck. She notices a figure poised at the edge of the orange grove near the break in the fence. The light of a distant lantern filters through the avenue of cypress and lights the lower portion of the figure's body. A man in heavy work shoes, standing still, as if waiting in ambush. She takes longer steps without actually quickening her pace, the way you would with a ferocious dog. If he doesn't sense her fear maybe he won't want to harm her. Only from the safe distance of the bunga-low does she turn her head. The figure does not move, as if nailed to the spot. There is light coming from Raheli's win-dow, and, even though it goes out just as she is beginning to quicken her steps along the concrete path leading to their rooms, she lets herself knock at Raheli's door. She puts a hesitant finger out toward her neighbor's door and taps very lightly. If Raheli doesn't feel like getting out of bed she may believe that it was nothing but the nighttime creaking of an old bungalow. But the door opens at once, as if Raheli has been standing behind it. "You!" says Raheli coldly. Her eyes flash in the dark and they reflect a strange sort of trepidation.

"Did you see it too?" she asks.

"See what?" asks Raheli in an irritated voice.

Raheli's face freezes as she tells her what she has seen.

"It must have been the night watchman," says Raheli, without curiosity.

"Then why does he stand there in such a menacing way?" she says, unconvinced.

Raheli's body still exudes an odor of toilet soap. She is jealous of her calm and of her courage. Only for an instant did Raheli's face betray fear, when she knocked at the door in the middle of the night.

The night watchman does not hide from another member of the kibbutz who crosses his path, she reflects. On the contrary, the monotony makes them talkative and friendly. But she does not contradict her neighbor. She would love to go into Raheli's room and let a little of the quiet self-assuredness rub off on her. Once reassured that that man is not up to something she would go to her own room. But the door to Raheli's room is open only a crack, and Raheli's face is buttoned up tight. For a long moment she stands before her neighbor with one foot on the bottom step and the other on the step above, until she notices the impatience in Raheli's face, who wants to shut the door.

"Tobruk has fallen," she says, to cover up for the too-long interval.

Raheli's face expresses nothing. She draws one foot back and inclines her head as if preparing to say good-night, the way a person would who does not get excited over an event that was expected at any moment, a woman of valor.

"Well, good-night," says Raheli.

"Some of our people are there too," she says. The impatience in Raheli's face is positively offensive.

"Good-night," she says, and is hurt that the door shuts so quickly.

She goes back to her own room but cannot find the matches. She wonders about asking Raheli for some, but decides against it. Raheli will think it only a pretext for bothering her with her fears, her loneliness, and her disillusionment. She undresses in the dark and gets into bed.

Her thoughts turn to the diary. Lies and nothing more. Vain exercises in the pretty, the acceptable kinds of melancholy; poeticizing, without any of the imagined, hysterical pain that stinks like a moldy straw mattress.

She forces her eyes shut and prays for the onset of sleep that it may deliver her from these unwelcome thoughts. But at the very moment that slumber hovers over her eyelids she hears the disturbance.

At first a sort of grating sound that becomes intelligible as feet on the stair. She holds her breath. She is not afraid. Her door is bolted shut and nobody can get in. Then she hears the latch in Raheli's door, which turns on its hinges very cautiously. And right after that a hurried whisper and the floor's suffering response to bare feet. And a kind of sigh of resignation, and afterward a dull thumping and a frantic whisper, like crying.

She focuses all her senses on listening. And with her heart pounding, tries to interpret every sound. Gradually things begin to fall into place: the figure at the edge of the grove, the light that suddenly went out, the door that opened so quickly, Raheli's disappointment and impatience, and even her questioning, worried look yesterday morning. That night it had not been Big Yitzhak either. Whoever it was that said Big Yitzhak hadn't been home the night before was right. And she congratulated herself on being above arguing with people who feel they always have to be right.

A sigh escapes her as she hears the steady noise. Suddenly there is silence in the next room. She feels sorry about the anxiety she has caused Raheli and her lover. She pictures them to herself naked, panic-stricken, clinging to one another without moving, like terrified animals caught in a beam of light. For a long time she breathes through her wide-open mouth to keep her excited breathing inaudible. A sharp pain takes hold of her jaws. She loses track of time. She seems to be like that for hours, like a dying person, with halting breath. Finally, a faint whisper is heard in the next room. This time she can make out the words. A man's whisper, "These rooms are like echo chambers." And Raheli's voice, "Sometimes she sighs in her sleep."

And then the same sounds all over again, but restrained, without the spontaneity they had earlier. As if they were slowly subsiding. She is sorry to be involved. She permits herself to breathe deeply whenever she hears a faint sound. Bare footsteps, the cautious tread of a heavy shoe, the latch, the hinges. Silence. The man is probably facing the slightly open door and surveying the path of his retreat from the bungalow to the avenue of cypress. Then she hears his feet tramping down the squeaky wooden stairs. She takes credit for not giving in to her curiosity and going over to the window. Sooner or later, she thinks, she will know. She only regrets that her restraint will never be acknowledged and that Raheli will not know how much she ought to respect her. From her face she won't learn a thing. Tomorrow she will be unable to look her in the eye.

[5]

The business of the night fades like a ghost at the ringing of the work bell. Not even the worst insomnia is an excuse for staying away from work. Daylight calls for cleansing the mind of all personal thoughts. The light of the morning is cruel, cold, demanding and indifferent.

They are both on the stairs. Brisk, businesslike, hurrying. Soon the wagon leaves for the vegetable garden, and they mustn't miss it. Raheli steals glances at her. She turns her head as if her mind is on something else. She senses that her face is pale and drawn. She is glad that this time Meir Avrahami is home too—and he is standing on his doorstep furiously brushing his teeth. As if hypnotized she looks at his hand, moving back and forth with raging speed and at the white foam that frames his lips and spills down his chin until he spits it into the basin with revulsion.

He is an irascible man, this Meir Avrahami, and he wears a serious expression at all times. He is close to the movement leadership and probably knows things that others shouldn't know, and this knowledge weighs on him. Night after night he sits up with his books and his articles until very late, and mornings he is always tired and irritable. Something has been left unsaid. Something is still unclear. Even though he doesn't respond to her good-morning, she is glad that he is there. This way she does not have to look Raheli in the eye, and she has time to pull herself together, so that the signs of the previous night are no longer visible. But the honking of a bus horn pulls Meir Avrahami up short. He wipes a wet hand over his hair, grabs his briefcase, and runs. Even though the driver is a member of the kibbutz and would wait for him, only last night in the dining hall in front of everybody he was bragging about his punctuality.

Once Meir Avrahami has left she goes about her preparations ponderously, and with trembling fingers undoes a knot that is not even tangled. Perhaps, if Raheli's door were open to her more than just a crack, she might have been able to speak openly with her and even to tell her that she does not condemn her.

Man to man, naked we remain.
Let us learn to forgive the one who has sinned.
Let us remember to forget
The moment of weakness of a comrade who has sinned.

Even a week of weakness. Even a month. A year. She does not judge anybody. She does not yet know what vice lies in her own heart. I abhor piety—and false piety as well. And the counterfeit virtue of the deprived and the wretched.

But Raheli's door is closed to her, and any chance of talk is doomed. She cannot even tell her that she doesn't mind if Big Yitzhak is hurt. She thinks of him with revulsion—a coarse loudmouth who gets everything his way. A greedy person who preaches to others to make do with less and who even treats his wife like a piece of property. With head erect, he walks alongside her, like a proud owner. He digs his fat, strong fingers into her shapely buttocks as he looks from one to another of his fellows with a sort of mockery that is not entirely free of malice. And he is always ready with some clumsy, witless joke. And whenever he has to listen to someone else there is a deprecating, self-satisfied smirk frozen onto his lips that becomes all the more evident when he disagrees with the speaker. He has a beautiful wife, and that gives him the right to insult girls who are homely. He undresses them with his sharp eagle's eye and stares in pleasurable revulsion at their miserable nudity. It is his way of getting even.

The silence weighs heavily upon her, but she is at a loss for something to say. Finally she gets up her courage, turns to Raheli with a tormented smile, and, in a cracked voice, drained of emotion, says, "Good-morning." "Great," says Raheli, and the forced breeziness of her voice makes it strange and harsh, quavering slightly. "I was beginning to think that we don't say good-morning anymore."

"It's because of Meir Avrahami," she says. "I didn't want to upset him."

The curious expression on Raheli's face puts her at ease.

"Why is it that saying good-morning to him is like stepping on his toes? His head is so crammed full of important things that our good-morning only disturbs him."

The long sentence embarrasses her, but Raheli laughs. "That's beautiful, the way you said that," says Raheli in admiration.

A light blush covers her face, but Raheli cannot see it, because she suddenly gets up and rushes to the dining hall with a childish, thoroughly captivating bounce. Something clean, pure, carefree is called to mind by Raheli's light step. Something freshly washed. Straightforwardness personified. Her perfectly formed buttocks, the slender legs, the winsome naiveté of the braid swinging from shoulder to shoulder. As if she had left the weight of her sin behind in her room and had taken flight. And now she has no choice but to bend down, to shoulder the burden, and to bear it in silence. The small joke made at Meir Avrahami's expense has determined her mission. Raheli is certain that the flimsy wooden walls protect her happiness.

[6]

In the morning, when she is not working in the fields and there is time, she goes into the empty shower house and looks at herself in the mirror. This is a kind of trial, a test of her courage. In the kerchief that covers her hair her face is coarse and her eyes sad, and this brings her to the verge of tears. The shower house is empty at such times. But just to play it safe she lets the water run. If anyone should happen to come in she will pretend that she has come to wash her face.

The face she sees in the cloudy mirror is both familiar and strange. A large, broad face. Soft, pouchy cheeks. An old woman's cheeks. A tense grimace at the corners of the mouth. But it may be that that exists only when she is looking at herself. The lips are thin and cracked. The chin is round, with a hint of a double chin. She loosens the knot in her kerchief and shakes out her hair with quick motions. But the limp hair clings to her head. She runs her fingers through it, but the hair doesn't fluff out. She ought to shampoo it more often, she thinks. But she doesn't like the shampoo that the kibbutz provides, and the kind she brings from her parents' house is expensive and hard to get, and she is ashamed of using it in the shower house unless everyone has gone, and by then the water is usually tepid or cold.

Under her clothes matters are even worse. Better not to be reminded. The breasts are small and pointed, the hips fleshy. The belly is soft and quivery. The buttocks are heavy and seem to be knit of bulky wool.

She sticks her tongue out at the face in the mirror. The sad, beautiful eyes awaken like two alert creatures with life of their own.

Some are uglier than you, but nobody is ugly in precisely the way you are, says she, murdering the words of a popular song. The thought brings a smile to her face, which suddenly seems to light up.

Maybe I'll forgive him,
Wipe the slate clean,
And start all over again.

She used to listen to her mother's advice. Good looks are not everything. Certain improvements are possible. The freshness of youth imparts a charm all its own. Her mother's remarks used to make her angry. Occasionally she would reply, but her mother's remarks always led back to the ache that instigated them. Facing the cloudy mirror in the empty shower house they cluster about her like a swarm of annoying flies.

She ponders the petit bourgeois oversimplifications that she is trying to shake off. Petty, cruel, embittered notions, always lying in wait for the pitiful moments of weakness, when she lets down the defenses that protect her from jealousy, self-pity, worry about the morrow, miserable fear for her own existence, and yearning for recognition. Even when she was young she had determined to conquer jealousy. With gritted teeth and compressed lips, never to give in to the bitter emotion. The Lord was not merciful—may His name not be blessed. Sometimes she secretly listened in on her parents' conversations. They were full of concern for her future. Her mother's words were harsh, frightening in their bluntness. Fear of an unsuitable marriage. "As long as they are on the kibbutz he can be a pioneer and what not, but on the outside he will only be what he is and not a whit more." "Free love is idealistic schmaltz that covers up for base lust." And other painful talk of similar nature. Her mother scolds her father. Why doesn't he do something? The silent despair in her father's face hurts much more. Her father's words are few and far between, and they emerge in an apologetic whisper. The same fear for her future. But expressed politely. He is afraid that her scrupulous honesty and broad-mindedness, "borrowed from foreign literature in translation," and her naive idealism that takes things at face value and demands an immediate personal commitment, and also her love of poetry and of emotional memoirs of "all sorts of writers who have emancipated themselves from the rules of original Hebrew syntax," that all these stem from the very same ache.

[7]

In the dining hall she scrutinizes the young men as they gather and tries to guess which of them was in Raheli's room last night. But she cannot guess. Many have tired, red eyes. Last night a few were mobilized for a secret patrol and didn't get back until dawn. And now they are standing in front of the work schedule, as usual. One, who has a secret glint in his eye, is ruled out because he isn't the type. Another—because his wife is with him, in work clothes stained with whitewash, clinging to him. And not even the whitewash can cover up her memory of the night before.

She goes to work in the clothing supply room with raised spirits, as if in possession of a secret treasure. What she knows others cannot even guess at. The other women, engrossed in stale gossip, are beating dead horses, things whose time is past, the same old stories. Her silence flushes her with a sense of superiority. She is overcome by a quiet, profound, secret, hazily defined pleasure. She will never be tempted to surrender Raheli's secret to the others. Not even though that would make her the focus of attention for a few moments.

Raheli's face is nothing but pleasantness, sweetness, and readiness to be everybody's darling. She enters the dining hall at breakfast time like a babe fresh out of the bath. A tawny rosiness envelops her like impregnable armor. There is no sign. No trace. No hint. As if nothing had happened. If she is at all worried she certainly hides it well.

Raheli smiles at her with a nod and comes to sit by her. She makes small talk. The faucet near their rooms is dripping. Will she be able to get the plumbers? If they see fit to come, she says. Somebody else complains. They are in demand, so they make themselves scarce. Somebody else says, "If Raheli calls they'll come running." Raheli laughs as if she were not the subject of these remarks.

There is never a free spot next to Raheli. Even if the table is dirty, someone comes along and sits down. The young men like to make wisecracks. She always listens and never tries to match wits with them. Only a quiet smile steals across her face. As if she knows that all the words are only messengers. Firmly but politely she sends them back empty-handed.

Somebody notices Raheli's pallor. Raheli smiles and remains silent. She is impelled to cover up for her, "Oh, but she isn't a bit pale." They make a joke at her expense, too. "You're just color-blind." What does she care? At least she isn't being left out of everything. She is part of something vital, and her connection to Raheli is not being questioned.

Somebody once again mentions the fall of Tobruk. They ask about Big Yitzhak and Raheli replies pleasantly that she doesn't know. You never can tell. Her voice suggests a yearning that is held under control, as is to be expected. If there is a correct way for these things to sound you can hear it in Raheli's voice: yearning, but not more than a woman of valor is allowed to show, nor less than a loving wife ought to.

Raheli's face does not give the lie to her words. Not even for an instant is there a shade of evasiveness in her expression. "He who conceals his wit is wiser than he who flaunts it. For the first it is a useful instrument; for the second, merely an ornament," her father used to say. Perhaps Raheli is wise. Whenever she does say something it is in Big Yitzhak's name. "There are hard times ahead, but one must not give up hope." And her words have a tranquilizing effect. She is close to the One Who Knows.

The need to put up a front is no problem. She is in the service of a cause. She smiles to herself. Raheli loves—and she lies to cover up for her. Her own love will be a thing of absolute honesty, she solemnly promises herself. She could never lie without showing it. She can only do it for someone else. In the brazen way she used to lie to the English policemen.

It is only with her diary that she discusses things openly. But with caution. One day the diary may fall into the hands of a stranger. Much later, when the whole thing is over and done with, and then it will come back to haunt them from the pages of her diary and mess up Raheli's life. Therefore she writes in the first person. As if it had to do with her. Into her room there steals a nameless man. On her doorstep he quietly takes off his shoes. He tiptoes over to her bed and, with a courage born of desperation, launches upon a dangerous adventure.

Once in her room he casts his lot with the god of fools, the patron of lovers, in touching supplication that the wall may absorb the sound, that the boards not lose their self-control, that the feverish panting be swallowed up, that the neighbors not listen and not talk, that morning may come without disaster, that a friend's face bear neither reproach nor witness, that life may go on as before. And tonight he will come again in secret, by the same hidden path, from the orange grove to the avenue of cypress, with the springy step of a panther, carefully, in order not to land on the treacherous gravel path, and he will dare to make his way into her room, with pounding heart, with flowing myrrh upon the handles of the bar, and none standing behind the wall, looking in through the windows, peering through the lattice.

It is all written in paraphrase and parable, with a sprinkling of facts, in the first person, and if anyone should happen to read it it wouldn't make any sense. Certainly there would be no trace of Raheli or of her nameless lover. A fertile imagination, the reader would say, without compassion. The vain meanderings of a girl who hasn't anybody to keep her warm in bed. But, of course, nobody will read it.

The following night he fails to come. She listens with

bated breath. Not a sound. On the night after that she puts her light out early. For a long time she lies on her bed without moving. As if engaged in a dumb ritual to placate the spirits. Her efforts are rewarded. Seemingly by dint of the tension and the stillness she has forced upon her limbs, he appears out of the dark. First an airy stirring, as of a ghost, and then the sound of footsteps, an incarnation. And the handles of the bar and myrrh flowing and the joyous rust and the lustful groans of the wooden floor and the innocent whisper coming through the flimsy wall, which resonates like a violin.

[8]

The darkened window summons, and he comes. As if risen from out of her imaginings. She knows of his coming and of his going, and that is all. She will not look out the window or peer through the cracks. Lest he melt away and disappear beneath her gaze. He is the man without a name. He is a lover and nothing more.

Behind her wall the smell of his countenance is like apples. Thy name is as ointment poured forth. One day she cannot take it anymore. She puts out the kerosene lamp and, with fluttering heart, takes up a position behind the curtain. Her fingers pick at the coarse jute while her eyes are fixed on the orange grove.

But something else happens that night. There is unusual activity in the orange grove. Figures come and go with rapid steps. The night watchman is positioned at the break in the fence, and his gun is at the ready. Two others stand by the gravel path. A pickup is driving along the dirt road with its lights out. From the side of the packing house comes the thud of pickaxes. The floodlights along the fence are out. Nevertheless, she can make out the gigantic figure of Big

Yitzhak, with a flashlight in his hand, directing the proceedings.

She understands what she sees and guesses at the meaning of the sounds: the digging, removal of the earth, hiding the weapons, the clang of metal. She goes over to her table and lights the kerosene lamp. As soon as flame rises from the wick there is a knock at the door. A member of the security committee eyes her suspiciously. "Why was it dark here just a moment ago?" As if she had been spying on them and their secrets.

"I was sleeping." Her voice is steady. In the weak light of the low flame you cannot see how flushed she is. Only her eyelids are burning.

"Then stay in your room and don't come out until you're told," scolds the man. His inquisitive eyes do not leave her.

"Can I go to the reading room?" she asks.

"Yes, but right away."

He walks with her for part of the way, as if to make sure that she doesn't look behind. The hint of an insult creeps over her as if of its own accord. Our weapons are secret and costly, she muses. But here everyone knows where and how. She is the only one they are careful with. They do not seem to have established full confidence in her. Her father writes articles in the newspaper of the independent farmers calling for moderation. They must be afraid that she will unwittingly blurt out things she shouldn't know. Still, they ought not to treat her as if she were trying to spy on them from a darkened room.

She accepts the incident as a kind of punishment. As she sits in the reading room, the letters dance before her eyes and do not make sense and she orders herself to unlearn what she knows. The man is nameless, and nameless he shall remain. Sound and vibration. Without body, without bodily image.

In bed that night she cries. She hates the sound she hears.

In Raheli's room there is a party going on. The job has been completed according to plan. Big Yitzhak and his friends are drinking and laughing and congratulating themselves on what they have done. And what was supposed to remain top secret is being mentioned out loud: machine guns. They are talking about them with a sort of manly love and in warm and resonant tones. She is angry with them for not being careful about what they say and for bragging. Isn't Raheli sitting there and another girl who came along with the regional commander, all of whose movements are supposed to be secret? She is angry that they were careful enough to hold her to the letter of the law and that now they are jabbering away like teenagers.

But most of all she loathes the sounds she hears afterward. Big Yitzhak is drunk and uses obscene language. Raheli's voice whines and wheedles. Raheli laughs at the vulgarity and enjoys it. Every now and then she mentions the neighbors. After all, they are supposed to rise at dawn for work. Big Yitzhak hushes her with slobbering kisses. Like an ox, she says to herself. Abstinence is not good for people, says Big Yitzhak. Nothing is so good for a woman as a good fuck from time to time. That's how he speaks to the bride of his youth. With that very word: fuck. And it's even good for the complexion, he says. Better than all the cosmetics in the world. And cheaper, and more enjoyable, he guffaws. And as for the refined lady on the other side of the wall, he adds, she's probably sleeping like a log. But if she should hear, it wouldn't hurt her. She's a big girl and it's time she found out.

Raheli's coarse laughter is what brings the tears to her eyes.

[9]

But the next morning there they are with their shoes on the steps and good-morning with bloodshot eyes and walking a little stiffly to work. Business as usual. The ability to say good-morning without overtones of the night before is required as a kind of denial of the self. Can it be that the criterion of maturity is this dulling of sensibilities?

In the communal shower house, as she combs her hair in front of the mirror, she steals a glance at Raheli's body. The shower head sprays her hard, glistening body with wasteful jets of hot water. Steam covers everything with a bluish mist so that a veil of modesty seems to envelop the bodies and move about with them from place to place. Better this than when the water is cold, and everything is bare and out in the open. Raheli's body is taut and translucent as a jar of honey. There are no freckles or pimples. The burning sun, the mosquitoes, the filth, and the monotonous diet have no effect on her. Not even love or lust or fear or anguish or guilt leave marks. Like one who has emerged from the bath. Perfumed with myrrh and frankincense. Raheli bears her childlike nakedness with supreme indifference, with a slightly careless gait, dragging her feet. The wooden clogs make a dull, sleep-inducing percussion. Raheli is complacent at all times, like one who knows neither her body nor her soul. A girl without pride or shame, unaware of her beauty, virginal in her round, firm breasts, her youthful hips, her firm belly, in the suggestion of a closed line over a gaping wound. In her own body it is a bloodcurdling scream, a den of lust wallowing in its own filth, and in Raheli it is a delicate flower of love. A bolted garden, a sealed well, a hard, unopened bivalve. You cannot tell from looking at Raheli that one day she sleeps with this fellow and the next day with that. It is all washed clean. She seems packed into her skin, ready to be sent somewhere else, there to be transplanted painlessly, without homesickness, without the torments of adjustment. A Bedouin gown, crepe de chine, it all looks right on Raheli: milk baths, mink furs, striped cloths of the yarn of Egypt. A beautiful woman come into the world, without time or place, whose beauty is her destiny, her home, her bridal canopy, and her grave.

In the evening she puts a light on in her room to keep the nameless one away. So that he shouldn't come before the other one has had a chance to leave. And that is not all. Her body is caught in that certain defiling function, so that all things having to do with the body are repugnant to her tonight. He seems to hover in the air, yet he does not come. She is grateful to him. And when Big Yitzhak, who has come home on leave, walks arm in arm with his wife in front of the dining hall she is angry with Raheli. Can't she see the grief of the nameless one who watches them from afar and has to swallow it all?

One clear, still night, when the air hangs motionless and no rustle of leaves is heard from the grove and the towel hanging near her window sill does not flutter and make its light snapping noise, she hears them talking.

"Are you sure she's asleep?" the man asks.

"I don't know," says Raheli. "Maybe she is, and maybe she isn't." Then she adds, "She's sleeping like a baby."

"Sleeping like someone who has never committed a sin in her life," says the man.

Raheli laughs. "Are we committing a sin?"

The man does not laugh. "I don't know. Are we committing a sin?"

"Yes."

A flash of light suddenly appears on her ceiling. A match has been struck in Raheli's room and the light seeps through a small hole in the wall separating the two rooms. Raheli objects with a weak voice. "I want to see," the man apologizes.

"What is there to see?" says Raheli. And laughter is heard. Admiring, happy laughter.

"Don't worry, nobody will come in," says the man.

"Aren't you ashamed of being so beautiful?"

[133]

His voice is familiar and yet not familiar. But she remains firm in her resolve. Nameless he has been and nameless he shall remain.

But not for long.

One night, on her way back from a visit to her parents—her father is driving her back, up to the gate of the kibbutz, for no other reason than to be able to spend a few more hours with her, because the last bus leaves in the late afternoon—she notices a shapeless mass on the steps of her room. For a moment she fancies that it is a pile of dirty laundry, but as she approaches the pile straightens up on all fours and arches its back, stretches, and growls. At first she is a little frightened because the terrifying watchdogs, which are always tied up, can inflict a serious wound. But then, even in the dark, she can tell that there is nothing to be afraid of. The gigantic dog stretches and comes toward her with a swaying gait. Two sad, marvelously beautiful eyes are set into his large head, and a contented expression, permanently concealing a guilty conscience, greets all comers, whether friend or foe. His long tail wags with a life of its own. With ears drawn back he extends his head for her to pet. It can't be, she says to herself, and her hand reaches out to pet the head pressing into her bosom, it can't be!

CHAPTER TWO

[1]

A dog can tell a great deal about its master. The kibbutz is poor and food is scarce and they are not much given to raising animals that do not have some purpose. There are the quick, effective shepherds who go out with the flock, and there are the watchdogs, trained to instill fear and to attack. Even the two poodles in the kindergarten are kept as creatures having educational value of some kind. One of the women working in the nursery came back from a seminar where she heard from an expert that it is important for preschoolers to exercise their emotions on dumb animals. One dog, a shriveled, ugly, mean creature, belongs to one of the elderly parents who lives alone and whose daughter is childless. Only one dog is unaccounted for. A mangy mongrel, without breeding or pedigree, strayed from the neighboring Arab village and used to wander around the yard. He served as a football for anyone without pity until he adopted the one person who couldn't stand to watch him suffer and yet didn't find it in his heart to put him out of his misery.

The dog is a point in his favor. His humility is reflected in sympathy for the underdog. The young man, as he asserts his right to scraps for the wretched parasite at the door of his tent, who doesn't even bark when you step on his big, tick-infested ears, is exhibiting the stubbornness proper to a true pioneer.

She tries to conjure him up and reconstructs chance meetings and stories she has heard. Once he sat down next to her in the reading room and copied sentences out of an issue of *Mibifnim*. When she glanced at them she couldn't understand what was so special about them. The standard local repertoire includes one story that involves him. Two Arab shepherds wandered into the orchard with their flock, and he got into a long discussion with them, trying to convince them that they shouldn't be there. Meanwhile, the flock ate a path of destruction in its wake. For a while he worked in field crops, until it became evident that the machinery wouldn't obey him. Without admitting to a loss of face, he went to work in the vegetable garden, with the girls. She even knew that in the youth movement he had a reputation as a dedicated, inspired leader. Once a year he is still sent on loan to head the Passover march to Masada. There he stands on a rocky crag and interprets the speech of Elazar ben Yair in the spirit of our time. When he is away, his dog pines and starves himself to death. At campfires, he sings solo. His voice is clear and resonant and seems like a hidden wonder, as if he is surprised at having had the nerve to sing.

She lets her thoughts turn to his appearance: a childish forelock, which is a bit unruly, sharp, inquisitive eyes, high, delicate cheekbones, with a tracery of blue veins, like a kind of heightened sensitivity showing through. An intelligent forehead, even though he never went beyond eighth grade, like any poor kid who has to go to work. His nose is long and narrow with prominent nostrils. His ears stick out, as if permanently cupped and listening. His narrow shoulders, caved-in chest, and thin arms hardly indicate masculine vigor and seem to mock the strength suggested by the set jaw and mouth, which look like they belong to somebody who has just expressed a definite opinion and will not retreat. She is pleased with his appearance. Poetic justice has been done. Big Yitzhak is good-looking, tall, solid, and his arms are strong and muscular.

In her diary he does not appear under his real name. She has made up a name for him. The strange name came into being completely by chance. At first she planned to conceal his identity in her diary by using initials: S and D, for his first and last names. Then she decided that that wasn't enough. She invented a double-cover. S became T, and D became E. While she was writing the pen fell from her hand and made a mark between the T and the E. Since she doesn't like to mess up her diary with crossings out and erasures, she turned the mark into an H and added an O at the end. It amuses her that this native of Palestine, living the Zionist dream by tilling the soil, should come to be called "Theo."

Under this name he will live in her diary from now on. It is a name that seems to her to fit the spirit of the way things go on next door: with delicacy, in secret, in silence. His real name—Shmuel D., as he is commonly called to distinguish him from Shmuel C., the kibbutz treasurer, who is ahead of him in every way—is inappropriate. When she thinks of his manners, his love of good music and sports, of his discretion, respect for older people, and the way he controls his anger when it has been occasioned, she concludes that the name "Theo" fits him much better than the name selected by his father, who hauls gravel outside of Tel Aviv.

[2]

The dog's sensitivity is also scrutinized in the diary, but separately from Theo's story, so that the dog does not cast suspicion on its master. Isn't it amazing how the dog took to her from that very first night? Whenever MacMaykhl sees her he wags his tail and wiggles his whole behind. These small motions help him to get what he wants. He stands on his hind legs and paws the air in front of him insistently, so that she will pet him. "A new boyfriend," she says to whoever catches them in the act. A pathetic joke. If anybody else said it she would be insulted. They share a secret, she says to herself. And this is not without irony. Big Yitzhak and the mysterious comrades who come and go in the middle of the night share secrets that they keep from her. Nor is she completely innocent of complicity in encouraging this sudden friendship. One Saturday, when the meat doesn't seem very appetizing she slips her portion to MacMaykhl. This arouses the ire of one particularly straitlaced woman. You don't give "people meat" to a dog. Especially not to a good-for-nothing dog who deserves to be poisoned so that he will stop eating and messing up. Idiotic, unpleasant words are exchanged. She stands up for the dog, and the woman gives her an inquisitive glance, as if she has just given herself away. Unfortunately for her, she blushes as if she were really guilty of something. In any event, from that time on the dog expects food from her. And she doesn't like to disappoint him. She collects scraps and goes looking for him in the yard, and sometimes this brings her right up to Theo's tent.

Thanks to the dog Theo no longer passes her by with the troubled look that says should I or shouldn't I say hello. He stops to ask her about his dog. He, too, has a private joke: MacMaykhl is careful not to offend anybody, but he only makes friends with very special people. She smiles humbly to show Theo that she appreciates the veiled compliment. When they meet on a narrow path they can stop and have a long conversation about dogs and their ways. Theo is sure she has a special thing about animals, and she doesn't bother to tell him that she has never in her life had a pet, not a dog nor a cat nor a parakeet, not in her room, not in her parents' yard, nor anywhere else. Not only that, but deep down she is actually afraid of dogs, and even a cat who gives her a dirty look and refuses to let her pass sends shivers down her spine. She realizes from Theo's evasive looks and the lapses that intrude on their conversations that Theo is probably not much more of a nature enthusiast than she is and that his interest in the dog is a projection of his own need. MacMaykhl is nothing more than a vessel into which he pours his compassion. There are moments when she suspects, without any ill will, that not even his contact with her is completely free of an ulterior motive. It may be that for all his talk he is only posing the one question he does not dare to ask: what does she hear from the other side of the wall?

Even his naiveté is a mark in his favor. After a long talk about dogs, horses, mules, and snakes, Theo's voice, coming from the other side of the wall, is louder than usual. She smiles to herself in triumph. Well, so this is what Theo has concluded from the cunning way she steered a conversation about animals. She knows nothing, and she hears nothing.

The wall is a real wall. It stops the voices and is not merely a treacherous partition that lets them filter through.

Theo congratulates himself to Raheli: as the result of a carefully planned effort to sound out the neighbor he now knows for a certainty that she suspects nothing. A person of her standards would be liable to judge them severely. And since her voice did not betray even a shadow of reproach or of evasiveness or of the strident tone of somebody who is deliberately holding back criticism but, on the contrary, was warm and pleasant and friendly as ever and since she was eager to talk about the things closest to her heart—books and animals—it is safe to assume that their voices do not carry. After all, she is too straightforward to be putting on an act.

"That's true," agrees Raheli. "She is an honest girl."

"But only a little too sensitive," Raheli adds and sighs. Her burden becomes heavier. Now that they are certain she knows nothing about what goes on they permit themselves to keep a thin flame burning, so that a pale chink of light dances on her ceiling.

[3]

A routine establishes itself. During the day Theo and Raheli pass each other by glassy-eyed, without greeting, like two ships in the night. And at night the noises they make are full of love and tenderness. Now she even knows the pet names they have for one another, Muli and Rali, and a few other secrets whose memory causes her to blush. Their faith in the flimsy walls increases from day to day, and often they do not turn out the light at all. Raheli's naked beauty brings cries of astonishment to Theo's parched throat. No longer does Theo wait around outside. He opens the door in a single motion— not long ago Raheli oiled the hinges—and he leaves with rapid steps, his head erect. Now that she knows who he is she takes the liberty of peeking out the window from time to time. Only in leaving Raheli's room does he face any danger. Farther along, on the gravel path leading to the main walkway, where his steps ring out loud and clear, he has nothing to worry about. At most, people will think that it's her room he is coming from, and that will probably be viewed favorably and people will take care not to tread on so fragile a plant. That is how the wretched of the earth savor their happiness, how the supersensitive experience their timorous, resigned love. And could it be that those very public talks about dogs that he has with her so often are only meant to explain the nightly excursions in the vicinity of her bungalow?

A smile flickered on his lips, in silent expectation,
A smile that was meant for another.

Sometimes she does mind being used as his cover. As if she were some kind of burlap whose only function is to wrap delicate silks so that they shouldn't get dirty or wrinkled. But at other times she basks in the role of guardian angel in a matter so fragile, so very vulnerable, where so much is at stake. If not for her own noble, carefully guarded silence the thing would long since have come apart as it traveled the grapevine to its bitter end. And then she sees herself as the heroine of a romantic novel of great souls and courage and refined sentiment without limit and self-sacrifice and dedication and altruistic self-denial, and deep dark secrets that formerly could have existed only in gorgeously frescoed marble halls, in immaculately starched muslin gowns and small, diamond-encrusted tiaras, with dark, mysterious perfumes and tiny feet encased in sparkling silver slippers and dainty hands, heartrending in their limpness, held out to be kissed. And here are all these things in her poor shack, permeated always by an odor of dust, with mice gnawing away beneath the wooden floor and a coarse mat covering it, and sweaty work clothes and big clumsy shoes waiting at the door.

Sometimes she wishes she could take it upon herself to warn the two careless lovers, who, because they think they have pulled the wool over her eyes, allow themselves to take foolish risks. It does not stand to reason that such a scandal can go on for many days without being uncovered. This is a small place with only a hundred and twenty souls, mostly people from the Palmah and the youth group. But she hasn't the courage to do it, fearing that she may do more harm than good. She crawls into bed stealthily, puts the light out early, snuggles into the cozy warmth, and listens with compassion and love to the emotion-charged voices reaching her through the partition. She is not too strict with herself about listening in on conversations not meant for her ears. She rests easy in the knowledge that she will never betray their secret, that even in her diary they are thoroughly protected. Only once did she suffer serious remorse and think harsh thoughts about her probity, her character, and her reprehensible curiosity. One night, unable to resist the temptation offered by the crack of light flickering on her ceiling, and full of self-loathing at being able to stoop so low, she put a crate on her bed, climbed up, and put her eye to the hole near the top of the wall. She did not see much. When Theo and Raheli tumble into one another's arms in bed, all she can make out is the opposite wall.

[4]

She is not concerned about things that should concern her, but things that do not concern her she makes her concern. Day after day they shift her around from one workplace to another, and it doesn't matter to her. They treat her like a complete newcomer, and she has been here a whole year.

Often in the morning when she goes to the dining hall she doesn't know what kind of clothes to wear: whether she will have latrine duty and need boots or whether she will be sitting in the clothing depot and be all right with sandals. She doesn't care. Sometimes people encourage her to stick up for her rights, but she continues to work where she is told without saying a word. All she wants is for the person who assigns the work to speak to her straightforwardly, without double-dealing and without avoiding her glance. But even these things she forgives. She bears no grudge whatsoever. Not even the petty discrimination practiced against her in the clothing depot—it is taken for granted that her parents will provide her with whatever she needs if she shows up at their house in tattered, ill-fitting clothes—moves her to insult or to anger. She can see the point of view of the head of the clothing "commune." The budget is limited and subject to many claims, and prices are getting out of hand. In the old days, when the kibbutz was wretchedly poor and all were in favor of carefree, barefoot indigence the income covered expenditures. Something went awry during the past year. Kibbutz members want to dress nicely and to eat well. At times she regrets that the kibbutz is not exactly the way it is supposed to be. But then she tells herself: what would be so remarkable about having a kibbutz made up of enlightened, selfless people? Such people would fit in anywhere.

But when Big Yitzhak comes home on leave there is no rest for her. She wanders about until late, as if her own room were off bounds to her. When he was transferred to Kurdane she was delighted.

At the "Electricity Festival" she is a wet blanket. Everyone is happy that the kibbutz has been connected to the national grid. She is mournful. Tomorrow the cold electric light will uncover all the secrets! With apprehension she looks over the toddlers, participating in a kibbutz festival for the first time, with little gold paper flames on their heads. The secretary's speech sounds to her like so much gibberish. The fireworks seem childish, the ceremonial unveiling of the transformer, tasteless. She is glad that for budgetary reasons they will connect only the workshops, public buildings, and children's houses during the first stage. She worries when they place a new floodlight right opposite the bungalow. "I'm not afraid of snakes," she says curtly to the electrician on top of the pole when he tries to make small talk with her. She misses the huffing and puffing of the generator and the steady beat of the pump. Other noises of the night become clearer and more distinct in the absence of these. She fears for the fate of Raheli and Theo. And so it is that a few days after the lamp has been installed opposite the bungalow she hears nothing at night but the sighs of the creaky bungalow and the dogs of the Arab village in the distance. In the reading room the light is cruel and blinding. Certain poems lose their magic. The warmth goes out of nocturnal meetings, no longer lit by a sputtering Lux lantern. "I am a woman of the twilight, of flickering lamps. Even my eyes are more beautiful in the dusk," she writes in her diary. "Can it be that Theo will return no more?" She is suddenly overjoyed when the bulb in the floodlight burns out. The shadow of the bungalow reaches all the way to the break in the fence and she looks forward to Theo's return. With difficulty she manages to suppress a cry of joy when she hears his footsteps on the stairs.

[5]

Only her father senses the change. But her father does not speak up.

A discreet man, careful where her feelings are concerned,

he only discusses topics that she raises. From time to time on his way back from a business trip having to do with citrus marketing or viticulture he drops in for a quick visit. He comes alone, without her mother, in order not to upset her. They are unable to hold a three-way family gathering. A silly quarrel always develops over something trivial.

Sometimes he rebukes her, but without anger, "It isn't right to raise your voice to Mama. She is a good woman, and she loves you. Why do you offend her?" She knows that he does not really hold her at fault and she is not cross with him. After all, he can never say that his wife is the guilty party. "Mama offends me," she retorts calmly. "She does not mean to," he says in the same composed, tranquil voice. "She worries about you." "Then it's ten times more offensive," she replies, and he smiles as if he has had a sudden insight.

He sees her being in the kibbutz as a kind of cleansing transition. He does not believe that she will stick with it. But he does not say anything, in order not to put her on the defensive. He keeps his criticism of this way of life, which is not to his liking, veiled and low-key. He passes over it, as an aside, even though he is an observant Jew and, as such, is deeply saddened by the prevalent show of apostasy.

"A few of your friends seem to me like God-fearing people," he says, "and I cannot see why they choose idolatry."

Idolatry is a term whose meaning is not all that clear. Sometimes it means sticking to a political line that is bound to yield bitter disappointments. Now that the Russians are at war with the Germans he is less infuriated when he reads articles about socialism. Kibbutz holidays sadden him. "Your festivals are profane, and your Sabbaths are desecrated. Inspiration is on the decline and in the end materialism will prevail, and then there will be no room for even the tiniest bit of the Sabbath Soul," he laments as if to himself, and she is not expected to reply. But once when she made the biting retort that "Sabbath Soul means working extra hours without compensation and without complaint," he gave her a look of astonishment and said, "For two thousand years redemption has meant one thing, and now suddenly it means something else?"

The only thing he permits himself to make fun of is her friends' language: "Every little bit of nonsense is a 'project' and jobs that are accomplished without any effort are 'operations,' and they make no distinction between one form of the verb and another." He says these things so mournfully that one might think the world was reverting to chaos on account of them, and she smiles to herself and forgives him what she would never forgive her mother, who says the very same things, but harshly and with impatience.

Her father hides a brown paper parcel under his arm. She gives him a look of reproach and says nothing. He puts the package on the edge of her bed, almost absentmindedly. Very carefully he sets it down, as if it contained explosives. And at one time these packages were explosive in a sense. "I didn't leave home so that you could send me food packages," she used to say. Her father would swallow the insult in silence. Now she is silent, too. She accepts his gifts without enthusiasm, but she cannot be so crude as to reject them. Her father does not wish to impose his will upon her and embarrass her with presents of a kind that the others do not receive. But his eyes, which avoid the parcel as if that could cancel its existence, positively implore her not to refuse it. He knows that for her it is a question of violating a strictly kept custom. But is it not his love for her that is tied up with the halvah and the salami, with the olives and the chocolate and the shelled almonds? Especially with the last, which he does not buy, but which he picks and cracks with his own two hands.

She is at ease with her father. Moments of absolute tranquillity light upon them. They converse at length without tension, even though they take opposing views on every topic under the sun. Even their styles are different. He quotes to her from the rabbis of old, and she cites him passages of poetry, which to his thinking lack "true Jewish feeling." But it is only in her father's company that she can use her little puns, minuscule inventions that defy interpretation, a private language that she would never resort to in the presence of her mother, who is of the opinion that "after twenty a girl has to stop acting like an infant."

Only as he takes his leave—a small bell rings inside his head so that he always knows how far parental love can go before it becomes a nuisance—does he permit himself a few words about the appearance of her face and what lies behind the tight line at the corner of her mouth.

"You're looking good today," he says and stops, in case she may want to tell him why. She is aching to tell him about Theo and Raheli and even to confess about looking through the hole in the wall. To test his love for her. She knows that it wouldn't shock him as it would her mother, even though it might cause him great sorrow. But she checks the urge to confess, because she is afraid that he may not believe in a happiness that does not touch her own being, her flesh.

"Starting tomorrow I'll be one of the regulars in the vegetable garden," she replies, and the shadow of a knowing smile flits across his wrinkled face, as if to indicate that he is able to understand and appreciate such an exciting thing. She is sorry at having deceived him.

"And you are happy, I gather."

"Extremely," she says, and even hops lightly on one foot.

"Well, don't neglect your health," he says, gravely. Her cheerfulness is not contagious. "And you don't have to be a better worker than the other girls," he adds, and she hears her mother's voice coming from his throat.

"Better worker?" she gibes at herself. "Any little girl from the youth group is a better worker than I."

Later she slowly unties the knots in the cord and unwraps the package that her father has left. She nibbles halfheartedly at the chocolate bar, scoops up some of the shelled almonds, and drops them into her mouth one by one. Tomorrow she will invite over some of the comrades, who do not set foot in her room on other occasions, and like hungry cubs, they will pounce on the goodies and demolish them. The more people there are who share in the enjoyment of the package, the less guilty she feels about her dependence on the favors of her bourgeois parents. She is not greedy or stingy and she will participate in the joy of her comrades without reserve. Only when they thrust their hands into the shelled almonds will she feel a secret twinge. As if she is breaking faith with her father by allowing her comrades to devour the nuts he has cracked so patiently, so lovingly. For aren't these people in fundamental disagreement with his opinions, and don't they call him all sorts of names? He is her father and even so he is a class enemy. He is religious and employs Arab laborers in his grove, and in the articles he publishes in the independent farmers' weekly he attacks the policies of the governing bodies of the Jewish community.

The salami, the breast of goose, the pickles, and the pistachio nuts he has bought with his own money. And it may well be that they represent surplus value to which he is not entitled. This is money that grew out of the toil of the exploited. But the almonds, he grew those and cracked them with his own hands.

She remembers with regret how once, in order to win her comrades' approval, she even sullied his love for her, suggesting that the love of a man of property for his daughter is a kind of "egotism extended biologically." When she remembers his sad face she is overcome with shame at the nonsense she has uttered. Not until she has finished all the shelled almonds will she be satisfied with herself.

[6]

The longer things go on, the greater becomes her fear. Things like this cannot continue without being found out. There is no hiding place from curious glances. She also senses apprehension in the noises that reach her from the other side of the partition. Troubled sighs of happiness, fretful silences, and once—a panicked escape through the window because of the sound of an engine in the distance. She could imagine their worry and their letdown when they realized their fear was unfounded. The next day she was afraid that the thing might so trouble Theo that he would not want to come again. But he did come back, two days later. For a long while there reigned in Raheli's room a tense silence, punctuated now and then by an unanswerable question.

Meir Avrahami's face is not the same as it was just a short while ago. He looks straight at Raheli, and it seems as if curiosity has been awakened in him, as if he has begun to suspect something. Raheli avoids his glance. There are times when she looks as if she suspects that he, too, has fallen in love with her. This flatters her, but she is afraid of complications. Her eyes flash a sort of embarrassed coquetry, and she smiles to herself in confusion. There are times when she looks as if she is troubled by another thought. Men fantasize adultery with a woman who has acquired a bad name. They are certain that because she has made herself available to one she is available to all, and they become insolent and vulgar.

But it is soon learned that Meir Avrahami has a girlfriend from another kibbutz who works with him at movement headquarters, and that she is planning to join him when she finishes her tour of duty there.

One day Meir Avrahami brings his friend home for the weekend, and she sleeps in his room. Raheli and she have a real gabfest. Meir Avrahami and his girlfriend are so serious.

They love one another with such deference and respect and talk down to everybody else so politely. One might think that the sun shines for them alone. Raheli says in jest, "Those two must talk about the split in the party even when they're in bed." She does not let on to Raheli what she actually knows, lest Raheli put two and two together and lose faith in the thin walls. She suppresses the smile that tries to form on her lips as she is reminded that Meir Avrahami and his girlfriend did, in fact, talk about the situation in the movement.

A great change comes over Meir Avrahami from the time that he sleeps with a woman. It turns out that it is not because of a mean nature that he was very moody and depressed all this time. Now that women no longer constitute a threat to his chastity nor force him to control his natural instinct, they can once again become his friends. That is not to say that he has become so friendly with her that he would come into her room, but at least he no longer passes her by as if she were a ghost. He now eagerly gets into discussions with her about books and authors. She is sometimes annoyed at the benign expression he wears at such times, which seems to say, Here I am, a serious person, who, for diplomatic reasons, has undertaken to deal with a nonserious matter. But, still, she is glad to be able to talk to him. He is a smart man and knows how to read between the lines. They are in disagreement, and she is always sorry when he goes, because the right answers always come to mind too late. The crux of the disagreement is a novel written by a member of a kibbutz. Meir Avrahami is not happy with the book.

"A personal bellyache. Who cares?" says Meir Avrahami.

"What's wrong with that?" she retorts.

But she is critical of the book, too. Its use of language seems undistinguished to her. Must even the language wear work clothes when it is used to describe working folk? But she takes issue with Meir Avrahami for the way he belittles

[149]

"marginal people," who are absorbed in themselves, in their sorrow and their isolation. Is not the kibbutz full to overflowing with another sort of people—stalwart, cheerful, courageous, persevering, dedicated, witty and, begging your pardon, more interesting? But even the miserable, lonely, morose ones, who are preoccupied with petty, oppressive longings, do exist. But they are insignificant and of no consequence "either morally or statistically," and there is no point in having literature "latch on" to them and blow them up out of all proportion, as if everyone were like them.

"We are engaged here in an undertaking that has neither precedent nor parallel anywhere in the world," says Meir Avrahami. "And this is nowhere expressed in the book."

A hurt smile hovers on his lips for an instant. He is an intelligent and sensitive person and regrets that he must, because of her inability to comprehend, state things that are self-evident.

In her room, at night, she has an answer that clinches the argument. Much too late. If the more important things always eat up the less important things no room will be left for dreams. Because in our dreams it is always the lean cows who eat up the fat ones.

Meir Avrahami does not care for Theo. In his opinion Theo is a person who takes a perverse delight in his doubts and enjoys playing devil's advocate. At meetings of the kibbutz the fellow has a sixth sense, he says. Wise are the skeptics. And that is a role he is ready to assume at the drop of a hat.

"Although lately he seems to have grown up a bit," says Meir Avrahami.

She knows why Theo is no longer anxious to play the maverick before the meeting of the kibbutz. But she won't tell Meir Avrahami. Not even feelings of guilt seem to count for him. But this is one quality in Theo that appeals to her especially. He is not certain whether he has the right to instruct his comrades in matters of personal conduct. Only in plainly political matters does he permit himself free expression. But he always sides with the minority, as if he were eternally committed to staying off the bandwagon.

She thinks it better for Theo that Meir Avrahami not know about what goes on in Raheli's room. Since they are at odds over politics Meir Avrahami's broad-mindedness could never extend to Theo. Human foibles shock Meir Avrahami not at all insofar as they pertain to people who share his views. But in this case he would even be slightly offended that Raheli, the apple of his eye, could give her love to someone who does not have both feet planted firmly on the ground. He would see it as a failure on the part of the kibbutz. Law and order can only exist as the result of group initiative. As the result of private initiative there is anarchy.

[7]

For Meir Avrahami the movement is all. Without it he ceases to exist. He is prepared to put up with anything, be it work that is not to his liking or the company of people he does not respect, as long as it helps to fill the ranks. His tastes are simple and his clothes look neglected and he does not pay attention to mealtimes, and the resigned smile of a beatific monk spreads over his face as they tell him that the boiler has exploded and there is no hot water in the shower. But she tells herself how sad his life would be without the movement, which permits his comings and goings via the South Judea Bus Line to be inscribed upon the pages of history. She wonders if he could really bear the company of the metalworkers, who tell each other dirty jokes all day. How would he feel if his life were nothing more than the kitchen, the orange groves, the laundry, and the other simple tasks he works at from time to time, on mobilization weekends, wearing the amused expression of a country squire who has happened upon a peasant feast?

Just before the council of the movement is to convene he recruits her to decorate the granary, which is to serve as the hall for the gathering. And for a few days even she is aware of the movement as a living entity, whose deliberations will determine the destiny of the Jewish people. She puts bunches of dates up on the improvised platform and uses asparagus ferns to decorate the national flag and the red banner and is caught up in the festive mood. She arranges for her day off to be the day when the council holds its discussions and is brought to the attention of the movement bigwigs. Meir Avrahami introduces her to them as "the person who worked magic and transformed the shed into a palace," and she blushes and loses her voice when she is expected to tell them her name. She listens to a long, inflammatory speech and goes away brimming with symbols whose meaning she does not entirely fathom, but which strike her as shimmering truths. She is very proud of her kibbutz when it receives public praise—"It is no accident that this fateful meeting is being held in one of our most courageous and precedent-shattering kibbutzim." For an instant she fills with indignation against Theo, who says that he is revolted by "words that repeat themselves until little by little they lose all semblance of meaning." She even says to herself that Theo would be better off if he didn't get carried away but, rather, got his own house in order first. But in her diary she retracts the tongue-lashing she has thought up for Theo, saying that it is the product of genuine disappointment and not of pride or of a holier-than-thou attitude. That same man, who has been delivering his speech in solemn tones, as if officiating at a sacrament, has little flames dancing in his eyes as he beholds Raheli seated before him in her shorts, which show off the roundness of her small buttocks.

After the council, Meir Avrahami becomes extremely

friendly toward her, as if she has suddenly become a part of the closed circle of the movement faithful. He tells her about the rotten state of affairs in the party and about a faction he and others have formed. She is surprised that Meir Avrahami feels the need to win her over to his faction, since she never speaks up at meetings, and her opinion doesn't carry the slightest weight concerning the fine points that divide people who are otherwise in basic accord about settlement and defense, but she realizes that he may see it as a personal failure if his neighbor, who lives in the same bungalow, does not share his views. She succumbs to his wish and, together with Raheli, goes to his room for a meeting of some kibbutz members to discuss the situation in the party. Everything she hears seems consistent and straightforward, and she nods her head in accord with what Meir Avrahami is saying. He is at his best here—a sharp polemicist, a master of irony, steadfast in his opinion, aware of what he wants. Within a short time she no longer feels out of place. It matters to her that they see her as typical, as a "rank-and-file member," or something of the sort, a figure without distinction, whose opinion nobody would really dream of consulting.

She no longer feels the sort of stage fright that she experienced in the early days, and even though it would not occur to her to get up in front of a meeting of the kibbutz and speak her mind, she accepts the suggestion of Meir Avrahami, who is trying for all he is worth to get her involved in something, and once a week gives evening classes in English—for beginners. Even though her English is weak—just what she learned in high school and picked up from British civil servants who used to visit her father's house—she is able to teach what she knows. Many people show up. Some are serious and write everything down in their open notebooks. Others drop in to have a look and absorb whatever they can without exerting themselves. She is embarrassed when Meir Avrahami comes to her lessons, as if to put his stamp of approval on something he considers important, for his knowledge is considerable, and in politics and sociology his vocabulary is far better than hers. For everyday words and phrases, the ones she teaches, he has utter disregard. As if he knows from the outset just which words he will need.

Theo comes to the lessons, too. He is an exceptionally conscientious pupil, and seems to be trying to make up for lost time. One night she can scarcely check her laughter as she hears Theo's voice through the wall reciting his lesson to Raheli. Raheli sometimes comes too. Her memory lets her down. But she manages to acquire a perfect English accent, like that of a certain actress.

At the English lessons Raheli and Theo sit apart from one another and seem to ignore one another's existence. But when they touch in the narrow passage between the benches, which were intended for seven or eight year olds, she, and not Raheli, feels a tremor of electricity pass right through her entire body.

[8]

The war in the western desert brings with it a certain amount of prosperity. The local bakery supplies bread to the army camps in southern Palestine, and the bakery builds on one wing after another. Her English suffices for negotiations with the soldiers who come to pick up the spongy white loaves, and she is asked to work in the office of the bakery. A British corporal with yellow teeth and acne all over his face signs the invoices and casts a hungry, tormented look at her breasts. A dark-skinned Gurkha driver comes with him and pays her court with charm, and when he laughs his white teeth sparkle like fresh corn kernels. "You are a very pretty girl," he says to her in an accent that tries to be English, and he gives an insolent look to his superior, who lacks his nerve. The corporal's language is clipped. He does not dare to open his mouth in her presence, and they all joke about it. He only spoke to her once, when they were alone, and then she had to admit that her English was not good enough for a conversation in cockney dialect. She only understood a little of what he said, and of that only bits and pieces. He told her a horrifying tale about a battle near Tobruk in which he was wounded and which was the reason for his being transferred to the quartermaster corps. It was enough for her just to nod sympathetically every time his injury was mentioned. His face glowed as if he had been awarded a distinguished service medal. Perhaps because of that she protests when one agile fellow who works in the bakery makes it his habit to flip the bread onto the scale while the corporal's eyes are fixed on her face. She senses that the corporal notices these shenanigans out of the corner of his eye and that he greets them with the aristocratic disdain of an imperial power used to letting the poor colonial beggars get their share of the spoils of war. The head of the bakery is very hard on her for having such scruples. The English are the enemy, and it will do them no harm to make a contribution of their own to our cause. All of their acts are directed against our settling the land, he says scornfully, and she feels uneasy. It is not a moral question, she retorts, but simply that she hasn't the skill needed to bring it off without having her ears get red, thus giving her away. The bakery head pays no attention, because everyone knows that the Englishman is in a trance over her and doesn't know which way is up. When she replies that that is why it is especially difficult for her, he looks at her as if she has been laughing at him. The thing infuriates her so, that she refuses to go on working in the bakery.

Word of the short-weight affair spreads until she comes to regret being at the center of of such a profound ethical controversy. Some are pro and some are con. Some respect and some scoff. And someone even thinks that it all has to do with a pathetic love story involving a British soldier. And even Meir Avrahami has an opinion, expressed in appropriately theoretical terms: arms yes, bread no. He justifies her position, even though she had no "position" at all, namely, that it is all right to mislead the British when it comes to the weapons we need to defend our own existence, but it is not all right to fool them just so that we may raise our own standard of living. After everyone has gone, at the end of an English lesson, even Theo puts in a good word: is it proper to be more ethical than the most ethical of societies? And she cannot tell from the look on his face if he is serious or joking, because sometimes he uses irony in such a way that she cannot completely fathom his intent.

Meanwhile things happen, and Theo stays away from Raheli's room. The Palmah division has been participating in some action and Kuti was wounded. He has been smuggled out of the hospital where he was taken right after he was wounded because the British were looking for him, and the fourth room, which is usually empty, is abuzz day and night. Theo cannot risk playing at cloak and dagger with those more experienced than he. For a few days she is assigned to help take care of the sick and comes to do up Kuti's room each morning. His head is wrapped in a great bandage, like a sort of turban, and his thin, peaked face is ten times more emaciated than usual. His appearance suggests an injured chicken whose comb is pale and bloodless. But his intelligent eyes twinkle with a happiness that is checked and waiting to burst forth. He radiates a new confidence, and there are times when he permits himself to let out chickenlike sounds of courtship within earshot of her. She savors these in her own way, with a benign, ambivalent smile. Politely, but generously, she bestows upon him the hero worship he deserves, even though she hasn't the slightest idea—and this despite the various hints he drops to her in violation of all the rules

—what exactly went on at that engagement with the British that earned him the sterile halo he wears on his head with such unassuming pride.

Sometimes she looks in on him in the evening as well and stays, along with his friends. To hear their jokes and boastful allusions to military actions that she knows never took place, she feels herself to be their senior by many years, even though a few of them are nearly her age and a few, people from other kibbutzim, are even a little older than she. She makes them coffee and is not put out by the fact that they turn to topics she knows nothing about, or that they keep using slang expressions that are intelligible only to them. A few of the younger ones openly snub anyone not familiar with the subtleties of their military lingo. But she is insulted and unable to swallow the hurt when they exchange glances and tumble all over one another trying to get out of the room, pretending to be consummately polite but insinuating clumsily, unforgivably, that they all know why a woman visits the man next door.

And then she slips away quietly, trying with everything she has got not to let her face betray her feelings. She goes to her room and writes long diatribes against the foolish pride of young people, who see no need to respect the feelings of a woman who is not beautiful.

She does not suspect Kuti of having given his friends encouragement, for in the morning there seems to be a shade of apology in his look. She forgives him his friends' coarseness, but, since he was one of them, she can no longer strike up a simple conversation with him without a note of discord creeping in.

One evening while he is convalescing she walks him to the monthly movie, which is shown in the dining hall, sits beside him in the dark, and listens with a tolerant smile to the wisecracks and put-downs that cover the innocent emotion men are not supposed to feel. She does not notice, in order not to give offense, the arm pressing against her ribs. But on the threshold of her room when he stands before the stairs, one foot firmly planted on the ground and the other on the lowest step, asking but not insisting, she does not invite him in. She wears an apologetic smile, so that he should not be hurt. At times she asks herself, "After all, why not?" And she imagines the joy that would shine on her from his face if she complied, but she says nothing.

She has no regrets, even though on the last night, before Kuti goes back to live at the Palmah camp with his comrades, he sits up in her room until late, lost in sad, weary silence. She feels sorry for him but has no word of consolation, and the thing distresses her greatly. But now she knows that she is not in love with him. Since he has gone, hustle and bustle are gone from the bungalow. She is no longer awakened in the night by the excited laughter of young people who are used to saying whatever they please. And yet, she does not miss these outbursts of joie de vivre or the good-natured chitchat. The sudden quiet brings with it no feeling of loneliness. On the contrary. For this very night she hears Theo's muffled footsteps, as he walks on tiptoe in the next room.

CHAPTER THREE

[1]

For three weeks Big Yitzhak stays home, having been hurt in an automobile accident. She works in the vegetable garden, and as they sit opposite one another near the pile of carrots she can sense Theo's distress. It is precisely at times like these that he grows talkative and is ready to start a conversation with anyone. The rows of carrots are very, very long, and a kind of mating game occurs. From both ends people work toward one another, pulling up the carrots until they meet in the middle, where they sit down two by two and twist off the tops. It is customary not to choose one's partner, in order not to make people who are less popular feel left out. Nevertheless, she follows Theo and secretly counts the rows. Frequently they end up in the same row. She pretends it was all an accident, and Theo's face doesn't let on that he thinks otherwise.

They talk about work, dogs, and politics. Theo speaks, and she listens. He laments that there is nothing to this democracy that everybody brags about. The leaders confront the members with faits accomplis, and nobody pays any attention to what the rank and file have to say. She does not disagree with Theo, but her accord is silent. Although, given the chance, she would have no constructive counterproposals of her own to make. But perhaps Theo has ideas of his own. She nods her head in embarrassment, but Theo is not aware of her embarrassment. He is glad to win people over to his point of view, and she is glad he solicits her approval. She suspects that he may be trying to get close to her because he has no direct access to Raheli, but that doesn't bother her, as long as he sits with her and talks.

Perfect tranquillity descends upon her as she sits with Theo alongside the piles of carrots. Nor is she put off when he teases her for her fastidiousness as she scrubs her hands before touching food. The sky is bright and cold and luminous, and a flock of birds circles overhead, forming a black muslin canopy. A herd of sheep climbs a rocky hill as if some secret joy were come to life in the stones of the field.

To be filled with this day, this passing one, this only one,
Upon our own soil here.

Theo does not like to play "Find the quotation." As if she were trying to impose upon him an intimacy that is not

[159]

appropriate. He is not ashamed to admit that he has no time for literature. A working man needs all his free time to learn the things needed in the struggle for existence, he says.

There are times when she tells him about her childhood and adolescence. To Theo's way of thinking, she is a little, spoiled bourgeois brat who has been taught French and eurythmics and piano in order to suitably grace the home of a doctor. He takes pride in the change that kibbutz living has wrought in her values. She has no objection to assuming the role his imagination has assigned her, even though she senses no change whatsoever within herself.

In the afternoon Theo is very tired, and fine pearls of sweat glisten on his forehead despite the cool breeze that has started up. Theo is the son of workers, but he is not up to working, as if something had gone wrong at his conception. His head is elsewhere, and it's perhaps for that reason that he has no trade and that he is shifted from place to place like the teenage visitors who have no fixed place of work. If he subscribed to Meir Avrahami's views perhaps he might find his solution in a suitable movement job, but he quibbles with the movement leaders over trivia so that they must prefer not to have him around.

Work that others do without giving it a second thought becomes a test of his endurance. He does not complain, but everybody sees that monotonous, stultifying field work wears him down, so that finally he is left with strength for only the most essential things, like those books that are needed in his struggle for existence.

One night in a dream Theo replaces a man who died on her parents' doorstep.

Every morning her father would go out onto the porch together with the foreman of his orange grove. Jewish and Arab laborers, some experienced and some recent arrivals, would gather in front of the farmers' houses seeking work. The foreman would select the strongest among them and her father would nod his approval. One day along came an older man, pale, with delicate features and thin, spindly arms. Narrow-framed spectacles straddled his nose and everything about his appearance was foreign to this gang of Bedouin and rustics and tried and true mattock swingers. "I would gladly give you some work," her father said to him, "but the mattock is not for you." The man's face grew ten times paler. Her father could not stand to witness his sorrow and invited him in for breakfast. That breakfast lasted a long time, and her father was amazed at the erudition of the man, who had formerly taught philosophy at a German university. Then her father offered him some money, but the man refused it with tightly compressed lips. In order to placate him her father let him work in his grove. A little while later the Arab servant arrived from the grove carrying the man over his shoulder. His body lay on the porch until an ambulance of the Red Shield of David came and took it to the morgue. In her dream Big Yitzhak appeared dressed as an Arab carrying Theo over his shoulder, helpless, with drooping head and dangling arms. Theo's face was pale and distorted, and a drop of blood glistened at the corner of his mouth. Raheli stood alongside of her father with frozen features, and a tear rolled down her father's cheek. She fell onto Theo's neck weeping bitterly and awoke.

Theo listens with relish to stories about her father's house, as if he stands to learn things from them that are not written down in books. Sometimes he provokes her by saying that to her good manners seem to be a true indication of human relationships. It is the relations of production that determine the connections between men; not empty ritual courtesies, he says. She has to admit that he is right, but sometimes she misses a certain touch of refinement, and she doesn't care a whit that it would not be an accurate reflection of the "relations of production."

She wonders whether he talks to Raheli about Borochov

and conditions of production and *The Family and the State* by Engels, but she keeps the question to herself. Sometimes she turns the conversation to Raheli, casually, touching upon neighborly matters and so forth. Theo's fingers flit nimbly over the pile of earth as if suddenly realizing that this chatter is taking them away from their work. He is only too glad to listen to the good things she has to say about Raheli, what a quiet, pleasant neighbor she is and how careful she is to avoid disturbing her neighbors, unlike many other people who think they can barge in on their neighbors whenever their boredom gets to be overwhelming. But he hasn't a thing to say in reply. He guards his secret with absolute control. When work is over and the wagon comes to take the workers back from the field, Theo sits by her. It's hard to talk during the ride, on account of fatigue and because of the bumpiness of the road, which has hardened after the first rain. At the bends in the road the wagon leans to one side and then she can feel Theo's bony, angular, hard body. Theo draws back a little when they touch.

Even though Theo has "sloughed off bourgeois manners," as he is fond of saying, he is polite and is careful to show her respect. When he feels the touch of her breasts on his arm he pulls away gently. When he straightens up he is a hands-breadth away. And at times she asks herself if it is really Theo who bounds along the gravel path at night and secretly steals into her neighbor's room.

[2]

Big Yitzhak is still at home and Theo whiles away long hours in the reading room. One night she peeks over his shoulder and notices that he is reading a book of poetry put out by the movement's publishing house.

"Well, so it isn't just ammunition in the war for survival?" she whispers. She smiles through fluttering eyelids as if to clarify the intent of her words: she is not making fun of him—heaven forbid—nor would she dare take credit for this departure from his normal practice. Theo does not smile. His face is serious, even a little grim.

He launches forth on a long diatribe. And is furious in his condemnation of the movement's publishing house. As long as the subject is economics or society, they are down-to-earth. Class warfare. Orientation toward the forces of tomorrow. Intensive cultivation. And there are even some among them who are not too high and mighty to contemplate a mixture of industry and agriculture. But when it comes to culture they suddenly reveal their hand as offspring of the upper classes. Descendants of an assimilated Jewish bourgeoisie. What have they to do with this decadent poetry? It has no connection with the lives of working people. And it bears no relationship to the values of Labor Israel.

"I read and I ask myself, whom are they trying to fool?" he says. "And these bourgeois diversions are published by a house that exists off the savings of people who are breaking their backs and living on bread and water. There is something wrong here."

She peers at the poems over his shoulder, reading a line and then another line. "To me they seem very beautiful," she says apologetically.

A flicker of affection lights up for an instant in Theo's eyes. The reading room is empty now. They are alone. Theo speaks a little louder. Now that he is not whispering his voice is pleasant, as if the impatience and urgency that the effort of whispering imparts even to ordinary utterances have suddenly vanished. Words were meant to bring people together, he explains, and his eyes sparkle with the light of a thought whose time has come. To bring *people* together, not unrelated objects like the moon and green cheese. Words must undergo a process of refinement until we are all able to derive the same meaning from them, without any margin for error. This is a long and complicated process, maybe hopeless, but worth attempting. These metaphors, analogies, and personifications are superfluous, wasteful, confusing games that stand in complete contradiction to the main effort. What is culture? To bring forth bread with honor; to rule over nature; to create clear, unambiguous, linear, perpendicular, cut-and-dried linguistic tools. To build anew that tower that was destroyed. To take the building stones and lay them out, each in its place. To grab people by the scruff of the neck and say here is electricity, here is manpower, horsepower, productivity, seeds, nails, ideas. They can be molded into a single entity: diligent working people, not interested in getting the better of one another, parts of one whole, without selfishness, without jealousy, without competitiveness; with honesty and loyalty.

She asks if honesty is that important. Theo nods vigorously, and his face gets worked up. For a few minutes he sounds like Meir Avrahami—the kibbutz, new society—but at no point is the zealot's spark kindled in his eyes. His voice is soft, pleasant, melodious. He uses the movement vocabulary, and yet the things do not sound familiar. A note of disappointed love comes through, like someone who talks about a loved one who has betrayed him, whom he cannot stop loving.

"You have to continue your studies," she tells him suddenly.

A sad smile spreads across Theo's face. A few days ago he was given some cause to feel sorry. It was decided to send another member of the kibbutz to the university, who would study to become a teacher of the continuation classes. Theo, who last year burned the midnight oil to pass his matrics, wasn't even considered by the secretariat as a possible candidate.

"They won't send me," he says. Without rebelliousness, without ill will. As if the decision of the secretariat were an immutable act of fate.

"They are preparing for a split," he explains to her, "and their sixth sense tells them that I am not one of them."

He is not shaken. He is a party man and understands that you pass over those who are not in step with the opinion of the majority. The coming split saddens him more than do his personal prospects. He just feels that it is too bad about the missed opportunity. Studies mean everything to him. He needs them, he explains to her, because knowledge to him is one of the tools of his work, ammunition. He is no Meir Avrahami, who is clever and shrewd and undisturbed by his lack of schooling. What does Avrahami know about economics? What does he comprehend of the social and political sciences? Not a thing. The numbers, the tables, the statistics, the hard, dry facts—all these he leaves to others. He, Meir Avrahami, has a few simple, concrete principles. He is able to give an irrefutable answer, breathtaking in its simplicity, to anyone who poses a difficult question, whether or not it is bolstered with stubborn, contemptible numbers. In this manner he is not even obliged to give recognition to people who have studied and who know, and who can be his teachers and masters. All they do is to complicate simple matters. He is a past master at this heroic science, that the late Arlozorov used to ridicule.

He, Theo, is not so shrewd. He must have a look at those boring tables in order to know where he stands.

"And would you have been ready, then, to up and go to Jerusalem for three or four years, and not to come home except for weekends?" she asks.

"And why not?" he wonders aloud.

[3]

She is bashful about asking at the library for the books that Theo has been reading. But one day a button comes off Meir Avrahami's shirt and he comes to borrow a needle and thread from her. She goes into his room and spares him a task that is not for him. She takes a peek at his bookshelf and sees that Theo has been unfair to him. Books that Theo speaks about with admiration are piled up here, one on top of the other, on Meir Avrahami's desk, which is covered with a green blotter. She checks her bashfulness and asks to borrow a few. A sarcastic grin comes to Meir Avrahami's lips.

"Are you planning to catch malaria?" he asks.

She blushes, but smiles to show that she understands the joke. Only a person who has time on his hands asks for two or three books at once, and, at that, only a person who wants to be taken for a scholar.

Meir Avrahami presents the books with a flourish, as if to show that he is playing a game and makes no attempt to hide it. She passes over the slight and takes the books, determined to read them through from cover to cover. But once in her room their tedium gets to her, and she puts them aside in order not to fall asleep before hearing Theo's feet on the stairs.

A little of what she reads leaves traces in her style, and her father detects this. Once, during a visit to her parents', she gets into a political discussion with him, one that she really did not wish to start. She says harsh things and then is sorry about what she has said. "It is somebody else's voice that I hear coming from your mouth," says her father, controlling his irritation. "You must have heard that from some loud-mouth who owes his entire education to party pamphlets." Her mother is delighted. This means that she has a boy-friend. She gets up from the table and storms out of the house. It is only when she reaches the bus stop that she discovers that the last bus has left. But along comes her father in his car as she is standing by herself at the dark crossroads, trembling with cold and with fear, and with tears running down her face.

"A person has nothing but his parents and his children," says her father in a voice charged with emotion. "And all the rest—friends, are fine for those who have them. But we must never allow ourselves to become enslaved to other people's ways of thinking."

From the depths
To the heights
Just like that
With a sad, devoted look.

keeps humming through her head as she gets to her room, and a mouselike sort of nibbling starts up in Raheli's room.

At kibbutz celebrations Theo comes and sits down beside her. She is vexed, because she sees that he is really longing for Raheli, but she knows that she wouldn't want him to sit next to anybody else. And especially not if his face were cheerful and if he were saying bright and witty things. Now she no longer minds it when he too loudly whispers in her ear clever, charming witticisms that are meant for Raheli. He tells her at length about an article he plans to write for the movement newspaper. He wants to see if they are ready to listen to the individual member's opinion.

There are times when they go for walks with the dog among the orange groves and the vineyards, and when nobody else is with them Theo is much more at ease and also gentler. He is truly and sincerely concerned for her morale and her opinion of the kibbutz and its members, and she senses that he is careful not to express all of his criticism of the kibbutz, since she is new and "without roots." He is apprehensive that the slightest breeze might shake her and transport her to a place where she is better off and has greater comforts.

One evening he even comes to her room to show her a draft of his article. Once she called to his attention the fact that two *lameds* of purpose cannot follow one another, and since then he considers her a woman of learning. But somehow the very fact that they are in her room does not seem to let the conversation get off the ground. They sit opposite one another—she on the bed and he on the chair facing it— in evident embarrassment. Raheli's voice, as she talks to Big Yitzhak in the next room, develops a slight tremor, a rising choking vibration that is so obvious that even Big Yitzhak, who usually drones on without hearing other people, even he takes notice. "Are you ill?" asks Big Yitzhak. "Maybe we should send for the doctor?" "No, it's just that I suddenly feel very tired," says Raheli.

"You can hear every word," says Theo, and his face darkens.

She comes to his support, "We can't be heard, because we're speaking quietly."

Theo is grateful. She adds, "It's only Big Yitzhak whose voice carries. He talks to his wife as if he were barking orders at a company of soldiers."

[4]

Big Yitzhak has gone away, but still there is absolute silence in Raheli's room. Theo's face is serious and tense and even Raheli's face is not the way it used to be. She no longer sings to herself as she cleans her room. One night he knocks at her door. Very gently, very cautiously Theo raps at the locked door, but it does not open. She peeks out through her window and sees Theo's sad, frightened face and his bent back as he retreats with chastened steps through the opening in the fence. A few days later the door opens slowly, and excited, trembling voices can be heard. But she is not able to make anything out. Torrents of rain are beating down on the tin roof. She snuggles up in her bed and abandons herself to lazy pleasures. Tomorrow she will not have to get up for work in the morning, because she is scheduled for the vegetable garden and they probably will not go out in such stormy weather. The drumming of the rain makes a monotonous din that quickly lulls her into a deep sleep. She is shaken out of her slumber by the morning bell. She is happy to be able to turn over. The downpour continues without letup. Suddenly she hears voices in the next room.

Her mind races feverishly. She dresses hurriedly and rushes off to the dining hall. They are surprised that she has come, and she savors her secret by herself. She volunteers to work in the kitchen in place of someone who has taken ill, and her generosity puts her in a good mood. She sings to herself secretly as she peels potatoes, and a hidden smile spreads across her face as she washes the dishes in a basin of lukewarm, greasy water. "I just love the rain," she tells the others. "Everything is so beautiful, and the colors are deeper and more vivid."

Raheli doesn't know nor does she guess. She could not know that the canvas tarpaulin under which Theo hid, ostensibly from the rain, had not been hanging there before.

She discusses next year's crops with Theo and laughs to herself at his credulity. His face is relaxed, the face of a man who is sure of his luck. He does not know that if she had not taken pity on him he would have been caught in Raheli's room like a mouse in a trap.

Theo has fallen ill, and the doctor will not let him live in a tent. He is moved to one of the new bungalows, in which young single people are housed two by two. His roommate is Yehoshua from the Youth Aliyah group. Yehoshua is a young man from a family of Talmudists, who has broken with orthodoxy as well as with good manners. Here he permits himself to use foul language as if he had no choice. Only in her presence does he observe the old courtesies. He disappears from the room the minute she arrives with the meal tray.

They take no heed of the fact that Yehoshua thinks she is Theo's sweetheart. Sometimes they joke about it. But she does not laugh when Theo guffaws as if it were the most freakish thing in the world.

They are all glad that Theo finally has a girl of his own. Around here Theo is thought of as a fellow who has no time to run after girls. All of his free time is taken up with studying, and he is used to burning the midnight oil. That, at any rate, is the reason he gives for preferring a tent, where he can be alone with his books, to a bungalow with two in a room. He would hate to disturb a roommate's sleep. And if not for the doctor, who has decided otherwise, he would still be living in a tent.

Every evening she brings Theo his supper and stays on for as long as decency will permit. Yehoshua cannot bring himself to come back to the room as long as she is there. She steers the conversation toward Raheli, but Theo does not let himself get involved in a conversation where he would risk giving himself away.

Raheli makes jokes at her expense, "They say you've adopted Shmuel D." She senses Raheli's desire to speak his name, as if by accident. Every day she informs Raheli about the state of his health. She is so careful to point out the slightest change, temperature, appetite, morale, that Raheli begins to think that she may have missed her calling. She could easily make a good nurse.

She is crestfallen when she sees Raheli pacing back and forth outside of Theo and Yehoshua's room. Theo is standing in the window, on the other side of the screen, pale as a ghost, his eyes looking and yearning. She sees herself as a sort of missive—a blank page, without words, with only their pain and longing upon it—as she leaves Raheli to go to Theo's room. She is their feverish desire and the sadness of their parting, covered with skin, with sinews. Their mad yearning for one another sears her flesh. A bittersweet smile covers her face at all times.

The day the doctor lets Theo get out of bed he hastens to move his few belongings back to the tent. She returns to her room in a fit of ill temper and does not leave it until the following morning. As she passes Theo's tent—"Maybe I can be of help. You're so run-down"—he gives her a look of icy gratitude, as if to settle their account. He seems surprised that she pauses to chat. Doesn't she realize that she's finished her job and is not needed any longer?

But that night Theo and Raheli do not fall into each other's arms.

Her heart throbbing and thoroughly ashamed of herself, she stands on her bed and peers through the tiny hole in the wall. Theo is sitting on a chair near the table with his chin in his hand. The flame of the lamp burns low in its chimney, and Theo's eyes are melancholy pools of blackness. She does not see Raheli. She imagines that Raheli is seated on the bed with her back to the wall and her arms clasped around her knees. She can only make out her toes on the edge of the bed. One big toe rubs incessantly against the toe next to it. There is an oppressive silence. A cough escapes from Theo's throat and he hastily suppresses it with his hand. Raheli's voice seems to rise out of Theo's cough. She cannot hear everything they are saying, but is able to pick up the main points. The rest is easy enough to fill in. "I can't go on like this," Raheli says, "I can't go on." The name of Big Yitzhak is mentioned, and the members of the kibbutz, and the tension, and the constant fear, and the faces of people, who may know and be hiding what they know. Raheli speaks in a whisper and very quickly, so that the words just come tumbling out of her mouth.

She gets down slowly and sits on her bed without moving. A stifled moaning is heard through the partition. Raheli is crying.

"I'm afraid I have no choice but to go away," says Theo quietly.

[5]

But Theo does not go to another kibbutz. He takes part in the annual excursion to the Galilee and skips lightly from rock to rock. Raheli does not go along. The work schedule has been unkind to her. They had to cut down the list and everyone was sure that she would be willing to stay behind. After all, Big Yitzhak is expected back from Egypt before the trip is over. She feels sorry for her friend, but is glad that Theo will be free to chat with her.

Of late he has been absorbed in studying the geography and lore of Palestine, and he is ready and willing to share what he has read with her. At night they go swimming in the Kinneret, naked as the day they were born. By the light of the stars she sees his lean nakedness, and this gives rise to feelings of maternal love. She tells him how she used to quarrel with her mother as a child, and he tells her about his parents and his family. In an unguarded moment she tells him how much she frets over her ungainly figure. He pays her compliments and says things that are nice to hear. Many men actually prefer girls who are well filled out and solid. Near the Wood of Ginossar he lays his hand on her shoulder and her head suddenly feels heavy. She wants to rest her head on his chest and weep with joy. When they get back from the trip she writes an enthusiastic report in the kibbutz newsletter, and Raheli expresses wonder at all the fancy, poetic words that go into the article. From Raheli's words she senses curiosity and suspicion and veiled anger. She assumes that she has gone a little too far in her friendship with Theo and that word of this has gotten back to Raheli. At night she pricks up her ears, but Big Yitzhak has come back from Egypt this very day, and it is his voice that comes rasping through the partition.

A day later they are to attend a ballet performance in the neighboring town, and she is overjoyed when Theo asks her to get him a ticket next to hers. But it is to Raheli's request that she responds when she takes four tickets in a row from the committee for cultural affairs.

She passionately adores these rides to town in the back of an open truck. The wind hits you in the face and brings with it other times, with their subtle, finely tuned expectations. Body touches body, and yet there is no contact, and the darkness covers up awakening lusts. She loves the entry en masse into the dimly lit auditorium and the folding seat that, for two hours, will be her preserve, a piece of private property within the public domain. And the fading of the lights and the sudden burst of the music, and the curtain slowly being drawn upward and the deliberate, inspired body movements of the dancers. There are times when she envies them, but without hard feelings, for she is reconciled to her fate. Now Theo's glowing face is beside her too, listening intently, with a faint smile of amazement. During the intermission he tries to undo the magic bonds by sounding off with cold, smart-alecky criticism, saying things like there are no more than four or five motions that keep repeating themselves, and similar remarks characteristic of a clever person trying to trivialize his excitement over the music. He has no use for luxuries and nonutilitarian pleasures. Her own pleasure is diminished, since sitting between Theo and Big Yitzhak, with Raheli alongside her better half, she necessarily feels that she serves as a kind of barrier. The drama, filled with internal tension and a frenetic musical undercurrent, is not being played out on stage, but alongside of her, touching her, and yet not touching her. There are moments when she envies Big Yitzhak his ability to guzzle down sensual pleasure, with an alert, appreciative smile twinkling in his eyes whenever a dress is lifted and panties show. He senses nothing; he knows nothing. He enjoys both what is his and what is not his, and lays a large, heavy hand on his wife's shoulder. His strong, thick fingers crawl possessively over his property and tap clumsily to the music, a little behind the beat, at the smooth of Raheli's swanlike neck, through which a small tense artery pulsates without letup.

The way home is extremely eventful. She loses Theo as they scramble onto the truck. Somebody jams into her from behind, and she does not dare to look at the face of this person who is attempting to use her to quench a wild and uncontrollable desire. But when the motions of the faceless one, aided by the swaying of the truck, become bolder, she wriggles away, as if by chance, without looking back. She now finds herself stuck between a man and a woman and cannot make out who they are until the truck passes under a light. Theo's lips are forced into a pained smile, and Raheli's eyelids are lowered, although she can feel the fury mounting in Raheli's eyes as she opens them and sees her. She tries with all her might to extricate herself but Big Yitzhak is blocking her way like a stone wall. Her body is squashed between Raheli and Theo. She can feel Raheli's supple breasts pressing against her back and Theo's thin, stiff body against her whole body, taut and raging and ready to burst. She wishes with all her might that she could get away from this trap that was not set for her, but the whole group is rocking like one mass, and there is no way out. By the time the truck reaches the gates of the kibbutz she is completely dizzy. As she jumps down from the truck she stumbles and slips and if not for

Big Yitzhak's hand, which catches her with a strong, swift motion, she would fall flat on her face.

In the yard she finds herself in the company of Raheli and Big Yitzhak. Raheli is walking quickly, as if wanting to run away from her, but Big Yitzhak's arm encompasses Raheli's narrow waist, thus forcing her to keep step with him. He has seen enough and is bored and is now ready for a little fun. He asks her deliberately provocative questions in order to amuse himself by condescending to listen to her pointless arty talk. Everything belonging to that good-for-nothing world of pretentious hot air called culture gives him a big laugh. "There were some fairly pretty girls, and one was a real nice piece," he sums up his own impressions. "But nobody looks as good as Raheli," he says and roars with laughter. His arm draws Raheli closer in a mighty hug until Raheli's feet lift off the ground and flutter in the air.

Raheli's face is somber and tense, and not even the suggestion of a smile crosses her lips as Big Yitzhak gently sets her down on the gravel path in front of the bungalow. She tries to free herself of his grasp but is unable to loosen the fingers from around her waist.

"Enough is enough," says Raheli in disgust.

"What's wrong? Is there a law against stopping a moment to chat with a neighbor?" says Big Yitzhak and lets Raheli slip out of his grasp. He follows her at a clip, with agile, nervous steps, into their room. A slight grin lights up in his eye, and she is annoyed at Big Yitzhak's thoughts as she coldly imagines them: he is amazed that his wife has stood up to him for starting a conversation with the neighbor, as if her being the neighbor actually meant something to him. Raheli doesn't understand that it is only to intensify his lust and to increase it that he is delaying the frenzied assault on the bed. For a brief moment they stand opposite one another, she and Big Yitzhak, until, once again, they have nothing to say to each other. The subject of the ballet has been thoroughly exhausted, and the savoring of Raheli's impatience can no longer take place without her there. And then a malicious, dirty smile spreads across Big Yitzhak's face.

"You write me a note that I didn't pinch you, not even when we were completely alone," he says and grabs her cheek with two insolent fingers. He gives her an affectionate pinch, as one would give a patient, devoted, slightly ludicrous beast.

[6]

At night she suffers an attack of malaria. Big Yitzhak hears her breathing and comes to help. He slips a pillow under her head and treats her with extreme tenderness. He brings the nurse running, and rushes off to the dispensary to get medication. He sees to all her needs and, despite her protests, carries her in his arms, wrapped in a blanket like a baby, to the infirmary. He also brings her books to read. But there is a hammer banging away inside her head and a blue-gray curtain descending over her eyes, and she is unable to read or write. She is barely able to eat. Big Yitzhak takes even this job upon himself. He is on vacation and is free to help take care of the sick, which is even more of a job after the trip to the Galilee. And he puts his muscular arm under her head and feeds her with a teaspoon, wearing the good-natured expression of a man feeding a canary.

The disease saps her strength. A sharp ringing constantly sounds in her ears. She is enraptured by her helplessness and enjoys the pampering she receives. She falls in love with the kibbutz and with each of its members all over again every time she sees the trays of food they bring her. Even though she is incapable of eating more than a mouthful she can appreciate the intent behind this lavishness, which the kib-

butz certainly cannot afford. Big Yitzhak shares her food
with her and she can tell how much he enjoys these nourishing dishes that never reach the tables of the healthy. Sometimes he permits himself a joke at his own expense and tells
her that some kind souls must surely attribute his daily visits
to her not to neighborliness but to leftovers. He gobbles
down the food and looks at her with amused affection. Even
Raheli comes with him from time to time, but she never
touches the food. She smiles an icy, forced smile, and it is
plain that she would rather be somewhere else. But she could
not stay away without attracting attention when Big Yitzhak
is making such a display of courtesy. They only say things
that are necessary and to the point, and she is sorry that she
cannot apologize or explain her actions. But she is not supposed to have any idea of the basis for Raheli's hostility
toward her. It is possible that Raheli has made her a symbol
of all that stands between her and Theo. At any rate, there
is something oppressive between her and Raheli, and it will
not go away. Even though they both do all that they can to
obscure the fact, it keeps coming to the surface in one form
or another. Each incident is pettier and more stupid than
the next. She senses that Raheli is resentful of Big Yitzhak
for forcing her to spend time in her company and that she is
even angrier because she cannot explain why he ought to
avoid visiting the room of a neighbor who is sick and in need
of support. Raheli sometimes brings certain necessities that
you cannot ask a man to get, but explicitly feminine matters
seem to be repugnant to Raheli, as if by their nature they
call attention to what she would rather forget. And ordinary
rags suddenly become symbols of tormented, hopeless desires.

Theo comes by in the evening. He stations himself in the
kitchen, fixes her a get-well salad, and fries her some potatoes.
He is neither neighbor nor family and knows that his behavior is open to any number of interpretations, but that
doesn't scare him. She is grateful to him for taking the liberty

of mocking her appearance—she is pale as a ghost, her face is fallen and thin, and there are black circles under her eyes— as if she were a good-looking girl with enough self-confidence not to be bothered by such remarks.

"Eat, eat," he implores her. "Soon we'll be able to stick a broom in your hand and put you out in the alfalfa field to scare off the birds."

Her recovery is slow, but her appetite returns. Big Yitzhak watches in disappointment as she polishes off the salad and the sour cream and the eggs and the cakes. But his benevolence does not forsake him. Now is his chance to show all the gossips that it wasn't the sour cream he was after when he obeyed the commandment to visit the sick. A pleasant warmth spreads through her limbs when she gets up and takes her first steps on the lawn in front of the infirmary. Especially pleasant is the feel of Theo's arm as he automatically supports her.

An influenza epidemic strikes the kibbutz, and she offers to give up her place to someone in greater need. She is glad to return to her room, both because she has grown tired of the pampering and because many thoughts that she had wanted to set down in her diary have been lost with the passing of time. In the morning and at noon she takes a slow stroll to the dining hall, but in the evening, under doctor's orders, she does not leave her room, and Theo or Big Yitzhak and Raheli bring the meal to her room. When Theo is in her room he is loud and speaks with emphasis, and this sets off a flurry of activity in Raheli's room. The sound of walking, or a thin, pitiful cough, or, occasionally, a bit of singing is heard, a line and then half a line trailing off in the middle.

One evening, while Theo is there, Raheli comes in with a tray holding an Arab coffee jug exuding an aroma of coffee with cardamom and three tiny porcelain cups. Raheli excuses herself for intruding and stammers something that doesn't quite make sense. Before Big Yitzhak left for Egypt, she

[178]

relates, he rode over to the Arab village and got her this marvelously fragrant and delicious coffee flavored with cardamom. Since her neighbor has company, it occurred to her to surprise them with this excellent coffee. She won't stay for more than a few minutes. She doesn't want to be a nuisance. She'll just have one cup and be on her way. But she begs Raheli to stay with them. She is not being a nuisance at all. They are both happy to have her.

"Speak for yourself," says Raheli and forces her lips into a smile.

A delightfully naughty expression lights up in Theo's eyes. He looks at Raheli with astonishment, gets up, and with a polite bow, like that of a ballet dancer, says in a warm, slightly trembling voice, "We would be very happy if Madame deigned to honor us with her company."

As if serenading his beloved. With calm assurance, beyond embarrassment. And a kind of curtain descends. Raheli sits at the edge of the bed with her knees together and her arms folded across her chest. Her white blouse sparkles with virginal whiteness and her blue shorts reveal hips as clean and as smooth as marble. Simple, chaste; nakedness without pride and without shame.

Spring is here in all its glory and the smells of blossoming fill the room. Theo understands the call implicit in Raheli's words and Raheli discerns from the look on his face that he has understood. It occurs to neither that she, too, shares their secret and has deciphered the message concealed in the story, which mentions in passing Big Yitzhak's departure for Egypt but makes much of the coffee with cardamom.

Her emotions swing from one extreme to the other, but she does not allow herself to say what is in her heart. She regrets leading herself on from one cup of coffee to another, until the pot is practically empty. She is aware of a gentle dizziness, which usually occurs when she has had too much coffee, but she must keep the faltering encounter alive, and that is impossible without the steady stream of her talk. Danger lurks in each moment of surcease, as if her talk were a curtain covering over their secret. In its absence they would be exposed without mercy, and the whole game they have been playing with one another and the sad little deceptions over which they no longer have any control would be revealed to the harsh light of the world with neither their charm nor their nobility intact. She talks on and on, about her illness and about the excursion and about the ballet and even about politics, in order to involve Theo. But he only says a few words, as a person would who is content with just being and listening to the unfolding of time. He is full to overflowing with the woman who sits opposite him in silence, and it is only out of politeness that he emits a few words that make no difference whatsoever. Finally, Theo gets up, as if reminded of something, and goes. Nor does Raheli stay on with her for more than a short while, just long enough to meet the demands of the situation. An embarrassed silence prevails. And then Raheli goes too, and all that is left are the coffee things, which she has forgotten.

[7]

Her fears are realized. In the small hours she awakens. The coffee has done its work. She dresses hurriedly and goes the long way to the toilets, which are near the dining hall. On her way back, exhausted and drained as a result of the effort—traces of the disease are still very much present—she suddenly notices Theo's dog, making his way to Raheli's room. She calls to him gently, and as he approaches she grabs his collar. But near Theo's tent he breaks away. The struggle with the dog wears her out and she feels dizzy. With her last strength she makes it to the shower house and sprawls out on the wooden bench. The blood has drained from her face and her legs are wobbly. Nevertheless, she decides to gather strength and walk back to her room. The yard is empty and all she is able to make out is the lantern of the night watchwoman floating over the earth. The night is cold and silent. Nothing is audible but the pained sighing of the animals and the crying of an infant from behind closed shutters. She manages to take a few steps before the sharp buzzing in her ears breaks out with full force. She leans her head against the electric pole and clings to it. She shuts her eyes in pain and suddenly hears the plaintive wail of the dog from near her room.

A soft hand touches her shoulder. The night watchwoman puts her arm around her body and leads her along. She wants to stall her, in order to give Theo time to get his dog out of the way, but all she can manage to produce is a rasping sigh.

"That's how it is with malaria," says the night watchwoman gently. "They let you get up a little too soon."

The night watchwoman's voice soothes and consoles, and her arms are strong and loving. Houses and shacks and guava trees fly before her eyes with dizzying speed. Even so, she marshals all her strength and when they approach the bungalow she manages to get a few words out, "From here on, alone. No need. I'll manage, thanks." But her words only bring a smile to the night watchwoman's face, who tightens her hold. Just as they reach the spot where the paths cross she is seized by a perfectly lucid revelation. As if all at once, the curtain of mist is torn away from before her eyes. A dim figure slips away from Raheli's room! Theo does not notice them. Bent over the dog, he is dragging him along with whispers of encouragement and does not look behind. A moment later he is at the break in the fence, and the dark orange grove swallows him up. For another moment footsteps can be heard and the howl of a dog, and these, too, are absorbed in the stillness.

For a long while they stand without moving. The night

watchwoman's body is taut with emotion. Her gaze is fixed, as one bewitched, at the spot where Theo has disappeared.

"Did you see what I saw?" asks the night watchwoman. There is a giddy note to her voice and a tremor.

Her head reels from side to side. The dizziness returns and takes over. Her body is suddenly heavy and drops into the arms of the other. She does not wish to hear.

"You're really in a daze," says the night watchwoman in an excited voice, the emotion steadily rising.

"It must be Meir Avrahami," she says.

"No," says the night watchwoman. "And I know who it is." She inclines her head toward her chest.

"From the dog," says the night watchwoman.

As they stand on the steps she steals a glance at Raheli's room. The window is dark. The curtain flutters and the wind pins it to the screen. Not a sound. Not a move. The night watchwoman puts her gently down on the bed. Inside the room she speaks in a whisper. Her voice is like a stifled breath.

"I wouldn't have believed it."

[8]

Until morning she tosses on her bed without being able to fall asleep. The next day she does not go to the dining hall. At noon the nurse arrives. But her temperature is normal. "Just a little fatigue," she says. She looks at her. Her face says nothing.

In the evening Theo comes along. His face is tranquil, at peace. She laughs, reassured. "You're all aglow today. What happened?" he asks. She lowers her eyes. "Everything is all right." She is happy. The night watchwoman has kept the secret to herself. And perhaps she did not correctly identify the dog.

The next day she does go to the dining hall. But the minute she sets her foot down inside she knows that the thing has happened. Nothing is said, but a black cloud hovers over everything. Raheli is waiting on tables. Her lips are compressed. Her face lacks expression. It seems gray, and a veil seems to float before her eyes. She sees the suffering reflected in Raheli's face and feels the heartache. She wants to offer some expression of sympathy but does not dare. Suddenly their eyes meet. She is alarmed. In Raheli's eyes she perceives hard, ugly hatred.

At night she hears Raheli's weeping from the next room, and tears escape her own eyes, as well. They are warm and comforting as they roll down her nose and her cheeks into the pillow.

That night I heard you weep into your pillow.
Choking bitterly you wept.

She gets up to go to the door and goes back to her bed. Wrapped in a blanket and shivering with cold she sits with her knees tucked up against her chest and imagines Raheli, in the very same position, on the other side of the wall.

CHAPTER FOUR

[1]

The night watchwoman's story has become the topic of the day. Everybody goes at it in his or her own way: like discoverers of buried treasure, eyes sparkling, nostrils quivering in anticipation of the scent of a scandal, rejoicing at another's downfall, with a nod, in sorrow, in disappointment—with a look of reproach, angrily, with jealousy. Who would have thought? That rooster of all the cocks! The men speak with contagious enjoyment, facetiously, with much rolling of the eyes, with moral indignation, and with coarse humor. Boy-girl complications, from a safe distance, of course, are great material for humor. What an appetite she has. If she wants volunteers, count on me. They all give themselves the right to discuss these delicate, painful matters in the grossest, most arrogant language. But there are high-minded words too. Holier-than-thou repugnance, self-righteous offense. Nerve, disgraceful, shame, disgusting, and when the husband is away risking his life on a mission of national importance, et cetera, et cetera. Some speak with an air of triumphant moral superiority, pure and innocent as the cheek of a newborn babe. Some make their remarks in Yiddish, that salty, peppery language that holds, in its attic, an expression for every occasion. They dredge up worn-out bits of gossip and weigh them and measure them and pass judgment and mete out punishment. With irony, with glassy eyes, and screwed-up noses. Not even she escapes a modest share of the sarcasm: under her very nose, on the other side of a thin plywood partition, went on what must have been a churning of earthquake proportions, and that one, with her head in the clouds and her nose in the treetops, saw no evil and heard no evil. It occurs to no one that she might have known about it and kept it to herself, that she went about on tiptoe as one would by the bed of a sick child. Discretion and tact do not seem to enter the picture. For adultery belongs in the public domain, and everybody is allowed to grope and feel and spit. Anybody who shies away is an accessory to the crime and denies the public its due.

She is alone with her diary. In her heart are words of the most bitter opprobrium for her comrades, but when it comes to writing them down her hands will not obey. One page is already filled with doodling. The one after contains a couple of disjointed words. Can an outsider be the judge? When it comes to setting things down on a smooth sheet of paper she can always see the other point of view. Suddenly she is defense attorney for the gossips. They are, in a sense, defending the sanctity of their home. One does not cast stones. There is no pillory, no punishment. Except that those who have transgressed are denied the right to be taken seriously.

[2]

Big Yitzhak arrives the next day. The secret mission with which he had been charged was canceled by the central authorities at the last minute. This in itself upsets him. To his friends he has harsh words for the commanders of the Haganah. He cannot be specific. But they all understand from what he says that a great opportunity has been missed.

They walk around him on tiptoe. Not even those who always justify the decisions of the Haganah argue with him.

Big Yitzhak seems his usual self. Within a couple of hours he is walking around the yard like a master in his house, making a snide remark here, telling a dirty joke there. She is amazed that he doesn't sense anything. Ever since he was so gentle with her when she was sick she is concerned for him. But she is afraid that one of his many friends will be unable to keep his mouth shut. He does not want for close friends, but not all are schooled in the art of silence.

The next day, at lunchtime, she can tell by looking at Big Yitzhak's face that the damage has been done. He stares straight ahead. He speaks to no one. He is bent over his plate, and he cuts with stiff motions. Raheli comes along stepping lightly. There is a smile on her face and her gestures are mischievous. She sits down by her husband and says something, but Big Yitzhak seems not to have heard. A moment later, her face is like his. Frozen, greenish, with reddish patches coming and going. Fear dominates Raheli's expression. She leaves her husband with a toss of her head and disappears. Big Yitzhak, eyes focused on his plate, devours his food with redoubled fervor. Until a friend comes and sits by him. All at once his expression is transformed. A smile appears. And there he is with a witty remark and a good story. You don't air your dirty laundry in public. And if for a moment you forget, you fix things up in a hurry.

She wishes she could help but doesn't know how. In the shower house she tries to send out sympathetic signals. But Raheli avoids meeting her eyes. An angry, hurt line stretches around the corners of Raheli's mouth. She showers quickly, without looking at the others. Shamed, scorned, as good as guilty, Raheli stands beneath the canopy of hot water as if the whole story were inscribed upon her flesh. With bowed head, she lets the water run over her, and it drips like tears of shame and humiliation from the tips of her saddened breasts. When she has finished Raheli gathers up her work clothes and leaves the shower house quickly, as if in flight. The women are silent, but their looks lash out mercilessly. Once the door has closed the talk begins. As if a steam valve has been opened. Now they do not discuss the thing itself. They await the reaction of Big Yitzhak like a storm gathering on the horizon. The man is tough and used to getting his way. He will not turn the other cheek. Even Theo is mentioned. That weakling would be better off packing up and getting away until it all blows over.

But things turn out differently. Toward evening Big Yitzhak and Raheli can be seen going through the break in the fence. He is agitated, his arms swing to and fro, and his large body seems bent a little under its burden of pain; she walks with a careful, moderate gait and wears an expression of quiet despair. Her arms appear stuck to her sides, almost tied there, and her gaze is fixed on some distant point deep in the orange grove, as if hoping for a redeeming coup de grace.

She stops where the paths divide and looks after them. Meir Avrahami joins her. For a moment they are silent until Big Yitzhak and Raheli disappear into the thick of the orange grove, their bodies first and then their feet. They mustn't be left alone, she ventures tentatively. But Meir Avrahami reassures her. Things aren't that bad. There will be harsh words, undoubtedly. But no more. There is nothing to be done. At least not by us.

For a while they stand and talk. Meir Avrahami does not usually have much use for gossip, except for an occasional nasty remark about some political figure. Affairs of the heart were never of sufficient consequence. The devil in the flesh does not seem so awful. That's how men are. That's the way it was, and that's the way it will be, forever. Man has a small member. The sex drive is mad and unbridled.

Only Theo's behavior seems somehow attributable to something else. Somehow when she is with Meir Avrahami she comes to terms with Theo's views. There she is: deep within her is the same quality that always makes him take the opposing view. She is not listening. She is listening for voices from the orange grove, but nothing can be heard except for the pump.

Big Yitzhak and Raheli come back late. At night there are no loud voices coming from their room. But Big Yitzhak doesn't know how to whisper either. His voice can be heard perfectly clearly, as if he were talking in her room. "We need a lot of time now," he says. Raheli's voice cannot be heard. Only quiet weeping. "A lot of time," Big Yitzhak repeats. He is talking to himself, as if Raheli were not there.

In the morning he gets up and goes away. Nobody knows where. A few days later it becomes clear that the secret mission is on after all. Big Yitzhak has succeeded in having his way with the leaders of the Haganah. They have agreed to accept responsibility for a dangerous adventure. He has disappeared inside Egypt, and for many days there is no word of him.

Theo, too, disappears on the following morning. Only Raheli does not escape her fate. As if resigned to accept the punishment that she deserves, Raheli gets up for work each morning. She doesn't speak with anyone except for what is essential. She does her work in tense, nervous silence and disappears into her room. The light stays on there until late.

A few times she would like to stop Raheli and talk to her, but Raheli passes her by in outraged silence. She does not dare to initiate the conversation. In the morning she gets up early, but Raheli's shoes are gone from the front steps already. Raheli seems to get up deliberately early, in order to avoid meeting her.

After a few days have passed, when she can no longer endure the tense silence, she tears a page out of her diary and writes, "I must speak with you." She folds the sheet in two and slips it under Raheli's door.

She sits in her room and waits. From Raheli's room there is silence. She sits up late waiting attentively, but Raheli is silent. She cannot be heard lying down or getting up.

The next day, when she gets back from work, Raheli's door is open. She looks in. A bed with a bare mattress and empty boxes. On the floor near the door—her note, folded just the way it was put there. The heel of a shoe has left its imprint upon it, a delicate, pretty design, that grows faint as she picks the note up off the floor.

In the evening she hears that Raheli left for Sodom the night before to cook for the combined work battalion of the kibbutz movement. Meir Avrahami is glad. He had been asked to take care of the matter and for a long time was unable to find anyone suitable for the job. He permits himself a sarcastic remark: "There is no sin that cannot be atoned for in Sodom."

[4]

Life returns to normal. Without Raheli, without Big
Yitzhak, without Theo. She awaits his return. She wants at
least him to know that the fault does not lie with her. But
Theo is in no hurry to return. She seldom visits the reading
room. Her life seems to have been emptied of its content.
Even jobs that she had learned to like have suddenly become monotonous again. At night she misses the voices on
the other side of the wall and during the day the accidental
meetings with Theo. Life is boring without the secret that
was guarded like a sacred trust. Now, as she goes from place
to place in silence, her silence is utterly empty. Only her
boredom is carried about in her bosom, like a wasting disease.

Theo returns, and she trembles as she looks forward to
their first meeting. But nothing transpires. Theo's face is
impassive; no spark is kindled. He seems to have lost his interest in her now that everything is out in the open. As if he
no longer cares what she thinks and feels. Only his dog runs
up to her with wagging tail. He is no longer tied up at night,
and when Theo is not around he sometimes dozes on her
doorstep. She lets him in, and at night he sleeps by her bed.
In a little while he will be her dog.

Spring comes and with it the first heat waves. Clouds of
gnats move through the air like a gray fog. On Saturday she
is unable to rest. Her room is like a furnace and even the
floor radiates heat like an oven. She goes to the irrigation
pond. Whoever is free is splashing about in its ever muddier
waters. As she comes out of the water she notices Theo
sprawled out on the grass in the shade of a bush. A girl from
a new youth group is lying by his side. Both of them are
laughing out loud. How well she knows that laugh!

The girl's breasts laugh with her and bob up and down in
simple desire. Her face is round, strong, and full of the joy
of the chase. It is the face of a young female who does not

waste time on fantasies. It reflects absolute certainty about who wants what and why.

The girl looks at Theo with curiosity, taking his measure, as if trying with one glance to determine wherein lie his strengths, wherein his assets.

Something in Theo has changed, she notices. He is calm and peaceful, and his look is a bit impudent. He gives the girl the knowing glance of a veteran hunter who is not afraid of evident dangers. Not even of that tanned, aggressive breast poking through the opening in her clothing. His happy look passes above her shoulder and is not fixed anywhere.

All of a sudden she understands where Theo's eyes are focused. Not even the girl is important any more. He gleefully takes in the glances of the men. His eyes do not miss a single one of the quick glances at his open nakedness. As if Raheli's beauty had become an inseparable part of him and enhanced him with its power.

She finds revolting in Theo that look of a man who succeeds with women. She is even hurt by the way he bears his head in foolish pride. Here is a man with a sensational adventure to his credit. As if his stature is derived from the pain he is able to cause others. A happy smile lights up the pupils of his eyes from time to time. A smile full of pleasure, of victory.

Is it possible that his love for Raheli was shallow and empty? Can love be something so stupid and degrading and selfish? Was it only in her diary that everything was so beautiful and so happy in its hurting?

Her eyes implore: let it not be so. She wishes for him to grant her one more look, an anguished cry from the depths. She will understand: this is only a mask, to conceal our wounded nakedness. Beneath the shell lies a pure untouched kernel. But Theo's glance, which comes to rest on her suddenly, obliterates her without even trying.

On the last page of her diary she writes: "Today, when I

saw Theo near the pond, so full of himself, like a man who has had an affair with a beautiful woman and is glad that everybody knows about it, and doesn't care a bit that a family was wrecked and that others were hurt and will remember it for the rest of their lives, suddenly a powerful hatred came over me."

She reads what she has written, crosses out Theo and writes Shmuel D. instead.

THE
SALT
OF THE
EARTH

When he awoke he couldn't remember where he was.

His eyelids smarted and his nostrils were on fire. There was a strange odor in the room. A band of light flickered in the window and there was a constant hum. Hot air was blowing in his face.

He dreamt. A forest. He is trying to move a heavy stone. One foot is in a stream. Sylvia is standing, laughing, and her face is burning.

Why Sylvia, all of a sudden? He hasn't seen her in six months.

And then, out of nowhere, two Indians appear. Kicking up their knees, complete with feathers, tomahawks, and wild shrieks.

[193]

Why Indians, of all things?

His head hurt and the furniture was spinning. He shut his eyes and opened them, and everything was back in place.

The lamp, the telephone, the desk, the dresser. The T.V.

The indistinct humming is the air conditioner. The screeching sound is the elevator. Water dripping in the sink is the distant beating of the tom-tom.

He is in New York. In a hotel. Angry, depressed, hating his loneliness. Disappointed in himself. He could have lifted the receiver and asked for room service. They would have fixed the drape, the faucet, the air conditioner. And then he wouldn't have woken up so early. There is a bitter taste in his mouth. From now until morning, outraged, he will just await the new day.

He would not have been capable of disturbing room service in the middle of the night. Some habits become second nature. The ingrown taboos of an old halutz.

The main thing is not to get angry, warned the doctor. It's not dangerous. But there can be a sudden change in his blood pressure. He ought to slow down. A man of his age should concentrate on learning one thing. Resignation. Nothing is the way it was. The kibbutz has changed. And so has he. All things change. Outwardly, of course. That which is essential never changes. Do you know French? It makes no sense to lose your temper. Anger never moved a soul.

The youngsters are just moved to laughter. Only the more sensitive feel any embarrassment. Their eyes implore him to stop. Rage has no effect on others. Only on himself. His body fills up with too much acid.

A philosophy for the old. A pill to deaden the pain. It's easy enough to say.

He can shut his eyes and cut off thought. A viscous thread flutters between tongue and palate. As if his mouth had been emptied of its teeth. You could play on it, with gentle breaths, as on the string of an instrument.

Three-thirty. Time stands still, heavy as a boulder. Six more hours until he can disturb anybody with the telephone.

He has always hated the telephone with all his heart.

Outside, a forest of buildings stands like a giant cemetery. Titans' gravestones soaring upward. A crossword puzzle of lit and unlit windows. A checkerboard standing on its side, with its head in the sky. At any moment mysterious rectangles of light go on or off. One man's night is another man's morning. At any hour of the day or night.

Not even for a second does this town go to sleep.

The building across the way is made up of offices. Empty lights stand watch over hidden treasures. A neon light dances its way downward without joy. In the street glowworms throw off shafts of light. Running. Stopping to sniff at intersections and hurrying along on their way. Maybe there is magic in the fact that somebody is looking and taking it all in. This is the way an electronic control panel blinks at the uninitiated.

You can't stand there forever. An old Eskimo, alone on a block of ice, facing the endless ocean. The bed absorbs him mercifully. Even time seems to subside with him. Without moving.

Last night he got to Kennedy. On American. He had not intended to stop over in New York. He had an El-Al ticket and a piece of paper with flight number, date, and boarding time. During the entire trip he was afraid he might be late. But his plane landed an hour and a half ahead of schedule. He could have gotten lost and found again. But he didn't go astray even once. He quickly found the departure lounge, the entrance, the El-Al counter. He was really proud of himself. In fifty years he had not been outside of Israel. Now that he was on his own for the first time he kept a cool head. He asked, in English, got an answer, in English. And understood. America had wrought some kind of change in him after all. Stepping lightly, even though the valises were heavy, he went up to the counter and presented his ticket.

Anna Steinhardt had said: You just have to get the ticket stamped. Everything's been taken care of. And he was ashamed of having been so jittery.

Anna had smiled at him radiantly: Dear, sweet provincial. In America there's no need to buttonhole one of the clerks. Far more important matters are settled over the telephone.

And the attendant put his ticket down and flipped through the passenger list. He was asked to spell his name. But it couldn't be found the second time either.

Sorry, you're not on the list, she said.

He was aware of a strange sensation. As if he had been violated.

But they told me in Boston that everything was taken care of.

Who told you?

He looked around. Passengers stood by their belongings, perfectly calm. Not impatient. Smiling. As if he were an obstacle that time would remove. He couldn't tell which of them understood Hebrew. Maybe all of them. Maybe not a single one. They waited politely. They didn't eavesdrop. Nobody offered help.

There wasn't a single small-town busybody there, to butt in, perhaps to suggest a solution, chat with him, tell him of a similar occurrence that had befallen him or another.

The attendant was courteous. You can make a reservation for another day. Over there, across from the corner. Determined to keep his composure, he compressed his lips.

Where?

Even the second time she was courteous.

But he said: I want it for today.

And he was surprised at his own voice. Too loud, tense, angry.

They're expecting me at home. They're coming to the airport to meet me, he apologized.

The attendant looked at him and an expression of despair spread across her face.

You can speak to the manager. This way.

He knocked gently but received no answer. He opened the door slowly. He saw one man with his back to him, another facing him. The manager threw him a glassy stare.

Wait outside, he said to him in Hebrew. With your valises.

For a moment he was glad that his face gave him away. Then he detected some slight condescension in what had occurred. And he was not pleased. But he didn't allow himself to get angry. He decided to forgive the man his poor manners. After all, in a few minutes the man would get him out of this jam. He guessed at his age. About the same as the youngest of his sons. And that gave him confidence. As if the fact implied some kind of promise. The man who came out said you can go in. But when he got inside the manager's ear was glued to the telephone. He waited meekly by the door until he got a nod of the head and sat down. A young man, brimming with happiness, health, strength. Certainty radiated from his face and the tie of the successful hung around his neck. And what was more: gold buttons. A gold pen. A gold ring. Glasses with gilded frames. The gold of this land and its happiness.

He waited patiently and only once glanced at his watch. There was time. The conversation went on and on. He didn't take offense. Something of the audible half of the conversation appealed to him. The joy of a reserve unit getting together again. The familiar words that his sons used with friends. *Salamtak.* Tell us about it. Some friend you are. So help me. We won't let you get away hungry. With the Missus, naturally. How are the little bastards?

A lingo that belonged to a certain time and place. And

a few memories of his own associated themselves with it for a while. Even though he was only a visitor to this idiom. The imitation that leads to assimilation. He had used it from time to time. With cautious irony.

After the receiver was replaced there remained a last afterglow of the conversation. Then little by little the eyes went dull and froze. He related his weary tale. In Boston. Over the phone. They said everything would be all right. Only to get the ticket stamped. And here we are. He may have made it longer; he may have made it shorter. The man said I can't help you, and he believed him. And he was suddenly very tired. And he was sorry to have been a nuisance. And didn't bother to ask essential questions. But at that very moment a curly-headed young man, almost a boy, came in, and the manager got up to greet him. They shook hands; they slapped each other on the back. And the spark was lit once again. They deliberately greeted one another in broken English. Long time no see. And they launched into a conversation loaded with childish jokes. Suddenly the manager realized that he was still sitting there and threw him an impatient glance. Well, that's that, he said. And dismissed him without further ado. And he got up to leave. He trudged heavily across the space separating the armchair, which was occupied at once, and the door. Meanwhile, he managed to catch a few words. And these fired his anger.

The manager said: You're a lucky sonofabitch; you always were. Just a few minutes ago we got a cancellation. I didn't know whether you'd make it or not. In a few minutes you'll have to board.

He stopped by the door. He spoke in a loud voice, and the other two fell silent. Something in his voice forced them to listen. I was first!

He did not recognize the voice coming out of his own throat.

The manager fixed him with a hostile gaze. As if unable

to believe his ears. Do you want to take over my job? Soon the position will be vacant. You can submit an application. He was pleased with his little joke. He even stole a sugary smile at the curly-headed visitor.

But he stubbornly repeated: I was first. His voice projected uncompromising purpose. An injustice had been done, and this time he would not let it pass. The anger served its purpose. The manager retreated from his irony and became polite once again. He explained: It is true. Sometimes there are a few last-minute cancellations. We keep them for the most urgent cases. And it is up to me to decide who goes and who stays.

But you gave him my seat, he insisted.

He was amazed at how quickly the manager's face changed expression. These were simple and unmistakable. Now the message was boredom. As if he were suddenly overcome. Up to this point he had still seen some use in the brief dialogue. Sir, he said, your name was not on our list.

But they told me everything was okay.

Who told you?

Could he really have said: Anna Steinhardt?

For a moment he stood there not knowing what to do. Through the open door he could see his valises, just outside, like faithful watchdogs. The manager looked at him impatiently. Even the curly-haired young man's face registered some amused curiosity. As if waiting for him to speak again. What would he say this time?

They'll be waiting for me at the airport, he said.

The manager's voice matched his facial expression. Now the tone was one of quiet desperation. As if a different string were being played.

Let them wait. When they see that you haven't come they'll go home, the manager said patiently, and got up to help move him along.

We live very far away, he said, and a gentle smile lit up

his face. He was expecting the question: How far? Where? But it did not come. The manager just shrugged his shoulders in annoyance and moved a little closer. Now his hand was on the doorknob.

He was a little disappointed that not even a spark of recognition was kindled when he mentioned the name of the kibbutz, of his kibbutz.

Do you know where it is?

I've been there, said the manager indifferently.

It's also a big expense, a special trip, he said.

This was the fatal mistake. Here the floodgates burst. A sneer lit the manager's eye. And a peculiar alertness came over him. Here was a topic certainly to his liking. He was ready to waste valuable time over it. The young man, with whom only a moment ago he had been trading slaps on the back, seemed to fade into the background. And you really couldn't afford that, said the manager. And in order not to leave any doubt about the intended irony, he nodded his head from side to side so that his forelock bobbed lightly to and fro.

He wondered where this hatred was coming from. You have a swimming pool? A public auditorium? Tennis courts? The man even had something to say about income tax. And he could hardly get a word in edgewise. We built it all with our own hands. The manager laughed. And the subsidies? And he wasn't well-enough versed in the matter to match wits with an economist, who could wipe him out with numbers. He just managed to say that he had worked all his life, and worked hard. He wasn't happy with the apologetic tone that emerged. And could one imagine living in the Jordan Valley without a swimming pool? Today, that he has an air conditioner, he is amazed at how he survived for so long. Fifty years without one. A hundred and ten in the shade, in summer, in the banana groves. In that sweltering heat. And it would be shameful to mention the wars. And what for?

[200]

And why must one hate so much, here in New York, in a plastic armchair, with gold buttons on a haughty blue blazer? And then, when he wanted to make one more irrefutable point in a disheartened defense of his principles, his life history, and even his honor to some extent, and the manager suddenly said with a smile at once amused and bored—even combinations were possible on his versatile face—you're wasting my time, at that point he got angry enough to kill. And he yelled.

You gave my seat to this man and you aren't ashamed of yourself!

And then the manager touched him on the shoulder, gently, but without respect, and said: Sir, we have nothing further to discuss. Get out please. If you want to file a complaint contact the head office.

It was that touch that caused him to fall apart. It had something coarse—cruel, he said to himself later—and degrading about it, and he couldn't stand it. As if it were that touch that knocked him down onto the bench with trembling lips, even though he had managed to close the door behind him and to move his valises away from the doorway.

He sat down on the bench and envied the passengers who were lifting their valises onto the scales. He hoped that none of them had noticed the momentary blackout that had come over him. But his face gave him away. An attendant came over and asked him what the matter was. He repeated the story for the third time. She asked for his ticket, and hope was reawakened. Her face was agreeable and fresh and while she was bending over him he was able to make out a slight dimple at the base of her neck. She spoke to him in English, but when she noticed that he was having trouble she switched to Hebrew. And then she had trouble. She told him more or less what the others had said. He should lodge a complaint against the person who had misinformed him in Boston. Tomorrow he would be able to go to the main office and try to make a reservation for another day. Chances are poor since demand is heavy before the holidays. But there may be a last-minute cancellation. Everything is booked solid on the other airlines, as well. Peak season, what can you do?

She said all these things with delicacy and out of genuine sympathy for his plight. She asked if he had relatives and even changed a dollar bill for him so that he might get in touch with them. She showed him where the telephones were. She expressed true regret that she couldn't call for him on the company telephone. Only from the manager's office can you make outside calls. She soothed him. Telephones in America are not like in Israel. Here you drop in a coin, dial, and speak. He dragged the valises a long way, up to the line of telephones near the entrance. This exhausted him. For a while he stood by the phone booth and panted heavily; he was unable to speak. Then he took out his glasses and read the directions on the instrument. He didn't understand everything, so that he lost two coins and the third was returned four times. Until a man came along who spoke with a completely incomprehensible accent and dialed Feinstein's number, and without realizing it pocketed the rest of the change. He was so happy to hear the telephone ringing in Feinstein's house that it seemed petty to ask the man to return his money. The phone rang and rang. He grew angry with Feinstein for never being at home when he was needed and went back to sit by his valises. In a little while he tried again. An hour later Feinstein was still not at home. The loudspeaker was summoning the passengers to the departure gate as he tried, in vain, for the fourth time.

It was the polite attendant who helped him find a hotel room. This time she dialed. He had spent six weeks, he apologized, in the United States and had never had the occasion to use a public telephone. Everything had been done for him. She smiled: an important visitor. He told her where he was from. She suppressed a kindly smile when he asked her in a fatherly tone of voice if she knew what a kibbutz was. As if this were an idiotic question. She had spent half a year on a kibbutz the previous summer. Yes, she had enjoyed every minute of it. The pool, the tennis courts. She even managed to say in pleasant fashion that "the Company" could not pay for his hotel. "The Company" could certainly not hold itself responsible for his being stuck in New York because some travel agent in Boston had made an error. Nor was it likely that the Boston agency would agree to compensate him. They would probably claim that he had not heard correctly. Or something of the sort. But he had not gone to a travel agent to change the date. There is no evidence of any such thing on the ticket. On the contrary, it bears a different date altogether. Somebody has made a mistake and he ought to lodge a complaint against whoever it was. She looked at him with compassion, and then her eyes lit up in a sly smile. Tomorrow morning he ought to call his relative and tell him the whole story. And if that man can take a hint—and what Jew in America cannot take a hint?—he will offer to pay for the hotel. He felt slightly humiliated. He wanted to say: I'm no schnorrer, but he didn't.

He felt a lot better when she helped him put his valises onto the bus and promised to give some more thought to the idea of settling in Israel, which he had broached with waxing enthusiasm. Israel needs girls like that. She said that the hotel wasn't far from the station, but that he would have to take a taxi. The valises were too heavy. She said that the taxi drivers were swindlers and that he ought to pretend to some familiarity with New York. The hotel was not especially expensive, but it was not the cheapest, either. Still, that was better than ending up in some third-rate hotel in a strange neighborhood. New York is not exactly a picnic. Especially not for people who are no longer young. He felt better now.

[203]

Maybe some Zionist purpose will have been served by their meeting. You never can tell which meetings with strangers will set hidden wheels in motion.

But once he was alone on the bus he began to worry. He had not noticed that the valises were being loaded into the baggage compartment. He was pushed along and only later heard dull thuds coming from the belly of the vehicle. It only remained for him to hope that his valises were there, too. Everybody was so quiet. Little by little the anger returned and wormed its way into his consciousness. He remembered the manager's words, his sarcastic smile, the quivering shoulders of the young man who so brazenly took his place and then pretended he no longer existed. Words came back and hung on, with all their degrading significance. He said to himself: Don't get excited! Under any circumstances. But the whole thing came back, and it got the better of him.

If not for his well-known temper nothing would ever happen in his life. And he would probably have gone up in smoke. If he had lived quietly and reasonably he might never have left Vilna in the first place. And it was the same when it came to settling on the land. As the result of a great outburst, and in defiance of the land office. And even the bananas—despite the rage and fury of the kibbutz institutions. It was all accomplished with his tried and true temper and without a care for his health.

Everything must be returned to its place. These grave but dormant matters must not be stirred up because of a new hate for an arrogant little man in a director's chair. But, still, he could not restrain his anger. His disappointment nourished itself on new facts. Each of them brought with it its own measure of anger. That the taxi driver had deceived him he had no doubt. The hotel clerks were disrespectful, as if they had sized him up with one look. In the evening he did not leave his room. He was mindful of the warnings—

New York is a city of bandits and murderers, and there is no respect for the elderly—even the radio let out bloodcurdling screams, and the television was not working. Maybe there was some hidden button. But he did not call the front desk. It was enough that he had disturbed the operator five times in fruitless efforts to call Feinstein. He positively loathed the cold touch of the shiny surface that still smelled of previous tenants' breath. He went out into the hall hoping he might bump into one of the employees, but the corridors were empty and silent, except for the noise of the elevator. A woman who got off passed him quickly and at the end of the hall looked back. He decided to forget about the television. He turned the knobs on the radio until he got some talk that he couldn't understand. By now he was quite hungry, but he was afraid that food prices would be too high. The lobby was too fancy—red carpets, velvet, crystal chandeliers, display cases all lit up with jewelry and gold watches.

He polished off the candy he had bought for his grandchildren and lay down on the bed. He waited for sleep, but it did not come. He fumbled around in a drawer but only found an entertainment guide, laundry tickets, an empty tampon box, the Yellow Pages, and a Bible. To his great surprise he understood most of what he read. It lacked the grandeur of the Hebrew, but it was clearer and simpler than the original. Stubborn passages yielded their meaning in a language he did not know fluently.

He read from the Book of Job and became enraged with Feinstein. A Jew from Vilna who never even bothered to learn English, or at least spoke it with such a weird accent that one couldn't help making fun of it, for whom the American Way of Life had replaced the Ten Commandments. He lived in the country and, even then, went away for the weekend to another place in the country so that no one should—God forbid!—catch him at home on Saturday or Sunday and think he wasn't doing too well.

By ten he had gotten over his reluctance to waste money on a long-distance call.

As he heard the ringing at the other end his anticipation grew. He promised himself that he would not gripe or grumble. He would simply relate what had happened. He would try to laugh it off, to show that he wasn't angry. He was just calling to let her know. This is what happened, but he's taking it like a good sport. It's just a pity that he has to waste these few days in New York. They could have spent them sight-seeing.

But this attempt, like the others, failed to raise a human voice at the other end. Anna Steinhardt was not at home either. He got angry with her too. She had conducted him to the departure gate, waved her handkerchief, which she then applied to her nose, regarded him with moist eyes, as if something had torn inside of her, and, after he disappeared down the corridor, wiped her eyes, applied powder as necessary, and went off in search of further emotional stimulation.

He was absolutely furious. And under his breath he even let out a curse in Polish.

Maybe that's why his sleep was fitful.

He turned on the reading lamp. Opened the Bible but could not read. His eyes smarted, and the letters jumped. Three-forty.

His mind turned to the others' disappointment. Bronka. And whoever volunteered to drive her to the airport. They would wait a long time at the customs exit. Bronka with a guarded smile of anticipation. Trying not to let her son or son-in-law see too much of her excitement. Her hair done with care. The color freshly touched up. She would stand behind the glass partition until the last of the passengers came out. A few times she would step outside. Maybe she had missed him and he had passed her by. Finally, they would ride home in silence. She worried. Her companion annoyed. Perhaps, too, something would be said about his well-known carelessness. Couldn't he have let them know that he wouldn't be on this flight? A waste of time, of gasoline. He likes it over there, in America, the driver would say. Greedy. He has discovered America. Making up for lost time. Bronka would swallow the insult in silence. And doesn't her excitement count? She might be ashamed to ask for a ride the next time. But in the evening, alone in their room, she would worry. She might even cry. And she wouldn't know whether it was out of sorrow, worry, or insult.

Maybe I should never have gone abroad, he said to himself.

He recalled the advice of a friend. You're in for a disappointment. They'll greet you like royalty, they'll fuss over you, they'll spoil you with silly presents, and be glad to get rid of you.

His valise was full of them. For himself and for others. He couldn't refuse. They fed him, they put him up, they flattered him. Now he was forced to carry it all. A disgrace, weighing him down.

The taxi driver was amazed at the heaviness of the valise. He warned: You'll have to pay overweight. A lot of money. They're very strict about that.

Up to last night he had thought that he would go back and say to his friend: no disappointment. Only a person who comes to America with preconceived notions or who is too concerned with appearances can say such things about good, warmhearted Jews. I saw a different America.

And now.

If he had not taken that woman's advice he would have gone home a happy man. Without anger. With a dream fulfilled.

That woman!

Now he was angry with himself for allowing a technicality to spoil his most beautiful memory of America. Even the dream belonged to her. The forest, the river, the campfire, the Indians. Sylvia had usurped Anna's place. It was the forest rangers who had entered his dream as Indians.

One was white, with a red face and a bland expression. The other one had the look of an Indian: a wild expression and a certain natural curiosity. Two old loonies, said the white fellow. But that is not what the Indian thought. He looked at the campfire and at the old woman singing her heart out and that seemed to awaken in him memories of yore.

Four. Even time has succumbed to her caress. A pale light can already be seen behind the tops of the buildings. And that oppressive feeling in his chest seems gone. He once lay that way for a few hours at the edge of the orchard. He bound his own wound and his fear went away. But he didn't know when the comrades would come. Whether in a few hours, or a day. He was afraid they wouldn't go out looking for him. Sylvia had gone off—one of those mental-health leaves of hers that had made his life so difficult in the early days—and nobody knew that he was in the orchard. There was every reason to believe that he had come back when darkness fell.

Now none of his acquaintances knows where he is, either. Except for that pleasant stewardess, who may emigrate to Israel. But she must surely have forgotten his name by now. By five he is aware of an unpleasant odor emanating from his body. A kind of ether materializing from his thoughts. As if the rot were spreading all over him.

The faucets taunted him. Boiling and freezing in turn. It was impossible to adjust them. Even the towel made him mad. It gave off a foreign smell. With great effort he dragged himself back to the bed. His eyes burned. Now he hated America with all his heart. And was furious with himself for having been taken in.

In twenty years he had not celebrated his birthday. In August he turned seventy, and they surprised him with a big party and presents. He used to laugh at the Germans for making such a fuss about personal celebrations. Now he was glad that a few things were left in their care. It is all written down in a book, and someone remembers to look.

In the kibbutz newsletter there was a congratulatory message. May you live to be a hundred and twenty. It was something he would not have understood a few years earlier. In the old days they were happy to be inscribed in the Golden Book of the Jewish National Fund and took comfort in the building up of the land. Even marriages were somehow tied to the national rebirth. At seventy he was alone, with his few remaining years and an unfilled quest.

For a few days he walked around like a bridegroom, surprised that everyone knew and remembered. Only a few weeks earlier he had had harsh words to say to his wife about the isolation of the elderly. Yes, even among us. Even more so among us, where you're always surrounded by people. And along came a personal milestone he had scarcely been aware of, and everybody was celebrating. People would stop him in the yard and shake his hand. The Good and Welfare Committee sent a cake and a check. The secretary of the kibbutz congratulated him at the general meeting, and a few members applauded. As if it were such a great accomplishment, seventy. And he could barely hold back the tears. Comrades who generally made themselves scarce, came to his room and sat down to an endless conversation that didn't make sense, with good manners that he could not grasp. People twenty and thirty years his junior even consented to listen to some stories out of the past. His contemporaries came to talk about themselves—their aches, their suffering, their old age. Bronka served tea and cookies and sometimes even wine. For the drinkers there was cognac that he got at the commissary, using a special fund whose very existence he had not known about.

Even the factory celebrated the occasion, after its fashion.

During the tea break, against a backdrop of machine noise, a few words, serious words, were spoken. The production manager, a kid of thirty-five, an engineer who travels to Europe three times a year, showed his sincere appreciation of a man who for fifty years, give or take a few, had been doing every kind of menial job. Then they clinked glasses and had some pretzels and chips, and he said a few words, too. Words of irony, in order not to show how moved he was. Playing with the traditional "He who works for the Sabbath eats on the Sabbath," he said, "He who works for the Sabbath works on the Sabbath." And "Aging does not do for a life what it does for wine." A few understood and a few did not. Those who did not understand thought that he had become too emotional. Perhaps they were right. Even he was sorry that he had made a joke. The subtleties didn't come through. They thought he had lapsed into bitterness. When actually he was happy. As happy as he could be. A holiday is a day when you're called upon to reckon with time. When we were young we added each new day to the one before. Now we subtract each day from those left.

He received many gifts. Books, flowers, liquor. The affluent society, he lamented in a sort of happy disappointment, when he saw the presents piled up on his table. One friend of his youth sent a set of the *Encyclopaedia Judaica*. A kind of peace offering. Forty years earlier that one had fallen for communism and they parted ways. As if he wanted to say: You were right, you youthful builders. The geography group brought him the Masada album. The orchard workers—a record, favorite old Zionist songs. The factory workers—a beautiful carrying-case, for glasses, pen, handkerchiefs, and the like. The youngest of the grandchildren, whose parents had left the kibbutz, sent letters of congratulation. A grandpa big as a house with a little tree alongside of him. Out-stretched arms and extended fingers, and legs like poles, and a blue stripe above and a brown stripe below, and a yellow sun.

He received a very special gift from his children. And it was really a surprise, the result of the combined effort of three families. At first he had refused to accept it as a matter of principle. I see that you have taken up a collection for a poor relative. As sarcastic as possible. But later he allowed them to tempt him. His children handled his sensibilities with extraordinary patience, like a medical team. They succeeded in proving to him that neither the image of the kibbutz nor its values would be hurt by a gesture of goodwill on the part of children who had left it. Altogether he would be taking a month's leave. He deserves it. After so many years. He is going to see relatives in America. So what? Many perfectly respectable people go and come back and go again. Is it better to take public money than the money of one's children? On the contrary, whoever travels at his own expense today is especially worthy. His daughter even said: Knowing him, even though it's a private visit once he's there he'll make propaganda for every worthwhile Zionist cause and will do it better than those who get sent there to do it at public expense. He listened carefully, and, since he heard love underneath what was being said somewhat thoughtlessly, he did not get angry.

A few days later he thought he detected some trickery that compromised his dignity. The words are true, but there is harmful intent, nevertheless. A kibbutz member is not a beggar who needs alms. If he wants to see relatives that he has neglected these many years—the kibbutz can pay for his trip. Although, at the time he did remove his name from the "list," because he felt that this "running abroad has something provincial about it that is beneath us." But if he changed his mind, he would undoubtedly be at the top of the "list." But he had to give up that idea, too. The Good and Welfare Committee recognized his priority, but the secretariat refused to increase the budget, and he was not willing to take somebody else's place. He still had the right to go next year, but in the meantime everything had been prepared and taken care of. The doubts he expressed to his children were far from clear. Both because he couched them in watered-down language and because they were voiced over the phone, and he has trouble talking to people whose faces he cannot see. At any rate, by the time they realized that he intended to ask the kibbutz for money it was all done. The travel agent had made all the arrangements, and the relatives in America had been notified. Meanwhile he held a passport and a plane ticket and a mimeographed sheet, in Hebrew and English, of a detailed itinerary, as if he were some big shot, every minute of whose time must be accounted for. With a deep sense of loss of face he was forced to explain to his children that if he were to go this year the kibbutz would not pay. They said there was no point in putting it off. People were expecting him. He was peeved that they behaved as if they had known all along it would come to this. As if it were all part of a script—the refusal, the doubts, the coming round. It was expected and made inevitable by his pedantry and his pestering. He was sorry that he had troubled his conscience for nothing. He knew what his children were saying behind his back. The old man has to go through the old song and dance. To soothe his conscience and so forth. This time he almost went too far. The lack of respect enraged him, but he forced himself to control his anger as the doctor had ordered. Sleepless nights can come even without anger.

For a few days he went about like a man disgraced. Accusations made against others, of wanting to enjoy the best of both worlds, abnegation on the one hand and acquisitiveness on the other, came home to roost. When he was reminded of things he had written in the kibbutz newsletter a few years earlier he experienced genuine anguish. But he was not able to retreat, either. Ordinary curiosity had become an obsession. The wanderlust, whose very existence he was loath to acknowledge, was let loose within him not as a force that had lain dormant but as one that had been actively repressed. And he it was who had been fond of saying: I have but one dream—to plant one Jew on the soil of this small land and to put an end to the frantic running from place to place.

Before his children came and surprised him with their gift he could have managed without America. After they said America—it became his dream. As if a dam had burst. In fifty years he had not been out of the country. Except for a short visit to Syria, a partial mobilization having to do with the illegal immigration from there, and two sorties into Jordan, in the days when it was possible just to up and cross a river and move about at will. Actually, in '38 he had been asked to go to Poland on an educational mission, but the orchard workers rose in opposition. In '42 he asked the kibbutz to let him volunteer for the British army, but they were angry at him for presenting his request as a matter of conscience and didn't let him go. All of us are ready to volunteer and to fight against Hitler, they said. But there is a quota, and it has already been filled. Are you the only one who can't live with that?

There was still another reason why the whole thing caused him secret annoyance. Somehow, in a way he didn't completely fathom, the children's present was like belated revenge from Sylvia.

When he allows his thoughts to wander he forgets that he has commanded himself to stop thinking about Sylvia. Things that happened many years ago are seen with clarity. Always it is the same picture: she wearing a white dress, with a curious smile, luminous. The parlor tent of the first family of the kibbutz, visited by the unmarried with a mixture of generosity and jealousy in order to mitigate their loneliness, to peek at the hostess's beautiful breasts, and to get tipsy smelling the last of the European-style soap, which is condoned in this exceptional creature. A Tent of Congregation. He, in an embroidered Russian blouse, a rope, riding boots, smiling. All are welcome guests. By way of an allusion they used to say that their tent flaps were well greased. They saw themselves as those Bedouin whose many guests would wipe their greasy hands on the entrance flap after a bountiful feast. They were the heart of the kibbutz. The first who dared to call that place home and to send barefoot toddlers out among the thistles and briers.

For the movement paper in Vilna he would write philosophical articles. The small happiness was expected to find its place in the shadow of the great happiness. That is, the exalted business of throwing one's life away in the service of a lofty ideal. In that little tent of theirs the two kinds of happiness seemed to mingle. When water was found as the result of an experimental drilling he took Sylvia with all the coarseness of a peasant, and she kissed the blisters on the palms of his hands as if she were continuing an age-old tradition. Sometimes they did it on the threshing floor. To give substance to the word. To give new life as in days of yore. She was always afraid of losing a certain primacy, which was theirs by right in those days of in the beginning. When he returned at night, on foot, from the convention of the Labor Federation, somewhat inflamed by his own rhetoric, which had won sympathetic response, she washed the soles of his feet. At the full moon they would steal away to the swimming hole and bathe in the nude, as if enacting some pagan rite. On Jewish holidays she would drape herself in a muslin curtain and dance in the shack that served as dining hall to music by Schubert, played on a hand-wound gramophone.

All those eccentricities that were so foreign to him he was able to endure. A girl from Danzig, whose head was full of crazy German ideas. He didn't mind it when she gave Greek names to the goats and sheep and sang, in a thin, quivering voice, themes from symphonies instead of folk songs. He didn't even mind the fact that he wasn't allowed to speak to her while she was reading. He had to wait until she inserted a finger between the pages and lifted her dreamy eyes to him. The quarrels began when she insisted on speaking German to the children.

He remembered the bad years in a different outfit, the one she was wearing on one occasion when they had words. A sort of kimono it was—a voice beckoning from afar—the gift of a relative of hers who was a perpetual tourist, a secret ally. They had a room of their own at the time, without indoor plumbing, and a real wardrobe closet instead of vegetable crates. A long soft robe caressing her beautiful limbs. A form of dress that is out of place in the ascetic kibbutz, which insists on humble ways. She wore it on purpose, a form of instigation. A kind of declaration of independence in blue and red and gold. A dragon unfurled along her back, and her head was its head. And her eyes, which always wore a skeptical expression, reflected an embittered hostility. She had already given up all hope of making things right between them. She only awaited the day when he would give in and admit that what he called "values" were nothing but a mask. A mask for tyranny and nothing else.

The glow of the first days grew dull, and a kind of chronic misery emerged in her facial expression. Sylvia cannot see small, they said, a few with compassion, others with hostility. She did her work as if impelled by a demon. But the monotony consumed her. The stars have been unfaithful, and the people are revealed in their shame—the village mentality will not be suppressed—she would say—and he had no response save for severity, for harsh, orthodox, ascetic words. *Feinschmeckerin* was the worst epithet of all. She spoke German with relish, but she refused to speak Yiddish at all, as if it might offend her aesthetic sensibilities. But the other girls were all drawn to her. They gladly came to that public worship, around the tinny gramophone, as long as Mahler or Brahms or Beethoven was on the turntable. She taught even the deaf among them to say Bach with reverence. She was quick to adopt any perturbing, unsettling new idea from afar, without distinction, as if her life depended on it. The slightest tremor in any world capital would leave its imprint on her just as soon as the magazines, bundle after bundle in two or three languages, sent by her parents several times a year, had been picked up from the nearby post office. She seemed to miss the "spirituality" that permeated life in the youth movement—the excited philosophizing of young people who wrote poetry in secret, reflecting ideas linking arms with the whole world, self-immolation in overblown language. Here these had been elaborated into a row of humdrum tasks whose only reward lay in the doing. No longer did one speak of socialism in our time or redeeming the nation or the Sabbath Soul or moral renewal or return to the soil. The people of the settlement spoke of workdays and nutritional units and the shoe budget and the clothing budget and petty cash. Only *Davar* and the movement paper still "nurtured the spark" and had recourse to those holiday words.

They couldn't forgive her princess-held-captive-among-the-plebes behavior and little by little she withdrew into her German novels, reading them even during the "children's hour." And her face, which had always worn a certain mysterious expression, took on an ironic, hostile look, as if everything going on around her were too boring, as if it were only intellectual curiosity that enabled her to survey it all with detachment, with a slightly amused air, like Gulliver in Lilliput, and saved her from succumbing to melancholy. He forgave her all this, and even more. He did not call her to account when she fell in love, right out in the open—maybe just be-

cause she did it in the open and with such characteristic
naiveté—with all sorts of "interesting" men, artists, poets,
and one man from the Stern gang, who had got away from
the British police and spent some time in the kibbutz. He
knew that these were nothing but insubstantial romances,
unconsummated and what is more, consummation would
destroy them—clearly a matter of the spirit meant to shield
her from monotony, a refreshing pick-me-up, good for her
health, frustrating for the men in question, who believed in
her love and fell in love themselves. He never confronted her
with jealous scenes and sometimes he got the feeling that
she missed them. She was trying to prove that principles were
nothing but hot air, without relevance to the things that
matter, and he never gave her the chance. Secretly, he felt for
her unfortunate "loves," who sought her company plagued
by murky, bitter feelings of guilt. His willingness to share
probably made it worse for them.

He really knew no jealousy. He felt that her attentive,
fascinating smiles, the tilt of the head, with her body leaning forward so that the tips of her breasts showed, were
nothing but preoccupation with herself, a deliberate attempt
to understand the secret of her own magic.

But not even these innocent pastimes helped to relieve
her boredom. His few attempts to penetrate her "terrain," to
read carefully and with much goodwill some garbled poem
that she admired with all her heart, and to say something
intelligent about it, and even the small "betrayals" of values,
as he acquiesced in the heretical opinions she expressed in
public, all these were met with the cold derision of a child
who knows he is being humored when his father deliberately
loses to him at chess. And when the first silver thread made
its appearance—in the matter of tinting the hair she was a
true pioneer—and the children grew up wild in the farmyard and refused to learn German—Hitler had come to power
meanwhile, and she gave up on that—and the bouts of silence

between them grew longer and longer, and the members of the kibbutz lost their patience with her—the tolerance of a happy collective for a soul in torment—she began to be visited by mysterious illnesses. Not even the doctor, who was on friendly terms with her, could say what was the matter. And even though her illness had no name, it was something real, complete with migraines and attacks of shortness of breath and a fine rash. For a few years, with ever-increasing regularity and in every kind of weather, he would bring her trays of food. They had no refrigerators then, and every meal had to be carried on a tray, in covered plates, and by the time the food got to the room it was ice-cold and tasteless. Sometimes he was humiliated by the nasty remarks of the less considerate members of the kibbutz. They imagined that this was nothing but the mollycoddling and seclusion and airs of a fake aristocrat, and she never acknowledged his predicament or his efforts, nor did she try in any way to make life easier for him. She didn't even say thank you as he came into the room with wet shoes and dripping jacket. She only gave him that scrutinizing, clever look, with her head at an angle, as if each trip of his with outstretched arms, in *hamsin* or rain or pitch-black night, were a test of loyalty and uprightness. She stood guard and watched impatiently for the moment he would let down his guard and "prove once and for all" that the high standards he was so proud of were nothing but a tissue of lies, empty words, like everything else here in her opinion, in this society that never stopped singing its own praises or patting itself on the back. But he never complained and even tried not to let his face show his distress. In silence he would set before her the tray loaded with whatever he could put together at such a late hour. He was often late for supper, because in those days he was waging a war of his own against those members who finished work on the dot. A long, drawn-out workday was, in his opinion, a sign of true attachment to the kibbutz and also a question of honor. "Responsibility is something whole," he would say. Sylvia would step out of character and blow up at him over his neglect of the children.

In a calm, controlled voice, without the slightest trace of anger, he would reply that there is nothing wrong for the children of tillers of the soil to know that working the land involves unlimited devotion. If she had not "put it into their heads" that they were being neglected they would never have noticed. And what's more, they would be proud of their father for being one of the mainstays of the kibbutz, a man who does not punch a clock. He did not grumble, nor did he get angry with her even when she withheld herself from him on account of her same vague complaints. He would lie on his bed and read professional literature until she asked him to put out the light, and then, sometimes, a certain wonderful smile would come to her lips, and he would get into her bed, and what they did gently, tenderly made up for everything. Only that she would often cry afterward, as if she had sinned against herself, as if by responding to the demands of the flesh she had strayed from some path of continual struggle whose goal was never discussed openly. She wanted to leave the kibbutz. A relative of hers had made him a very attractive job offer that would mean getting away from the parched fields and would include an apartment in Tel Aviv, where, in those very days, a Philharmonic Orchestra was being organized. The quarrels over the souls of the children troubled his life. Especially hard on him was her sarcastic tone when she spoke to the children about kibbutz values. Concepts that were sacred to him were in her view conventional lies and empty chatter. He never raised his voice to her, only implored her insistently, "I beg of you, not in front of the children," and she would have no consideration for his feelings. Anything critical that occurred to her, whether a child's mind could grasp it or not, she chose to air in their presence.

When the first reports began to filter out of Europe and they did not let him volunteer for the British army—and he would work day and night at all sorts of tasks, as if to atone for enjoying pastoral tranquillity in time of war—a serious rift developed between them. She would speak of her boredom, as if it were the worst of tortures. He became enraged that she could speak about imaginary mental anguish when millions were suffering real tortures. One day he said, "You talk as if you had been sentenced to a lifetime of forced labor." She replied, "You said it!" He opened the door. "You're not a prisoner here." And she got up and went out and disappeared into the night. His pride didn't allow him to go after her, but when she had not come back a week later he picked himself up and went to where she was staying. He asked her to come back "for the children's sake." But she said, "Especially not for the children's sake." It would be better for them to have two happy parents, one here and one there.

The struggle over the souls of the children went on for a few more years. She did not acknowledge it. "They are adults and will choose when the time comes." And they chose, one by one. The two boys decided not to come back from the army after the War of Independence. He respected their decision, seeing in the army a pioneering goal in its own right. But the army, it turned out, was nothing but a stepping-stone. A year or two later they were out of it. One in the Foreign Ministry, the other at the Treasury. His daughter left a few years later. Her husband, a brilliant journalist, refused to live "far away from where it was happening."

He lay the blame with Sylvia. Even though it was she who had left home, they did not bear her any ill will. On the contrary, they admired her courage. For a few years she lived in a one-room rooftop apartment by the seashore and supported herself by giving exercise classes. She decorated the former laundry room with the most fascinating rags and created an atmosphere of restrained tranquillity. She endured her solitary state for quite a number of years. The ailments all disappeared. Reconciled with herself and with the whole world, she received her guests in that Chinese robe of hers. Even his visits were welcome there. A few of them ended in curious probings.

After she left she stopped voicing criticism of the kibbutz. Just the opposite. She discovered all of its advantages, once she had distanced herself from it. It was simply that she had not been meant for that kind of life. And if the children left, she said, it was on account of him and not on account of her. The zeal, the asceticism, the constantly pursed lips, the cruel silence of a tormented saint, these and nothing else are what kept the children from following in his path. These words made him very angry. With seething emotions he would think over what she had said. It is true that he was strict with others and with himself in matters great and small, but he never was mean. Nor did he speak harsh words to his children. It was all in silence and tacit reproach. He would try to smile. To show that his love was still there. Actually, at the meetings of the kibbutz he would sometimes say sarcastic things directed at the anonymous whole. But he never used the expression "betrayal of values." Only in private conversations did he express sorrow and disappointment. He was unable to impose moderation on himself in matters requiring unqualified enthusiasm and dedication. The Age of the Titans is past, the members said; the Age of Man has arrived. Does not the strength of the kibbutz lie in its ability to make little people grow? So many times in his life it was proclaimed that a period had come to an end, that a new period was beginning. And he just didn't understand what had changed. All he did understand was that the new times were not his times.

In what was he so disappointed? Working people saw the fruit of their labor and could afford to buy a few things?

What was so bad about that? When others criticized the materialism of the younger generation he rushed to their defense. We are not a holy people. We are simple folk and have the desires of simple folk. For many years we were the cream of the nation and the cream of the working class, and they have skimmed off of us whatever they could.

Sylvia was wrong about his bullying, he said to himself. At least the children certainly had no cause for complaint. Did we not see ourselves as the fertilizer that would make the morrow bloom? What did we not lay at their feet? The butter and the cream and all our dreams. Every peep out of them was a tiding that the Redeemer cometh. Childish prattle we accepted as words of wisdom. And we did not attune our expectations to a distant morrow, but to their lifetime. As soon as today is over. Quickly, in our time. Not dreams of a far-off future or the Kingdom of Heaven at the end of a dark tunnel. It would all be right here, tomorrow. This little acre. This mule. This child. The redemption will come here and now and not in a generation that is all saints or all sinners or on the day that the tears of Jacob and Esau cease.

And yet, in spite of everything, the children picked themselves up and left without acknowledging his sorrow. After all, he had never expected them to build their lives around him. His argument was only with the kibbutz. In his first days he had founded it. In his youth he had put up its doors. And now it had all been broken through. There was no wall. There were no doors. And who would listen to him? The young ones thought he was a grouch and an idler. Only among us does it seem that the old are the enraged ones and the young defend the status quo.

On the eve of holidays, more than at any other time, does he feel his loneliness. He is not alone. He is with Bronka and the members of her family. And they see to it that he does not feel out of place. They see to it too much. This sensitivity to his feelings spoils his holiday mood. He sits, uncaring, among her offspring, a captive audience. A mourner among merrymakers. Things he had never paid any mind to bother him now. It seems that they overdo the eating a little, and the program is uninteresting, and there are too many outside guests, and the young people's manners are revolting. He would never dare go back to his room and pick up an interesting book. Bronka would come after him all worried and perplexed, and he would have to explain. What would there be to explain? Better to submit to an hour of boredom and to feed one's face a bit. And if there is something strong to drink, better yet. Then one can get a little tipsy, and what was aggravating becomes entertaining.

He will never celebrate with his own children. Once he went on a picnic with them to Hurshat Tal. The unrestrained gluttony of private enterprise. Each one hates his neighbor's smoke. They say all the right things about the mountains and the scenery, and if a bird should come along, about birds, too. Only his grandchildren are a source of comfort. But he prefers to see them at the kibbutz. The feeling of dependency creates a kind of closeness. And for a few hours Bronka walks on tiptoe, and only her cakes are welcome.

The isolation is closing in on him. Even anger—which used to be his stock reaction to the "slanders" he read about the kibbutz—is ebbing away. As if the last thread binding him to others has been broken. No longer does he seethe as he reads the papers. He even reads the gossip columns with a kind of icy impassivity. His friends of old, who have become the movers and shakers, are given the once-over there. What they said, with whom they dined, and all the other insipidities. And he would say to himself: Maybe there is no other way; maybe it is impossible to drive this flock without gossip. Lately he has even let Bronka buy a women's magazine. For the recipes, she says. But she doesn't skip what comes in between. Sometimes even he glances at it. The happy smiles on the faces of the people in the photographs make a mockery of his life. Not even the new style of writing is to his taste. Self-important professional jargon. As if it were common knowledge that the old words had lost their validity: self-realization, manual labor, loyalty to values, and all the rest. With whom could he talk about Jewish existential angst? The children have not been branded in their flesh by the degradation that continues to flourish around them. Youth without a history who have read many history books. Youth without culture who have stereo sets. Could he ever say to them—culture is bread with honor and a Jew beneath a tree? Even from the war they returned with shoes that pinched, a personal bellyache, heavy eyelids, and dreams of going abroad. But one musn't grumble. They are good people, workers. Only it is a pity that they are clearing a field of stones and cannot see Jacob's dream. They pick olives and no saying out of Jewish lore occurs to them as they climb down from the tree.

He is careful. He will never again write in the newsletter what he once wrote. The niceties of bourgeois culture may have a certain refinement about them, but this complex life that we are trying to build here is a more delicate matter still. For this a very subtle grasp is needed. Speaking to closed ears is a kind of obscenity. Only in silence is there true honesty. Like prayer. There is no point in carrying on about how times have changed. The kibbutz is not the way it was. And I am not the way I was, either. And then there is Bronka, and the word *loneliness* may hurt her. Bronka's face is the comfortable face of loneliness.

Fifteen years he lived by himself and did not want for anything. He withdrew into the habits of a bachelor, indulging in unreal victories, famished, humiliated loves complete with swollen eyelids and confused gestures and lies that only approximated the truth.

Bronka had been the wife of a friend. While her husband was still alive he had been fond of her because she was conscientious and understanding and realistic in her expectations. Sylvia in reverse. He found in her the folk-humor, the generosity, the tempered curiosity, the unassuming simplicity of a Jewish mother. He felt comfortable with her and with Avreml, her man, a repository of Jewish learning, who was always ready with an apposite saying, now in Hebrew, now in Yiddish. She was completely free of the airs of those women who are objects of desire. A good soul, people said. A perpetual candidate for the Education, Good and Welfare, Health, and Conciliation committees, in short, for any job where a low-key person was needed who knew how to keep a secret. When Avreml died he sat with her for an hour and a half. Her only friend, it turned out. For five years they said hello to one another and went their separate ways. Until it happened that they were on the same committee. They realized that they had similar opinions about certain people. They began inviting one another over for cups of coffee. When she fell ill he brought her some fruit. What others had seen all along finally dawned on them.

For a long while he hesitated. He remembered love as a great turmoil, and now he was in the grip of a sort of exaggerated calm. An occurrence of no import caused him to make up his mind. On a kibbutz outing he watched her opening cans of food with her steady hands, and he was reminded of the books lying in his room in disorder. About the real issue he said nothing. Nor did she call it by its rightful name. But one day he dozed off in her armchair as they were listening to a radio program together, and when she woke him he was too tired to go back to his own room. He said: These apartments are too big for one person. And he laughed: It's a messy life without a wife. Was this just a joke or was it an attempt at justification? Sensitive matters were discussed later, with great modesty and roundabout language. And these, too, worked out well, in keeping with her style: calmly, in relaxed fashion, with a show of gratitude. In the end she picked up her few belongings and moved in with him. She took over immediately and made the neglected room look like new. A bit of friction occurred shortly thereafter. From earliest youth she had a clear notion of what a family ought to be. Every last little thing down to the tiniest detail was to be shared. Small joys, inconsequential hurts, passing slights. He saw the family nest as something else. She was a little hurt when he failed to concentrate on her summary of the day's news: things that had happened to her in the kitchen or the clothing depot. He had no interest whatever in the sore spots that had developed in her co-workers as they approached old age. At times he was touched by her efforts to read his articles on technical matters in the *Farm Journal*. He couldn't understand why she was angry with him when for three days he concealed a mysterious pain in his chest. Pain is a private matter, he told her, and she regarded him with reproach, as if at that very moment she understood why Sylvia had left. He refused to raise family customs to the level of ritual. He tried to build a wall around himself without giving offense. He welcomed the onset of deafness, which enabled him to shut himself off from words for which he had no reply.

During the days before his trip he was beset with doubts. Fear of travel fatigue, foreign food, the English language, change. Whatever appeared unsettling was bad for his health. He also noticed a strange piercing sensation in his chest. And even though the doctor reassured him—a cold, most probably—his mind was not at rest. It was hard for him to tear himself away from his job, as well. Some foreign order had come in and he suddenly became indispensable. And he was the one who had spoken of export as the command of the hour. The minister of Finance had said it, and he agreed, for he had fond memories of him from days gone by. The matter of the archive weighed on him, too. A few months earlier he had taken it upon himself to establish order in the kibbutz archives, and the job took him over as if the collective memory had been put in his hands. Nor did he wish to leave the matter of his health to chance. It was a responsibility and there could be no overlooking the little things that might decide his fate: morning exercises, swimming, salad with onion and garlic, an afternoon nap. He also had a dentist appointment and tickets to an important performance of *Habimah*, with the old-timers in the leading roles. And a crucial discussion about the kibbutz economy. If he went he would miss the opportunity of making a resounding condemnation of hiring labor from the outside. The young ones, unfortunately, did not understand how serious this was. His contemporaries no longer dared to express forthright opinions. And then there was plain inertia. Going abroad just wasn't worth the trouble. There is nothing better for a person than a regular schedule, his own bed, a caring spouse, a strip of lawn, meals on time, fences to protect an old man's life. But his thoughts returned, from time to time, to the main point. And to Sylvia's victory. He was irritated by the weary expression on his children's faces, which seemed to indicate that this was all to be expected and that not even a last-minute refusal could surprise them.

But in the end the spirit of adventure prevailed. A trip of this kind, that the young undertake so easily, is a shout of defiance against old age. Anyone willing to learn something new is not truly old.

The world of the old closes in little by little, like a coffin, he would joke among his friends. Sad jokes. They contribute to the pain without adding wisdom. Sometimes he would worry about becoming confused and being overwhelmed by trivialities. A phenomenon he had observed in others. The minds of the unlearned, it is well known, deteriorate with age. But he considered himself a scholar, or at any rate took pride in his intellectual curiosity. Even so, he was afraid of the things that intellect cannot control. Just lately he had been experiencing a sense of powerlessness. As if suddenly nothing mattered anymore. And gray monotony covered everything like a fine shower of wheat rust. He could no longer open favorite books without being amazed that he had ever found wisdom and guidance in them. Silly suspense films and quiz shows with obvious answers served to kill time each evening until sleep took over. His finger would mark the place in a book, but his eyes were glued to the screen. An increasingly circumscribed life. Only work still held a few surprises, unexpected snags that could be anticipated by being alert. After work nothing new ever happened. Not even the newspapers had anything new to say. Their family discussions revolved around the selfsame things. His ailments. Her ailments. Things that had to be done. Sunday was for cleaning the room. Wednesday for picking up supplies. Friday, clothes. Occasionally, there was a concert. They would go with great expectations and then fall asleep, disappointed. The boredom was a kind of self-betrayal. But perhaps even that was a sort of minor victory for Sylvia.

The trip promised a great deal. First of all as a test of his ability to withstand small nuisances. Especially for such a person as he was, who had not ridden a train in thirty years and had never flown. And for him English was a written language that his ears were unaccustomed to. He had never in his life given a tip to a waiter or a porter. Concern for property was despicable to him, so that in anything having to do with money he was a babe in the woods, an easy mark. And in one other respect the trip was a good thing. Far from home and friends you learned to recognize them for what they were. And if you were really lucky you learned something about yourself, as well. And seeing America was a must. And this, too: his last chance to be a bearer of tidings. American Jews loved to hear stories from the Holy Land.

At home, it seemed that they did not listen anymore. Or at any rate—not willingly. He even had trouble speaking at the meeting of the kibbutz. The young people didn't listen. And sometimes they interrupted without any shame. They had no time for an old man's trouble. A generation passes; they owed him no respect. The best of them listened quietly, but with impatience. As if he had been condemned by his age to espouse outmoded views. Any error in judgment was a consequence of his age. Not even at the anniversary of the kibbutz, where he came to remind them of things gone by, were they ready to hear stories out of the past. These were tolerated only as jokes at the expense of some poor schlemiel. And even Bronka's children, who had been properly warned and listened like children at school, would fix their gaze high above his head, as if old age were a contagious disease that could be caught by looking a person in the eye. One evening, while watching television, he saw an old man, like himself, get into a shiny, big car, and he was jealous of him. His clear-cut features, glowing with health and decisiveness, projected confident, understated power. This film was no less stupid than its predecessors, and there was nothing in it that could win him over to the American way of life. Nevertheless, that evening he made up his mind. The next day he announced that he was going, and that was that. Nobody was surprised. They had known all along that he would go.

But on the last night he got cold feet. The packed valises threw him into a sudden panic. As if they, and not the strength of his own decision, were forcing him to go. In the evening some friends stopped in to say good-bye, and their stories only heightened his fears. On the face of it they had come to give him last bits of advice, addresses, phone numbers, and other useful things, but they were unable to resist the urge to tell their own tales of foreign travel. With great relish they spoke, and whole countries came to life before their eyes, complete with geography, history, and episodes of lewdness. Along with the rest they saw fit to relate terrible things that had befallen people they knew, forced landings, kidnappings, lost valises, navigational errors, and like adventures. The thought that on the following night he would be on the other side of the ocean, far from all these pestering friends, caused him to marvel greatly, but it also frightened him to no small degree.

At night he tossed and turned. Favorite pieces of furniture looked on in silence, and he was sorry to be leaving them. And even disturbing noises from outside—dogs barking, the rustle of a loose tarpaulin, the vehicles of the watchmen, a cow moaning, crickets, frogs—grew close to his heart. A leaky faucet bothered his conscience. He ought to have fixed it before going away. For a while he entertained himself with an idea that he hadn't the slightest intention of carrying out. He would stick out his hand and press the button on the alarm clock. In the morning he would startle the others by showing up in work clothes. I lost the desire, he would say. Like rich folk. Who buy a ticket and change their minds. They can afford it. On a grand scale. Isn't it enough just to feel that the whole world is out there waiting? Why must one endure the inconveniences of travel and crowding and fear of heights and tiresome conversations with strangers?

When the alarm clock rang Bronka was already dressed and the coffee was on. She checked his pockets and put everything back where it belonged, as if she herself were used to long trips. At the airport she was excited, and she stuffed some handkerchiefs into the pockets of his jacket. He kissed her timidly, as if all the great mob in the departure lounge were looking at them.

He was amazed at the look of recognition he got from porters, security staff, and ground attendants. Even though he was properly dressed and had a respectable valise, they knew that they didn't have to take him too seriously. If not for his son, who had come from Jerusalem, he would have been at his wit's end. Some of his son's manners startled him, but he kept his amazement for another time. He behaved too aggressively toward the policemen and the El-Al personnel, and he handled Bronka with amused politeness, as if an old lady were something intrinsically funny. His baggage was searched quickly, perfunctorily. The young security guard surmised that he was a member of a kibbutz and treated him as a trustworthy person, but was unwilling to hear a little story about how he once smuggled a pistol under the nose of a British policeman. Even in the lounge reserved for passengers only, his son acted as if he owned the place. Traits he got from Sylvia, he said to himself. He was angry with his son when he pressed two hundred dollars in small bills into his hand, but could not refuse, in order not to attract attention. He had never broken a law and was amazed at an employee of the Defense Ministry permitting himself to deceive the officials of the Treasury. Even if everybody did it, as was suggested, he would not have wanted to make light of the laws of this state, which up to a few years ago had only been a dream. Maybe the time had indeed come to talk prose, but that did not mean that all sorts of fraud could be condoned. Sylvia used to say: You and your principles! Children come before principles. And he would say: That only means raising children without principles. Sylvia's victory seemed complete.

Takeoff was delayed for some reason, and he bought a paper and read it from end to end. He was surprised at the tranquillity of the others, who did not seem bothered by travel fever. People he tried to converse with did not know Hebrew. His solitary attempt at English raised dark suspicions in him. He had never imagined that he lacked fluency to that extent. The flight was postponed again and again, and for a while he embraced the monotony like a kind of routine, as if he were already an experienced traveler. Finally he managed to strike up a conversation with a bespectacled man, carelessly dressed, a professor of mathematics at the end of his sabbatical. The man spoke pidgin Hebrew and asked naive questions about the kibbutz. By the third hour he was worrying about not finding his relatives at the airport. He was glad that he now had at least one acquaintance in New York. The professor. But when the plane landed the man disappeared without even saying goodbye.

The takeoff was not at all frightening, contrary to his expectations. The calmness of the others extended itself to him, as well. Tel Aviv disappeared in a flash, and then he saw nothing but water and clouds on the horizon, and sometimes it was impossible to distinguish them from distant mountains. An awe-inspiring spectacle he wrote to Bronka on the airletter he found in the folder provided by the airline. At lunchtime he caused himself a little embarrassment. He was sure he had to pay for the meal and asked for something simpler. The names of cities in France sounded over the loudspeaker, but nothing was visible. London, bathed in sunshine, delighted him, and he added a few words about it to the airletter. Flying over the ocean he set aside the frugality that was second nature to him and asked for earphones. Three times in succession he heard the same symphony by Mahler before falling asleep. Through a somnolent haze he watched a movie of which he didn't understand a word. When the lights went back on he began a diary of the trip. From the archive he had learned about that. Things that are not written down have no existence. For a long time he sat with pen in hand and didn't write a thing. Many details seemed unimportant. Things that had seemed exciting in the airport were forgotten over the sea. That evening he would probably have more interesting experiences. A new country, new people. In the end all he set down was an outline and a few thoughts, which he could have done at home just as well, except that at home he would not have written anything at all, because his mind was elsewhere. Writing one's impressions is one of those occupations that seem to grow out of idleness.

Petty nuisances were not wanting. His back ached from sitting too long. The toilets were occupied whenever he needed them. His neighbor overflowed his seat and stuck his elbow into his ribs. Over Newfoundland he experienced momentary panic that his valise had not been loaded onto the plane. Suddenly the earphones fell silent and he was afraid to bother the flight attendant. His address book was not in his handbag. In his haste he had packed it into the big valise. If it is sent to the wrong destination he may find himself at the airport in New York, that jungle, from what he has been told, without friend or relative. Sudden turbulence shook the plane and for a few moments real fear eclipsed his concern for his belongings.

The encounter with America was as he had expected it to be. Like something being discovered for the second time. Everything was new and yet familiar. As if America had been dormant within him even when it was far away. And was now being roused into an active state. A promise being fulfilled.

At first he saw only a strip of water between two great expanses of fog, and didn't know whether it was ocean or river. Through a quivering wall of mist he could make out vibrantly colored strips of green. But there was no time to assimilate the impressions, as there had been when first he encountered the Promised Land—Jaffa at dawn, slowly unfolding from the deck of an almost motionless ship. Here everything happened with dizzying speed. Manhattan appeared and disappeared in a flash: gigantic, silent monuments, one taller than the next, and proud bridges, astounding in their powerful delicacy, and he could find no words to write to Bronka, except that he was dumbfounded. New impressions pushed aside impressions grown old instantly, and again the ocean lay bare and ships could be seen, each patiently drawing a long white line in the gray-green water, and a minute later a sound of contact, and then bumping and rattling and from the loudspeaker the calm voice of the stewardess. Lights went on and off, and for a while he could not keep his eyes from the other planes landing one after another, and then he found himself pulled along by the flow of the throng. The professor suddenly appeared, nodded, and rushed on his way. The customs examination went on and on, but in the arrivals area no one was waiting for him. He was overjoyed when he saw his valise moving on the belt. Even belongings have the power to light up one's face. Somebody mistakenly took him for somebody else. For a while he stood with his valises near the information desk not knowing what to do, until a young woman he did not know came up to him and asked if he was he and dragged him along behind her to a gigantic automobile, which she seemed to drive almost without a thought, certainly with none of the triumph or celebration visible in his son's face when he bought his first American car. It turned out that they were not going to New York at all—the girl said Nooyawk, and he tried to imitate her accent—but to New Jersey. In New Jersey he discovered that he had flown halfway across the earth just to go from one country village to another. The relative, whom he hadn't seen in twenty-five years, stood there in a soft silk jacket, with open arms and an aggressive smile and showered him with greetings and declarations of affection in a broken American-Yiddish from which any trace of Vilna had long since disappeared. By the time he was ready to respond he was seated at a table with a cold alcoholic beverage in his hand and plied with questions. General questions and personal ones, peace in the Middle East and news of relatives, and about a few of these he did not even know whether they were living or dead.

Nooyawk was put off for another time. Anything bad that

could be said about it was said by Feinstein, who stayed away from it as much as he could. In order to breathe clean air, play golf, grow flowers and fruit trees, and keep a wolfhound "with a goyish soul." New York is hell, he said. A city of gangsters and murderers. You never know when you're going to run into a mugger, anti-Semite, psychopath, or just someone who doesn't care for the way you look or the color of your skin.

The next day friends were invited over for an evening of questions and answers of the kind that he would encounter during his entire stay in America. Strangers came, clinked glasses, had a bite to eat, chatted with him, one after another, in no special order. Some of the talk was just chitchat, but sometimes there were serious questions. And afterward they would sit around in a circle, and he would be asked to say a few words about the situation in Israel, as if this were a party or movement cell, in the spirit of days gone by. As if he were a representative of central headquarters visiting the local branches, the way he had done when he was a member of the movement secretariat in Vilna. Except that the youths seated before him drinking in his words, with their warm, sad Jewish eyes, were now fifty years older, and full of hope. A few had already been in Israel and saw whatever they saw. Others read the papers. A few posed questions just to show how much they knew. Others—in order to give him a chance to say something. He gave them solemn assurances that war was not in the cards. People who want to wage war do not make threats. He did not thoroughly believe every word that he said. But what was wrong with planting a few false hopes? After all, he had not come to America to sow seeds of despair.

And a few American things turned out as anticipated. Whatever he expected he found. The materialism, which was symptomatic, as the Good Book says, but also excitement of the kind he saw in people twenty or thirty years younger than he, who had come to hear the tales of an old man with nothing new to say. What he had read about in books he actually experienced here. Everything—the loss of individuality in the unending landscape, solitude in the crowd, alienation, simple fear for one's livelihood, it was all here as expected. Even his provincial qualities were exposed to the light of day. His children would probably have liked that. Wasn't that one of the reasons they wanted to send him to America, to deflate the pride of an old bumpkin who was too tired to fight back? That he might cease to believe that in some wondrous way the circumscribed life he had led in a small cooperative settlement was a triumphant rebuttal, although not adequately publicized, of all the world's ills; as if by his very existence, as a man at peace with man and beast, he were a response to the challenge presented by New York. Well, let him go out into the world and see that there are taller trees and broader rivers and even decent, honest people who do decent, honest work without a guiding *Weltanschauung* or dancing the hora until dawn.

And so, he saw and saw. And came to realize that he did have the reflexes of a country bumpkin. Wherever he gave a tip he embarrassed both himself and the recipient. Anything in a store that he touched he bought, in order not to seem a pest. Any salesperson could intimidate, cajole, cheat him. At airports he was like a child. And he never got used to them, not even after he had flown many times. A drop of alcohol would loosen his tongue. Any easygoing fool could become his friend. They even managed to impose a sense of family that was completely foreign to him. Every relative of a relative was like a member of the family. As if they were weaving a net across this vast land. And how easily he put his stamp of approval on the lives of the most distant, noisy, sentimental people, drunk with their own success.

An insane voyage. And suddenly he was like a superhuman glutton. Eating, drinking, jabbering, acquiring new friends on every hand, storing impressions at once hard to digest and yet necessary as a kind of justification of his idleness. In Israel a day with nothing accomplished would not have counted as part of his life, but here he got worked up over nothing. He choked on his words in one language he was no longer used to and in another that he had not yet mastered. An emissary from the Holy Land. Who had sent him? What for? What tidings did he bear? With a sense of disgrace he recalled a letter he had written to Bronka as empty boasting: something to the effect of his having brought the message of Israel to "American Jewry" more effectively than those paid to do the job, who demolish more than they build. He was ashamed of having fallen into the linguistic trap of those dignitaries who go to America to confer with two or three individuals and return to Israel as pleased with themselves as if they had sown seeds of hope on foreign soil.

They were attentive as people are whose manners are impeccable. They listened as they might have tasted fruit from Israel on Tu bi-Shevat. They did not even mind hearing the story of his own life. And he was able to give expression to an old man's thoughts with an old man's understanding and not have to pay to get an audience, not have to pounce on every new idea the way some of his cronies did, in order to impress the young. He could even bewail the passing of the generation and the shrinking of the core, and the lessening of stature and lowering of the flag and debasement of values. Sometimes a local organizer of the United Jewish Appeal would also be invited to one of these get-togethers, and in those cases he would only make a few opening remarks, and afterward the guests would sell one another raffle tickets and conduct smaller-scale fund raising for some cause serving the larger purpose. Sometimes he would be at a meeting with a younger person, a local intellectual or student who had been in Israel, to whom anything Israeli, even an old man, was dear. And then he would be flooded with well-informed, bothersome questions and would not be let off the hook until he admitted that the issues were too complex for a simple stock answer. And the next day he would move on, happy in the knowledge that what his lips had imparted, in Yiddish bounding forth out of his memory with all its resonant vitality, or in his touchingly limited English, had become part of the collective memory of some American town whose name he would forget tomorrow.

Relatives of whose very existence he was ignorant waited for him at airports or bus stations. Distant cousins, the brother-in-law of a grandnephew, the uncle of a *landsman*, would greet him with a bright smile and an air-conditioned car, and along the way would show him all the local sights, buildings, bridges, museums, and monuments to local heroes. The outward signs of Jewish life were never omitted, an old *shul* about to cave in, now a pool hall in the black part of town, and the coldly imposing new synagogue, more gorgeous than its predecessor, and the Hebrew school. At no small risk to life and limb they even showed him one cemetery, complete with Hebrew inscriptions and a Star of David chiseled in marble, right in the middle of the red-light district. In the tailors' synagogue—the tailors are now owners of a flourishing chain of retail clothing stores—he came across a spry old man who remembered the few words of Hebrew he had learned from Brenner in the Labor Battalion.

With a gin and tonic in his hand, through sparkling cubes of ice, he saw himself as the wandering *maggid* who used to preach in the Zionists' Synagogue. He remembered the man's great height, his emaciated face, his prayer shawl, his parables, stories, legends. When he spoke many melancholy old men would smile with joy. The power of the word and its sweet sounds. And on the other side—those dignitaries and functionaries with their renowned wit and their sad jokes turned inward against their people, doing to English what their parents had done to German, except that here people were not eager for stories about Hasidic rabbis. Gossip about leaders, writers, and names in the news were what they wanted to hear. And state secrets that are better forgotten.

Sometimes he caught himself relating stories he had read in the papers as if he himself had participated in the events. He boasted having firsthand knowledge of things he only learned from hearsay. Something corrupt emanated from all these stories. Something that infected even those things of which he had thorough, firsthand knowledge. A sort of encroaching stain, as if he were being forced to be what he was not, the representative of a kind of grass-roots Israeliness instead of just a tired old man. Only very late at night, when all the guests had gone and the members of the family called to mind relatives who had perished in the Holocaust, only then did things seem to fall back into place, with a feeling of authenticity, without pretense. Then the strange living room, filled with Chinese paintings and African sculptures and Mexican blankets, would become, for a few moments, like his father's house. In all its innocent poverty and quiet gravity. As if he were suddenly not in America, but in the Old World in times gone by.

A few of his relatives were met and forgotten within a day, their meeting like a snapshot interrupting a life laden with other cares. A few words blurted out in haste by each of them, following an almost standard formula, like a sort of prayer, and soon the guests would begin to arrive, and he would have to take up his role—that of the old pioneer, the country Jew in whom even a bit of crudeness was all right. It seemed as if two kinds of victory over Exile were facing one another, without Jew-fears or the equivocating of the underdog, proud in their strength, their wealth, their uprightness, with everything that America and Israel do to Jews, with everything that America does to Israel and Israel to America. And then they said Amen, and he moved on. Sometimes he didn't even know, and was ashamed to ask, which was his relative and which the neighbor whose birthday they were celebrating. They all seemed to like company; the houses were spacious, and the food abundant, and the offspring were invariably in another part of the country. They received him with generosity and sent him off with ease, as if he were a wandering minstrel or entertainer, who makes one day less boring than the rest, a shriveled old carob from the Holy Land, making their lives a shade less bland. With a handshake they made friends, with heart and soul and moist eye, and then they parted on schedule, ·so that nobody else would be left out. Tomorrow he was expected in another city. A few he detested profoundly. He could not bear the overweening pride and complacency of property owners who believed that the whole world operated according to their values. He hated those smug faces and the lady-bountiful expressions glittering forth out of covetous eyes. As if they were assaulting his own values—life without competitiveness, or class symbols, or the drive to dominate, life on a modest scale. He would let them brag about their wealth and shrewdness and resounding victories on invisible battlefields: banks and insurance companies and stocks and bonds and real estate, things he knew nothing about. And he would remain silent, as if in awe, and would have to agree that this big house, in which he got lost on his way to the bathroom, and the crystal chandeliers, and the swimming pool, and the horses and dogs and Japanese servants and Chinese cooks, and the private road and the private woods and the parties written up in the local paper, were all a valid way of getting back at the goyim. He ate their palate-tickling foods as if he were betraying a faithful wife and could not find the strength in his heart to take a stand of his own. After all, it was only to strengthen ties that he had come to America and not to make converts. Even the very wealthy who held progressive views made him angry, they and their Sartre and their friend Marcuse and all their up-to-the-minute gurus. They put their hand on the latest book and declare themselves the ally of so-and-so, who has devoted all of his efforts of the past fifty years to a particular issue of social justice, fair distribution of wealth, and human brotherhood.

In one place there was a relative wise in the ways of the world who sent him a friendship offering, right up to his hotel room in the form of a call girl, and he didn't know if this was generosity or a trap or an attempt at ridiculing the humility he had touted in his speeches. Even though a painful curiosity stirred within him, he sent her away after a ludicrous conversation, which the girl found so funny that, as she was leaving, she planted an affectionate kiss on his forehead. In another place he listened with unstinting admiration to the economic advice of a cousin he had known in childhood, and it was only after discerning clear signs of paranoia that he realized that the man's flawless logic was part of the disorder.

In most cases he would get on well with his hosts but would be a little disappointed in himself when called upon to make the effort necessary to maintain his humility. He could easily have conquered the vain pride, the drive for prestige and adulation felt by public figures, but he was easily won over to the simple creature comforts like alcoholic beverages, steaks, and even Coca-Cola, which up to the time of his trip had symbolized all that was shallow and empty in the consumer society. Once he had even smoked a cigar and felt a pleasant sort of intoxication, but was ashamed of his enjoyment once he knew how much the cigar had cost. The tolerant attitude that he had developed over the years, that enabled him to accept trite rhetoric and inept platitudes as long as they came out of the mouths of people who spent at least eight hours a day in greasy blue work clothes, extended here to characters foreign to his spirit, who had previously represented to him the parasitism of an exploiting class. And this only because they had said Israel with trembling lips and glistening eyes and bathed him in admiring affection and had sung his praises in two or three languages with the stammer of a bashful lover. Even though he despised them at times, he was touched by their Jewish pathos, Jewish pride, Jewish exaggeration, Jewish compassion, and even a new kind of modesty. Their humility proclaims itself, but they have lost the will to bring redemption to the whole world. Now it is enough if they extend a hand to one Jew and say welcome. If you need our money, it is there. And if our love is enough, it is certainly there.

At eight the telephone rang. He stretched forth a shaky hand and, with trepidation, put the receiver to his ear. He expected Feinstein's voice and Yiddish, which would have been a consolation. But this was not Feinstein. The operator, officious, tired, slightly irritable, asked if he was Meisels and connected him with a third person who, it transpired, was looking for another Meisels staying at the same hotel, but in another room. For a while this brought on a sense of amazement, as if he had discovered something truly wondrous. Every Israeli has a double in America, and it would be possible to start all over again if God forbid . . . He grew angry with himself for thinking such thoughts.

He took a shower, brushed his teeth, shaved. He was homesick for his own little corner, his towel, the medicine chest, the smell of Bronka's face creams. Simple faucets. One for hot and one for cold. The cough of a neighbor from the other side of the wall. Birds. It would be ridiculous to hate America all of a sudden. He hadn't come here just to confirm prejudices.

If he had not met Anna Steinhardt he would have been home by now. At this time the day before yesterday. He would be sitting around with friends, talking about things American. An expert. Actually many had been to America, but he had seen things through the eyes of an old man. A person who has not been bought, who does not have a chip on his shoulder, who does not need to seem young. Years ago it had been fashionable to go to America to see how wealth corrupted and how the blacks suffered. Now people went and saw what they saw.

Maybe he would set down a few impressions for the kibbutz newsletter. Corruption? The Watergate affair only points up a certain vulgar naiveté. The agents of the Cheka would have died laughing. He might also write down some of the things he had heard. Attention-getting ideas. A few words about violence, even though he hadn't seen any with his own eyes. Air pollution—he had felt it. The awakening of the blacks—he could illustrate this by telling about the elevator boy who made fun of him when he looked to press a button that wasn't there. And he could say a few words about the decline of the city.

In any case he could not say that wealth corrupted. People worked for a living.

For some time and with deepest reverence he had followed the activity of construction workers perched on thin steel beams near the street corner. Fifteen stories above the street they did their job as if it were the most natural thing in the world. As if there were no gaping abyss below. The sight enthralled him, but it also weighed. He felt the need to furnish them with a lofty purpose that would justify the risk. He recalled his article on cultural affairs. Culture means bringing forth bread with honor. Living by the sweat of one's brow. Everything else is just window dressing.

Would their bread cost them their lives?

He forced himself to turn away his glance. Idle curiosity leads to the anticipation of calamities.

He fumbled with the knobs on the television set and this time it spoke. Very quickly a picture appeared. A nice-looking lady was speaking in an engaging manner while behind her there appeared a backdrop of horror pictures. Suddenly on came a map of Israel and the prime minister's face. He laughed with excitement. But an instant later the screen was filled by a frisky pup who stuck his muzzle into a bowl piled high with something that looked like sheep turds.

Next he watched a yoga lesson and some cartoons and a preacher's sermon. By then it was nine, but Feinstein's telephone still rang unanswered.

Nor did anyone pick up the phone at Anna Steinhardt's house. Now he was glad that nobody answered. The sound of her voice would have left him breathless. And what could he have said to her? Could he have complained? Could he have muttered some confused words of friendship? There was no turning back the clock. Theirs had been a marvelous meeting. Time's boundaries were fused, and old mingled with new. But now it was all over. The circle was closed. She was there and he was on his way home. Words could only detract. Especially over the phone, where you have to shout and repeat everything twice and your voice is not your own.

Before leaving the room he counted his money. He was pleased. Up to now he had managed it so well that nobody could possibly find fault with him. The fear that he might have to pay for the hotel room depressed him. Once again he became upset with Feinstein. He railed at his luck. This time the telephone operator got annoyed with him. Better to try again later.

He took enough money for breakfast and went out. In the elevator he looked at the menu. The prices seemed too high. He decided to eat somewhere else.

A fine drizzle hovered in the air and sprinkled the glass door with glistening droplets. People in summer clothes shook the water from their umbrellas. The wall of the building opposite had turned gray, as if painted over with a thin wash. For a while he stood and looked, but the rain kept falling. He pressed himself against the wall and walked under the overhang as far as the corner. He remembered having seen a coffee shop there.

The greasy odor repelled him, but the prices were reasonable. He found it amusing to sit at a counter, resting his feet on a metal rail. An adventure of sorts. He remembered that at home whenever there was a film about the Wild West they would go their separate ways. Bronka would return to the room to read. As if it were not respectable for people their age to waste time on nonsense. And he would be all the more insistent on seeing those friendly giants gallop about on their magnificent horses. And, anyway, who said that a person had to be respectable all the time? The movies she liked best he found boring. Pretentious melodramas. And she would imagine that she had witnessed an intensely moving human conflict.

He waited a long time and then got angry. He was not being served in his proper turn. When he stood up for his rights he was regarded with indifference. The omelet was greasy and had a funny smell. The coffee was bitter and he didn't know how the sugar dispenser worked. By the time he saw how the others used it his coffee was too sweet. He went somewhere else and ordered pancakes. But these, too, were sickeningly sweet in their viscous bath of imitation maple syrup. It was his own fault. He ought never to have nodded his head when they asked and he didn't understand.

Meanwhile the rain had stopped. A heavy, silvery gray fog had settled around the tops of the buildings. He bought a colorful umbrella, for Bronka, and started walking. The map in his hand told him that the El-Al office could not be far. The city now appeared very different to him from what he had seen through the window of Dr. Webster's car.

That was on his second day in America. Feinstein had sensed his disappointment. It was not a craving for rustic simplicity that had brought him to America. That very eve-

ning a volunteer was found. You haven't seen New York yourself until you've shown it to an out-of-towner, said Dr. Webster. The next morning the doctor appeared, a tiny man with
a huge car. He made up his mind not to like this guide.
Everything sparkled and was oversized. What did a little
Jew need such a big car for? Even Webster's love of New
York was suspect. It made him want to boast about the
raciness of Paris, London, Amsterdam. But as time passed he
learned to like Webster, even though a few of his affectations
did seem ridiculous.

He finally resolved to tell the folks back home about the
doctor. As a sort of parable. He even wrote to Bronka at
length.

Webster tended to speak disparagingly of Feinstein. To
the latter every venture into New York seemed a life-
threatening experience. But this was just not so. New York
was at the crossroads of the world. And, in any case, it was
a great center of Jewish life. And, as for all the talk about the
population explosion and the decline of the city, ten million
people lived in that seething underworld and would not
trade it for any other place on earth.

But what Webster showed him was actually a Jewish city.
True, they did go up to the top of the Empire State Building, but that was while they were involved in a lively discussion about Mendele Mokher Seforim.

Webster rejoiced to see his jaw drop at the sight of Manhattan from across the river. Taller than tall. A wall at the
end of the earth. The beginning of another world. Those
were words that struck a chord in Webster: the beginning of
another world. Once you're there you'll get used to it. As
long as you're over here, in New Jersey, you'll never be
able to.

Across from Ellis Island Webster parked the car with the
air of one reciting a prayer for the soul of his departed
father. His eyes grew moist. As if seized by longing for those

bitter times. The fear, the poverty, the strangeness, the disgrace of being hungry. He had been a sickly child, Webster related, and on his account his parents were detained for many weeks.

He thought: That's how I get whenever I see the abandoned embankment of the railroad that used to cross the Valley of Jezreel. I am reminded of other journeys. A Russian blouse. Boots. And Sylvia dressed in white, standing on one foot at the very top of Nebi-Dehi. The doctor also showed him bridges and buildings, and they even passed through Harlem very quickly with the car windows rolled up, but they stopped only at the YIVO Institute and in front of a couple of old buildings downtown. One of these had been the home of a Yiddish newspaper. The second had been a theater and the third was the site of a sweatshop fire in which Jewish girls had been burned to death. Webster's sister had been among them. In front of the Biltmore Hotel Webster slowed down and looked at him to see what kind of impression the plaque was making. As if it had all started here. At Lincoln Center they got out. Webster indicated the names of famous artists. Jews.

They drove around all day. They had four cocktails and his head spun. They had lunch at a Jewish restaurant. Gefilte memories. Fish. Horseradish. Polish vodka. Meatballs. Strudel. Mitteleuropa. Gypsy music. Yiddishe Mame. The Blue Danube. Webster leaned over and whispered the names of some of the diners. How disappointing his reaction was! He had never heard the names of these celebrities before. To Webster this was sad evidence of isolation from the mainstream. These Jewish personalities that the whole world esteemed were unknown in Israel. Later Webster spoke of having heard Ben-Gurion and Golda. He himself was not a Zionist, but was broad-minded. Proud to be a Jew. They had late-afternoon coffee on top of the Pan-Am Building. Webster looked out over his beloved city. Behind every fourth window dwelt a Jewish family. And perhaps just now they were reciting the evening prayer. Webster said that he himself did not pray. Only on Yom Kippur. Weeping moved him somehow. But when evening came there was a surprise in store for him. For a few moments the Jew seemed to disappear, and an American face floated up to the surface. He had been all set to hear a lecture by some Yiddish author when the car ground to a halt in a neighborhood of glaring lights and other enticements. When he saw the lit-up figure of the nude girl he said to himself: Dirty old man. But he was careful not to criticize. He, too, was struck with curiosity. He was glad that here these things could be done out in the open. Two old men could go to a burlesque show with their heads held high and walk through the main door.

There were few spectators in the hall. They were scattered here and there. There were more individuals than pairs. And he sensed an atmosphere of painful solitude. But on stage the show was proceeding at a frenetic pace. Naked girls. Insolent breasts bobbing up and down. Swinging legs. Hips making coarse insinuations. Until the master of ceremonies came on stage, an old Jew in a straw hat. The connecting patter was full of Jewish jokes. Then he understood. And Webster confirmed it: this had once been a Yiddish theater. And now this was all that remained. This man. An old comedian. Earlier, he had played here in *Yoshe Kalb*. On stage he was born and on stage he would die. Even the burlesque somehow belonged to Jewish New York.

Most of the audience, Webster said, are blacks and Puerto Ricans. They don't understand the jokes. Maybe you and I are the only ones who do. But he isn't speaking to them. He's dredging things up from inside.

The nudity began to bore him. He couldn't take his mind off the old comedian. A person his own age. Clumsily tottering about on his old legs while his mouth never stopped pouring forth a stream of witless jokes, nasty barbs, vulgarity.

And these seemed to be propelled by a sort of convulsive action.

When they emerged both were in low spirits. So this is what Jewish culture looks like in America, he said sadly. An old Jew running around among bosomy girls for as long as he can hold out trying to be witty. Webster smiled. He liked wit even if it lacked real substance. The only hope for the Jewish people lay here. Israel was raising soldiers and peasants. In America we had been liberated. In America there was no such thing as one kind of work being less worthy than another. Whatever led to freedom and prosperity was respectable. Only in America could Jews be unafraid of the same things as the goyim.

He did not argue. He only asked: And in Israel? Israel is the only country in the world where Jews are killed because they are Jews, said Webster.

As they were about to part company he permitted himself to ask a question. Where did Webster come from? He could not have been born Webster. And if things Jewish were so important, why must he cut himself off from his forebears?

Webster was not embarrassed. It had not been of his doing. His father had been certain that in America every Jew could make a fresh start if only he had a new name. He took the first name he came upon in the dictionary. Now he did not know which name to select: his father's or his grandfather's? Is the Slavic pejorative assigned to his grandfather by an anti-Semitic clerk necessarily a more intrinsic part of his heritage than this reminder of his father's naiveté?

A few times he bumped into people absentmindedly. He wasn't used to walking about idly during the morning hours. All his life he had risen early for work. Not even in the evening was he capable of complete idleness. Only an open book could justify an early-evening snooze. If he was not producing anything let him at least add to his store of knowledge. Even watching a film on television had to be explained as a learning experience: getting into step with the spirit of the times. The cultural environment of the younger generation.

But now he was on his way to getting things set straight. And it was only fatigue that caused his pace to slacken.

In his whole life he had never seen so many people. People going about their business seemed to be moving on a conveyer. Irritability seemed waiting to be unleashed. They became impatient with anybody walking too slow who did not have a dog. And the ceaseless din, as if there were a gigantic engine causing the sidewalk to tremble.

His were the reflexes of a country person. Sometimes he imagined that he saw a familiar face. His imagination playing tricks on him. As if by looking at him the person were challenging him to remember. And then he would be sorry that in another instant he would be incapable of remembering. A new image blotted out the one that had preceded it. Nobody would have a lasting place in his memory.

When he worked as a herdsman he had thought he would never be able to tell the cows apart. But within a short time he got to know each one separately, by name.

But now this was overwhelming. His forgetfulness was killing these people off one by one. As if they had never existed.

Tomorrow he would go away and he, too, would be blotted out. Maybe he would stick in the desk clerk's memory: that rube who went into the bar and asked for a glass of milk.

He entered the El-Al office with a sense of belonging. The flag. The Hebrew letters. The politeness of the security man. The wall decorations. The scenes of Israel. He waited patiently, as if time alone would solve his problem. He didn't bother anybody. He didn't pester anybody with questions. He didn't go up to the counter until he was called. He stood humbly by and held out his ticket. He told his story for the fourth time. They told him in Boston. Everything was all right. He just had to get the ticket stamped. At which office? He didn't know. A friend had it done for him. Over the phone.

The girl said: The matter has not been settled. He could see for himself from the ticket.

She studied the ticket, as if able to read his story written between the lines. He asked when he would be able to leave, and she looked through her papers and said: There is no possibility for this week. As for next week, perhaps. He could be sure of getting onto a flight within ten days.

Later he found himself in a side room. When he came to two pair of eyes met his. A man's and a woman's. Serious expressions that betrayed worry. The woman was wearing the uniform of a stewardess. She asked if he had any medication on him. He was confused. It was a sudden weakness. He did not take medication. He drank some water and raised himself onto his elbow. A man came in and looked at him with reproach. In his condition he would not be able to fly. At any rate, there could be no question of it without a doctor's note. The stewardess said that there was no room for him anyway. And his story was told for the fifth time, by the stewardess now and as succinctly as possible: Some woman took it upon herself to arrange the flight for him. And the way she did it was over the telephone, without confirmation, and through some unnamed travel agent.

The man spoke with the voice of authority. Let him leave his address. We will get in touch with him if there is an available seat.

The man did not address him. It was as if he did not exist. Nevertheless, he was grateful. Haltingly, he asked about the hotel expenses. The man looked at him in amazement and shrugged his shoulders. Meanwhile another man, in a tweed jacket, came in and introduced himself as the doctor. He immediately picked up his wrist, looked at his watch, and peered into his eyes. The doctor said: It's nothing serious. Just a little excitement.

He said: I told you.

Afterward he explained: It had happened before. A few days earlier, in Maine. There, too, the doctor had said the very same thing: Nothing serious, just a little excitement. At home, too, the doctor had told him: Don't let yourself get angry. The stewardess said: But you have nothing to be angry with us about. We will do everything we can. Somebody gave you the wrong advice. We are not at fault. They kept him for a long while. They told him he was pale. The manager offered him coffee. The doctor said: Okay. It's all right. Why don't all three of us have some? The manager posed a few questions, politely. Seventy years old? Really? He didn't look a day over sixty. A member of a kibbutz? Really? What brought an old-time kibbutznik to these vice-ridden shores? Relatives? He had been in New York for three years and had so far managed to steer clear of all his relatives. The name of the kibbutz was not unknown to him. As a teenager he had attended a work camp there. One of the people in charge, a rigid fellow, had given them a hard time. Some people can think of nothing but work. But now all that has changed. The Arabs work and the Jews supervise them.

He tried to keep from getting angry. After all, he himself worked. He was not a supervisor. The manager said: *Salamtak*, it's not such a great shame. I'm a supervisor too.

Since it was lunchtime the manager drove him back to his hotel.

He was glad not to have to spend money on a cab. He had two hundred and fifty dollars left and he could have afforded it. But he wanted to return to his son those two hundred dollars that he had taken out of the country illegally. And he still did not know how much he would have to pay for the hotel. Unless Feinstein picked up the tab.

Those two hundred dollars bothered him. The act so surprised him that he had not been able to return them on the spot, tactfully but firmly. During the entire trip he had tried to economize so that he would still have them upon his return. It was never too late to educate one's children. It is imperative that we observe the laws of the state that we ourselves have brought into being. He knew that he would not get any thanks. Only a look of incredulity. And yet.

People who deal in millions are unable to understand such niceties. And his hands trembled as he frittered away dollars that Israel needed desperately. He ate lunch in the street, standing. At first he had wanted to eat at the hotel. If Feinstein paid it would be part of the bill. But he changed his mind at once. It was not nice to be calculating with relatives. Not even a wealthy person should have to pay outrageous prices for the smile of a disrespectful waiter, amused at an elderly guest's ignorance of the fine points of menu reading. Popcorn is nourishing. Ice cream even more so. A little hunger only sharpens the senses.

An odor of disinfectant permeated the room. He went to the window and watched workers walking about on steel girders. This complete idleness was not pleasant. He lay on his bed. He pushed the button on the radio and outdoor noises filled the room. He turned the dial and listened to classical music. Something he had once heard and couldn't place. The melody made him drowsy. He decided to have a nap first and to try Feinstein later. As if restraint were the virtue that would bring results. If he were patient he would get an answer.

The music divided the time into shorter intervals. Each one led to the next. He did not have to cross endless expanses of monotony. The waiting was filled with sound, punctuated by drumbeats, distant messages without meaning. He was tired, but sleep did not come. He was sorry that he had given away the few books he had brought. Reading the

Bible tired his eyes. Once again he picked up the *Playboy* that a relative had bought him while he was waiting at some airport. The girls were already familiar, and the sense of novelty had worn off. He tried to read the jokes, but never understood the punch line.

He wondered what Anna Steinhardt would have said if she had seen him lying on his bed looking at naughty pictures of girls young enough to be his granddaughters. It might not have upset her at all. It, too, must be part of that human condition to which she was no stranger. Even the old were human. What she saw under the microscope in a drop of water was equally true of larger creatures.

This time again Anna Steinhardt's number yielded the same nervous, monotonous ring. But by this time it was a betrayal.

They had met at the yearly gathering of old-timers from Vilna in that enchanting New England university town. Unlike the others present, she was not from Vilna. But her husband, a well-known scientist and perpetual Nobel candidate from what he had heard, had not missed a single meeting in forty years. After his death she kept faith with his memory and continued to attend.

She sat on the side, belonging and not belonging, and did not take part in the general discussion in which various individuals were singled out for acknowledgment of their roles in a local charity campaign. Her very way of sitting might have suggested certain reservations. At the edge of an armchair, as if closed in upon herself, legs crossed and arms folded, insinuating that her presence was a gesture of goodwill and not actual attendance. Only her eyes—curious and alert—were all there. At first he had not liked her. A strange irony echoed through her voice, and she listened to him with her head inclined, like Sylvia years before, as if waiting for him to make a slip. Not even the smile that covered her face looked nice to him. A knowing smile that barely concealed a touch of condescension. Later he said to himself that even her too well preserved face put him off. The self-satisfied smile of a girl framed in an old lady's face. Like a plastic surgeon's masterpiece, with only two tiny telltale scars alongside the ears, that permitted her to smile like the Mona Lisa. Even the bluish color of her hair exercised a certain repellent fascination. Like a fake halo setting her apart from ordinary mortals like himself. Long-term efforts to outwit old age did not generally earn his respect. Erasing a few of the more blatant, painful signs, the way Bronka did, was tolerable. But to paint oneself in the colors of an imagined youth he found revolting.

Although later on he did change his mind. Most of those present were tipsy, and he promised them all, with irony directed at himself and amazement at his newfound manners (it no longer bothered him to make promises, with a sweet smile and no seriousness whatever, that he had no intention of keeping) that he would come back to visit them the following year, and that in any case he would be very happy to have them visit him at his home if they ever got to Israel. A peculiar kind of excitement came over him. It was his last day in America—by now he was careful to say the United States—and he didn't know whether he was happy to be going home or sorry to be leaving a great big party that was over too soon. He was a little tipsy too, not from drinking but from the abandon of striking up friendships with nameless people. For over fifty years he had been true to a small nucleus of friends, made ever smaller by death and bitter disappointment, and suddenly, during the course of one trip, he had made legions of new friends, who liked him wholeheartedly and without reservation and sometimes carried the ritual of admiring him as a pioneer a little too far. Some even treated him with the reverence and awe reserved for an ancient relic from the Holy Land.

As soon as the early departures, those who lived far away,

had gone he sat down to rest a bit from the excitement and the commotion. The minute he was alone she came over and sat down. As if she had been waiting for the right moment all along.

She introduced herself by name and was surprised to find that he remembered her name from before. She would not have been happy to learn why her name stood out in his mind. He remembered it because of its very Germanic quality, which contrasted with the New England feistiness that was stamped on her features like a badge. As if the primacy of the New Englanders had rubbed off onto these refugees from Germany, who had been the last of all to arrive. She told him, in English that was above and beyond his comprehension, that his words had touched her deeply. She spared no effort, in the manner of a teacher enamored of her calling, and explained the expression she had used: "to strike home." She went over its origin and all its nuances and opined that the expression, with its strange combination of opposites, had been borrowed from baseball. But perhaps for that very reason it contained warmth. Later she spoke Hebrew in the Ashkenazic pronunciation. Her language was somewhat halting, but accurate, and it showed that she had studied grammar and some literature. Sometimes she had difficulty in choosing a word, and then her slender white hands would fly about in front of her face as if trying to catch the word that was about to elude her. She said that she sometimes grew a little tired of the kind of Jewish solidarity typified by the emotional talk of the other members of the group, who were otherwise rational, practical people. Love of the Jewish people had become linked in her mind to a form of self-indulgence. A sort of adorable defect, like the affected stammer of the British upper class. Or perhaps it would be better to call it a disease imparting to these tough individuals a certain sympathetic humanity. This weakness, she stated sadly, invites all kinds of fraud. It is a crack in the wall through which many Israelis, present company excluded of course, brazenly charge with outstretched hand. And then she had heard him speak, and it was like a breath of fresh air. The same love of one's fellow Jews, but without the whining. And without using rose-colored glasses for everything that goes on under that harsh blue sky. And then suddenly, without stopping for breath as if ready to continue in the same vein, a sweet smile broke out on her lips and she asked: Did anyone ever tell you that you look like Uncle Sam? The same elongated features and angular face and deep-set eyes, and strong nose, and even the beard. At this point she let out a little laugh; and he was not certain that she was not laughing at his gentlemanly attire, which wasn't really him: all he needed was the high hat and the old frock coat.

They spent a long while together, just the two of them. She asked what he had seen of America, and he asked for her impression of Israel. And then it emerged that she had never been to Israel. As a girl, she told him, she had belonged to a pioneering Zionist youth movement. Israel was a distant dream. Her parents had immigrated to America before she was fully grown, and here she was now, an American woman, afraid of losing her childhood dream. A few of the things she had heard from people who went there and returned were less than encouraging.

It turned out that they had both belonged to the same youth movement, and he was somehow sorry that he had not been sent back to Europe at the time to do educational work in the movement; as if by not having been sent he had missed a chance to meet her. They chatted easily and with steadily growing confidence, and once he even laughed out loud, which was unusual for him, and a few people turned around in surprise. She was very good at telling innocent little jokes with a straight face, and he was glad to be free, if only for a moment, of the need to be serious all the time, in the manner befitting an emissary from the Holy Land. Later on she asked what he had seen of America, and his answer left her unsatisfied. She felt he had only been shown "Jewish America" and declared enthusiastically that there was another America out there, too, an America of magical primeval landscapes and of marvelous tranquillity and of a simple, strong tie to work and the soil. He was a little sorry about the deep love for America that shone through her words, but he did agree that he had noticed in the course of his travels, to the extent that it is possible to notice anything when one is on the run, some positive American traits, like a healthy attitude toward work and a certain understated but vigorous efficiency, and these were qualities he certainly valued and appreciated. And then came an unexpected proposal that they take a trip, just the two of them, through that "other America." She told him that she had just retired and had plenty of time and would be happy to serve as his guide. With a clever smile, indicating that she appreciated his predicament, she added that he deserved to spend a few days in America without tiresome discussions on the future of Israel. He thanked her for the sudden, intriguing invitation and expressed his regrets at not being able to accept. At this time the next day he was supposed to fly to New York, and from there, a few hours later, on to Israel. She looked at him with amazement and said that planes would still be flying the day after tomorrow and even after that. He replied that his flight had already been set for the next day and was a little shamefaced when she laughed aloud, as if he really were an old man from out in the boondocks. That's what the telephone was invented for, she said. He stammered that he had already had his flight confirmed by the travel agent and that he didn't think it was possible to change plans at the last minute, just like that, without a valid reason. She realized that she had offended him and this time managed not to laugh, but only to smile and say: In the first place, why do you insult me by saying you haven't got a valid reason? And in the second place, some last-minute traveler will be very happy to get your seat. Unless a person is very important the only hope he has of getting a seat is that somebody like you will feel like staying in the United States for a few more days. He stammered, and, besides, they're waiting for me at home, and she retorted, that's what telegrams are for. You just sit here and give me your ticket and the address and what you want to say in the telegram you're sending home, she said. Even though he wanted to refuse, his fingers went into his pocket. He handed her the ticket with the grin of someone taking part in a prank that has no chance of being pulled off, and wrote on a slip of paper, in Hebrew in Roman characters, the text of a telegram to Bronka. A joke in itself: Found new relatives stop staying few more days stop. As she came out her face showed determination, but the naughty spark twinkling in her eyes made accomplices even of them, and his mind was set at ease. He had been certain that she would not be able to fix it, in the middle of the night. Not even in her efficient, hardworking America. But when she stayed in the other room for so long there rose in him both apprehension lest she carry it off—everyone spoke of her as a person with connections in all sorts of places—and also a certain spirit of adventure. The thing took hold of him in all its obvious idiocy: the hasty decision, the spontaneity of his reaction and the fast, insolent acquaintance with a woman rich in both charm and a sense of humor. He saw the thing as a kind of diverting return to the foolishness of youth, with its license to fall in love at first sight and to take all kinds of eccentric turns. And what, actually, was wrong with that? Even old people had their right to an occasional harmless fling. This was his first and last trip to America, and he ought to see as much as he could. And there was even independent justification for doing so—to live for once without keeping tabs on himself and without a sense of obligation bearing down from every side, like a man who had plenty of one thing at least: his own time, his own life. A sense of adventure for its own sake was something that his strict way of life eschewed. The guiding principle required them to discover the light concealed in a humdrum life of purpose. And sometimes it had been necessary for them to deceive themselves and to disguise the yearning for adventure. In his day he had fought for the right to help smuggle illegal immigrants from Syria, as if that represented his last chance to go to heaven through good works and lofty obligations. They barely admitted to themselves that what they really wanted was a chance to run around at night and to quicken the pulse through exposure to danger. And now he had the chance to introduce some adventure, albeit in a somewhat peculiar fashion, into his life—without any real danger and with a certain excitement as yet undeciphered—which smacked of cloak and dagger even before it had begun. He had just written things down on a slip of paper that could be a lie and could be a delightful joke. For Anna Steinhardt was no relative, and yet, she was already closer than a real relation. Every adventure probably implies a game of hide and seek with the truth.

When she came back radiantly waving his ticket he was in for a disappointment. The thing had not been completely resolved. He would not know until morning whether he would have a seat on the plane leaving the fourth or the sixth. But it was already too late to retreat, both because she was in such a festive, happy mood, as if she had managed to do the impossible, and because he did not want to look like an old fuddy-duddy, a stick in the mud. At any rate, his flight on the first was already canceled, and the cable to Bronka had already been sent. He was a little annoyed with Anna at having canceled his flight before she knew for sure that he had a seat on another one, but he did not show it. It seemed that there could be no true adventure without a little uncertainty. This little adventure was taking on an individuality all its own. They had to attend to a few things like a pair of conspirators. His host was supposed to drive him to the airport early in the morning, and she offered to do it under some pretext or other. They smiled at one another secretly as the last guests took leave of him, as if this were his last day in the United States. He just barely got out of a promise to send a cable saying that he had reached Israel safely. The next morning the game went on. She prodded him as he said good-bye to his hosts, as if she were worried that he might miss the plane. He played along and looked worried as he rushed to load the valises into her car. Only after they had turned the corner did they permit themselves to laugh. Quietly. But before long there was an awkward moment. Where do we go now, he asked, and she replied just leave everything to me. And he didn't ask any more questions, but let her point out what was worthwhile and pass over what was obvious. He wasn't completely at ease until she had called the travel agent and been told that he had a seat on the plane leaving Saturday. A five-day excursion in the company of a strange woman now seemed completely out of character for him—but he had undertaken to abide by the rules of adventure, which do not admit of any prior restraints. One more thing was worrying him, but he was ashamed even to hint at it. He had every intention of paying his own way, and he hoped she would understand that he could not afford to stay at very expensive hotels. But by the time they had finished breakfast in a small, neat restaurant overlooking the river, a convenient if embarrassing arrangement had been suggested. She scolded him when he tried to take out his wallet. You're my guest, aren't you? He was grateful to her for having turned the whole embarrassing issue into a joke. And you can see that I'm not really paying, anyway. All I do is show them a magic little card. She was ridiculing the Old World, where cash was still the rule.

When, nevertheless, he insisted on paying for lunch, which they had at a roadside restaurant on the shore, she reprimanded him with mock seriousness. Everybody knows just how much foreign currency an Israeli is allowed to take out of his country. And when he acquiesced and put the wallet back into his pocket she said with genuine affection and without a trace of irony, here is a real man. He is not afraid that his manhood will be compromised if, by pure chance, it happens to be a woman who foots the bill for a joint venture. She would have been bitterly disappointed to learn that a man from a kibbutz, an egalitarian society in every respect, was a male chauvinist. She let him pay only for the second cable to Bronka. She stayed outside the telegraph office as if this were something personal and not a question of simple information, as if delicacy of feeling required her to keep out of it. In fifty years' time he had hardly ever sent a telegram and now he sent two in one day, like a man of the world whose every whim is broadcast to the ends of the earth.

Since they had plenty of time, they turned around and headed south, instead of going north as they had originally intended. There was something adventurous even in this. Without a definite plan, without a timetable and on the spur of the moment, and without a thought for what had already been decided. In a few hours she had shown him all the sights south of Boston, including a life-sized replica of the *Mayflower*. At that point he regretted having thought, only the evening before, that she partook of a kind of New England arrogance, as if she had really wished to belong to the offspring of the Pilgrim Fathers. She poked fun at the Americans' efforts to bestow a dimension of antiquity on buildings that in Europe would be the homes of ordinary people. She showed him lakes and rivers and bridges and well-known factories, as was to be expected. But she surprised him by driving him to a scientific institute—for the study of the ocean and its flora and fauna, as he gathered from the sign at the entrance—and it turned out that they all knew her here and addressed her with obvious deference. In an offhand manner she mentioned that until her retirement a few months earlier she had been the director of this institute and that even now she engaged in some research in collaboration with certain promising younger colleagues and that as a result of the sudden change in their itinerary, she had had this marvelous idea at breakfast. He was glad she was trying to impress him—that is the way he saw the exaggerated modesty and the joy that flashed from her eyes when her prestige seemed to manifest itself out of nowhere, as if her trying to dazzle him with accomplishments he had no way of judging implied the possibility of a deeper friendship. Up to now he had the feeling she was sizing him up in order to formulate some sort of hypothesis. As if she had in mind some kind of image that he was supposed to live up to and she were checking to make sure she had not been mistaken about him. He noticed that even when she was showing him the large fish and the marvelous underwater plants she tried not to sound like an authority showing around an absolute ignoramus. Moreover, at certain moments and with great subtlety she led the conversation around to things about which he might be expected to know more than she. But it became apparent that she even knew more about the coast of Eilat, which she had never seen in her life. Or at least about the flora and fauna and climatological phenomena and the like.

The question of accommodation resolved itself, since they stayed at the home of a colleague. It was a cottage set off by itself amid greenery near the shore: a fourteen-room house for two people, two dogs, and a cat. There was another colleague staying there, from Finland, but they were received with genuine hospitality and with a generosity that was taken for granted, as if anybody coming to stay with them, to eat and drink and make himself at home, was bestowing a favor on the people of the house. His room was on the second floor and had its own bath, and for a while he sat by the window and gazed at the ocean. A lone sail bobbed gently up and down on the surface of the water and for a few moments he saw himself as the nameless sailor in that faraway boat. As if he, too, were gliding gently along on the waves, far from any other living soul, at peace with himself and with the world. The sweet solitude called him to take stock of things, but he did not know where to begin. The day's happenings merged in his mind in a beautiful, flawless delirium. Even that telegram to Bronka, though in the morning it had contained a white lie, by afternoon was the truth. He might even have written her what was actually happening: I met a fascinating woman and we're traveling together through an America completely different from the one Feinstein introduced me to. Bronka would say: If you're enjoying yourself and looking after your health, I'm happy. Bronka was a woman with a healthy knowledge of the world, and even her emotions were worldly-wise. It would have been hard to say that he knew Anna Steinhardt. He certainly was in no position to judge her contribution to oceanography. But even though they had met only the night before, he was as much at ease in her company as if she had been an old friend. Perhaps it was only a matter of coincidence that they had not met in the old days, and now along came a new coincidence and put things aright. Even if this hasty decision turned out to be a silly caprice, it was a good thing that there was still room in his life for one more bit of foolishness. Really, a person who had some crazy cause was lucky. But he had passed his whole life in painful, efficient moderation. He didn't even grow cacti with relish. Only once, for a year, had he participated in somebody else's cause by joining in the fight against poisons and chemical fertilizers. But, as soon as the yield of the experimental plot turned out to be lower, he withdrew even from that.

For a few minutes during dinner they spoke heatedly and enthusiastically about a certain professional matter, and he did not understand a thing. Even this was to his liking. He was tired of being the guest of honor. Now he was freed of the need to entertain his hosts. But they quickly changed the subject, as courtesy demanded, and drew him into the conversation. The lady of the house, who had visited Israel earlier on, when she was active in Protestant charity work, asked him to bring her up-to-date. But Anna Steinhardt came to his rescue and said no politics, please. He's on vacation and already they've tried to squeeze him dry at all the Jewish "command performance" dinners he's been forced to attend. The young oceanographer from Finland, who had probably been mulling over some scientific problem discussed a few minutes earlier, awoke from his trance as soon as "kibbutz" was mentioned. The young man besieged him with questions as if in urgent need of an answer to something that was troubling him. He managed to say a few things in English and sometimes Anna Steinhardt had to help him out. He was amazed at how much the man from Finland knew, even though he had never seen a kibbutz in his life. He spoke of the malaise of the younger generation, those who come after, as if he were personally involved. For a while his hosts entertained themselves with the idea of establishing a kibbutz of scientists in order to support a beautiful cooperative style of life right here in America by exporting know-how, but by the time the dessert was served they had given up. They agreed that kibbutz was a noble form of insanity that only Jews could maintain. And he was unable to disagree with them because of the language.

Nor did the question of hotel expenses arise on the following night, since they stayed at Anna Steinhardt's summer house in another town by the shore. On that day they didn't move around much. He was glad that she left him to his own devices for a few hours and shut herself up in her room to prepare the outline of an article for a scientific journal. He wandered through the streets of the town and was delighted by the tastefully decorated shops. He even bought a few small trinkets in the hope that Bronka might find some use for them. In the evening they sat in a spacious living room, made somber by the wall-to-wall bookcases closing in from every side. They drank dainty liqueurs that went straight to his head, and she asked him questions about himself.

He was not able to give her the stock answers he gave to others. He did not conceal his distress from her. In the harvest of his years he had everything, yet he had nothing he could pass on to others. He had nothing to leave behind but his mistakes and lessons that were no longer needed. There was nobody to follow in his footsteps, neither his children nor anybody else's children. He had no material things to bequeath. The younger generation was not interested in reading old books and, as for other property, they possessed it during his lifetime. And they even had a little more than he, since their work was needed more than his. Nor did he refrain from giving expression to the depression born of bitterness that had become a part of his life of late as it now entered its concluding phase. Those that used to respect the perseverance and stubbornness had come in recent years to see him as a kind of natural obstacle to the liquidation of unprofitable enterprises within the kibbutz. Thus he was forced to leave agriculture, his first love, and to sit on an assembly line doing stultifying work that subordinated the workday to what came after it, and this went against his principles. He also admitted to her that recently he had begun putting down a few things out of his memory "in order to free up a little room in the moldly warehouse inside his head," filled as it was to overflowing with "recollections of historical vintage" that nobody wanted anymore. But once the things were written down they seemed impoverished and empty and sometimes even a little pretentious.

He even told her things he hadn't admitted to himself before, and a few were things he was ashamed of. But it was not the kind of shame that blocked expression. Rather, it was a cleansing shame. As if, while he spoke, things became clearer and were chastened by the light of day. And this took the sting out of them. He told her how, during the difficult years of adolescence, he entertained the hope of someday becoming a sort of guru, like Aaron David Gordon in his day, but within a smaller frame of reference. A man whose attachment to labor and whose fidelity to the values of the kibbutz would be an example to others. This wish made him both arrogant and bitter. Sometimes he would harass the founding fathers of the movement who went off to congresses with the foolish conviction that each word they uttered would find its way straight into the holy writ of future generations. He always judged them by the dirt under their fingernails—the more the better—as if all the Zionist congresses were nothing but an excuse to bathe in the waters of Carlsbad and to drink French wines. When he awoke from his dreams he discovered that he no longer had a wife or children. His confidence in always being right waned over the years. In recent years a great silence had come over him and he no longer dared to speak up at meetings of the kibbutz. Issues that used to be matters of life and death for him he now passed over in silence. For a few minutes he had wondered if a strange woman, who had never lived on a kibbutz, could plumb the depths of grief felt by an old kibbutznik whose children had all left him, but Anna Steinhardt knew how to listen and not one single time did her eyes betray the smugness some people show when hearing a confession. He even told her how disappointed he had been when, at the establishment of the State, he learned that he would only be given the rank of sergeant, despite long years of service in the Haganah. As if all his exploits in the magical days of the underground were unworthy of the mystic aura that had sprung up about them. Once he stopped in the middle and said with a kind of embarrassment: This is my life, boring as it actually was. And she remained silent and just looked at him affectionately, as if she understood even the things he was not trying to say.

And when they spoke about matters that were clearly political he used different language from what he was accustomed to. He told her about something that had happened to him many years earlier. His daughter had fallen ill and the doctors said there was nothing physically wrong with her, that it was the result of a depression whose cause was to be sought in the troubled relations between him and Sylvia. Somebody recommended a pet and he went to Haifa and bought a pair of rabbits and was coming back on the train that used to cross the Valley of Jezreel when the rabbits jumped out of the sack. The engineer stopped the train. Dozens of Arabs in flowing robes spread out across the field like black ravens and didn't come back until they had caught those two rabbits. Anna Steinhardt understood on her own that his story contained a certain message of peace.

He was glad to be speaking the absolute, unembellished truth. As if by making confession he could atone for all the nonsense he had spoken to others. A few things, intimate things, that he told her without hesitation, gave him a strange kind of satisfaction. And it seemed amazing and peculiar and at the same time appropriate for him to be documenting himself in the memory of an unknown woman. In America of all places, far from his home, would be the one woman who knew him thoroughly. Everything he had kept hidden from others and managed to conceal even from his wife, with the exception of physical matters, which no longer had the importance they had once had, but which could probably be surmised from the other things.

At night Anna Steinhardt stayed on in his room for a few minutes after having made up his bed. She asked if he needed anything, and he wondered if this ought to be taken as a hint. But he put it out of his mind at once as an intolerable thought. He feared disappointment. That was the very reason why Anna Steinhardt had never visited Israel. For a while she stood by the door until, suddenly, understanding seemed to dawn. She bid him good-night in clear and cordial tones.

It was only on the following day that Anna Steinhardt spoke about herself. He held it to her credit that she had not done so the night before. If she had he might have assumed that he had gone too far with his confession and that in order to spare his feelings she saw fit to tell him a few things about herself. She, too, had been married twice, but both of her husbands had died. The first in an automobile accident a few years after the birth of her only daughter, who now lived in California, and the second—of a serious illness a few months earlier. She spoke with admiration of Sigmund Steinhardt, a humanist who had very vigorously maintained his moderate views. An enthusiastic music lover who, on Jewish holidays, would double as cantor whenever the need arose and who found no contradiction between the exact sciences and religious belief. Once, she related, he drew her a molecule of a certain protein, a complicated diagram, and said: Here, this is how we are joined to God: each person by means of his fellow to God and each person to his fellow by means of God, whether we will it or not. Unlike the other members of the Vilna Society, his tears were not always at the ready. Not for him easy displays of emotion. But it would have been too hard for a person not to belong to some kind of small group, a kibbutz of sorts, guarding shared memories of a Jewish metropolis far away. He got gooseflesh when she told him about her childhood in Danzig. He mentioned, as if he were giving a kind of password, that his first wife, too, had been born in Danzig. At that moment he imagined that he found a certain resemblance between her and Sylvia: the accent and a searching look that suddenly appeared and was gone. Except that Anna Steinhardt was calm and sure of herself, as Sylvia might have been if she had chanced to come to America instead of Israel and if she had not felt the call in her youth to undertake tasks that were beyond her endurance.

For two days they were on the road, passing through breathtaking scenery, as Anna Steinhardt liked to call it. They saw pretty, manicured small towns. By the time they got to them he regretted leaving them, and also a few cities and nature reserves. He jotted down a few ideas in his notebook for the kibbutz landscape gardener. He tired of trying to remember the names of the places they passed along the way, but his eye never had enough of seeing the clear lakes with giant evergreens reflected in them, a picture he retained from one of the movement's summer camps as a vision of pure beauty.

The question of accommodation never arose, since they spent the first night at a motel, which was not at all expensive, and for the second night Anna Steinhardt had planned something that he looked forward to with mixed feelings— with belated youthful enthusiasm and with some misgiving about catching cold—a night in sleeping bags under the open sky.

Two days of happy chatter. Only rarely did he feel his age: when he found it hard to keep up or when he got the runs from eating too much of an ice cream sundae, which she had offered him as a belated birthday present. He was intrigued by the fact that no one, save Anna Steinhardt, knew where he was. He was like a man on complete vacation, even from himself. A delightful woman drives the car and all he has to do is turn his eyes this way and that. The stories about the kibbutz sounded, even to him, like descriptions of some imaginary utopia, and more than a few notions seemed to have been refuted from this vantage point, at the edge of a sparkling lake with a snowcapped mountain towering overhead: the renunciation of beautiful things that have no use-value, the inability to enjoy complete idleness with the lazy thoughts that fill the void, as if there must be no contradiction between the vase of flowers and the book alongside of it, as if the picture on the wall must express the sum of all our values. For even the enjoyment of leisure time was supposed to serve a higher purpose.

Serious talk gave way to gentle fun when he tried to imitate Anna Steinhardt's accent. To his amazement his Hebrew was slipping back into a pattern of penultimate stress, and by the third day his speech emerged in pure East-European Ashkenazic pronunciation, as if he had never in his life spoken in the modern Israeli "Sephardic" style. He was also at ease with her because now for the first time since setting foot on American soil he was freed from the mantle of serious objectives—Israel and Jewish rebirth and justice for all Mankind. The kibbutz became once again a place where people live. "America without Jews," she smiled at him and permitted him to indulge in the simple pleasures of the elderly. Anna Steinhardt laughed heartily, and her laughter contained more than a hint of affection and esteem, when he told her right out how happy he was that with her he could be just a plain old Jew, a Chaim Yankel or Gimpel Beinish, with no pretensions of being a saint or the most righteous of his generation or of bearing the cross of American Jewry. With her he was freed of their torment, their suffering, their anguish, nor was it his responsibility to infuse them with pride. Here he was an ordinary Jew, content with what his life had been despite all the failures and the disappointments evident in the younger generation in that village of his, which was managing to carry on even without ironclad rules. A village that had good people in it as well as peculiar and ridiculous people, and even a few damned chiselers, may the devil take them. He no longer needed anybody to praise, laud, adore, or uplift him and his kind for their role in building a home for the Jewish people. It was enough to be himself, the self that he knew. The kibbutz brought out his good qualities and concealed his bad ones. Today it no longer mattered that he had not become a guru to Jewish farmers of later generations, that his name would not be engraved in marble in some national palace. It sufficed that he had learned to make a tree grow, to combat pests, to drive in a nail properly and to live alongside both horse and mosquito, who had taught him how things really happen, without pressing buttons, without throwing a switch in order to destroy an old world and make way for a new one.

On the last day they even spoke about things he usually preferred to keep hidden. But even talk about marital questions, old loves, and silly stories sprang from his lips like newborn babes, as if on the way from his mouth to her ears they lost their foolishness as well as their wickedness. She did not hesitate to ask about his wife, and he told her about life with Bronka, the watered-down joys of the elderly, everything with moderation, every day like the day before. And he even told her a few stories about Sylvia, how she had come to the kibbutz expecting an extended celebration of youth and how a cruel nature had had its way with her and left her with all kinds of allergies to grape-picking and grain-harvesting and olive-gathering, and how the arrogance she had brought from her parents' home caused the kibbutz to seem pitiful and disappointing. What others saw as recognition of duty or a sense of responsibility or acceptance of necessity took on an entirely different meaning to her. As if everything really were petty-mindedness and provincialism and the miserable aspirations of unlovely young women.

Anna Steinhardt was amazed to learn that the separation from Sylvia had taken place so very many years before. From the way he spoke of it she assumed that it had happened only a short time ago. He was unable to explain why now of all times—perhaps because of the trip to America, the children's present, and maybe on account of Danzig—it returned and erupted from his memory.

The last night was spent in a state park in Maine, and he did not even try to remember the name of the place. The hub of the universe, he said to himself as they unloaded Anna Steinhardt's car. Forest and river and snowcapped mountains off in the distance, familiar childhood scenery that he had brought with him to the very ends of the New World. They gathered wood and lit a fire on the riverbank. They devoured sandwiches and made ready to sleep under heavy-topped firs on weightless foam pads in soft, clean sleeping bags. Anna Steinhardt assured him that the birds would wake them at dawn. She burst out singing in a clear, tremulous voice, and he was put in mind of one summer encampment in Lithuania. Sylvia, her eyes asparkle, was singing a Polish folk song, and small, whitewashed stones marked a clear path up to the Jewish flag at the center of the campground. At this point he wondered what made Anna Steinhardt, an intelligent, even wise woman of proud, dignified bearing, want to be alone with the likes of him in this faraway place. After all, such old people as they ought to be as careful as possible of colds and their attendant complications. Perhaps she was a romantic soul in quest of some memory: a forgotten adolescent love, some well-endowed young man who had neither an American visa nor the courage to go to Palestine, and who perished with all the others. He regretted having to find meaning in everything, as if unable simply to enjoy a clear autumn evening with the moon of Canaan reflected in other waters and the glory of the forest in all the shades of its autumn splendor.

Why aren't you singing? asked Anna Steinhardt. He cleared his throat of something that seemed to have been stuck there for years and brought forth some choking noises, which little by little turned into a melody. Jewish tunes he had not heard in many years and which, even so, he remembered well, echoed in his heart.

Suddenly they noticed that they were not alone. Two forest rangers, one tall and blond with a marvelously calm Nordic face, the other shorter, with the sharp, chiseled features of an Indian, stood and looked at them in amused wonder. No fires allowed here, said the blond man in a voice without reproach. Please put it out. His partner mumbled something, too, but neither of them moved, as if the sight held them in its thrall. Two crazy old-timers, said the white man to the Indian. A faint smile broke out on Anna Steinhardt's lips, but she kept right on singing as if they didn't exist. He got up to put out the fire, and the slightest shadow of disappointment flitted across her face. As if by being in too great a hurry to obey the law he was breaking the natural law of the forest. As if she had expected a rebel to prove more faithful to the song. But he was already on his way down to the edge of the river. Still, he managed to see the Indian's startled eyes fixed on Anna Steinhardt in a hypnotic gaze, the vision of the woman singing to herself evoking lost memories of tribal life.

When he came to he saw the Indian's face and he saw Anna Steinhardt pouring a liquid into a handkerchief.

At the motel they registered as man and wife. By the time the doctor arrived the dizziness was completely gone. Nothing serious, said the doctor. Just the excitement.

He lay alone in the double bed and Anna Steinhardt slipped into her sleeping bag on the couch by the door.

When she came out of the bathroom enveloped in a light robe and delicate perfumes, there arose one more time a certain quiet expectancy, but he was glad that things had to transpire as they did. A promise without fulfillment.

The following day she drove him to the airport. On the way they climbed up to a lookout point for the last time. A spray as fine as mist rose from the base of the cliff. A distant vessel left a divided wake, like two soft locks of gray hair. Anna Steinhardt looked as if she wanted to say something. But it was only in the passenger lounge, when they took their last meal together, that she spoke. Offhandedly she said: I expect that I shall miss you when you are gone. He became a little confused and mumbled something and then said that he also hated good-byes and that he had very much enjoyed the last few days in her company. He thanked her, too, and she scolded him. He invited her to come to Israel and assured her that Bronka would be happy to meet her. But he was not really sure of that. In her stance, in a certain look, and in the way she inclined her head she bore a striking resemblance to Sylvia. And Bronka certainly did not like Sylvia.

At five he decided to go out for a walk again. It was rush hour and New York was a different city once again. Huge mobs, shoulder to shoulder. Some proceeding slowly, others dashing madly ahead. Countless people gliding along the walls of buildings, like cattle in disarray before the natural bullying order of the flock has been established. The gigantic buildings spewed forth people, too, as if there were an earthquake under way with everyone making for the outdoors. He was completely calm as he walked through the surging mass, and all of Feinstein's warnings faded away. This seemed the only way to see the real New York. He was glad of this chance to see the city in all its commotion. Only at Forty-second Street was he able to detach himself from the flow and for awhile he stood in front of a store that sold pornography, wondering at the vision of emptiness within. He imagined that he could tell from people's eyes whether they were headed home to dinner with the family and well-deserved rest in armchair and slippers or whether they were up to mischief.

When he got to Times Square he tried to read the moving letters, but he couldn't understand what he was reading. The word *Israel* appeared twice, but the rest of the headline was cryptically abbreviated. A police car flew by with heart-rending wails, but he seemed to be the only one who turned around to look. A black woman collided with him and cursed, as if he had bumped into her huge breasts on purpose. For a while he meandered along in the glow of lighted shop windows, until he grew tired. He decided to rest a bit and return to the hotel, but the coffee shops seemed packed. Everybody seemed to be eating hurriedly on the way to somewhere else and nobody was having a cup of tea simply in order to rest. He was suddenly overcome with a strange curiosity and went into a movie theater with quick steps, as if all the great crowd streaming past the entrance were watching. The theater was almost empty. Here and there people sat singly in the dark, and the pictures lighting up the screen only emphasized their loneliness. The overtness of the acts on the screen excited him a little, but he was soon profoundly bored. Even this must be seen once in a lifetime, he said to himself, and better that it be in the dark and in a foreign country. When he emerged it was completely dark. He was dazzled by the lights shining from every direction and was ashamed at being seen on his way out by a woman with a child. He told himself that they couldn't possibly know who he was—a dirty old man who looked a little bit like Uncle Sam—and that he would never see them again, but, nonetheless, he could not help feeling ashamed. For a minute this absolute anonymity made him feel uneasy. People passed him by glassy-eyed, and he had the impression that they would have been glad to see him get run over, that that would have diverted them from the monotony of their day.

When he decided to turn back toward the hotel it was seven. On Fifth Avenue he left Forty-second Street, which had acquired a sinister air. Each storefront sneered at his old age with its loud, funky clothes and nasty, erotic toys. He felt better in the bourgeois glow of conspicuous wealth. In the vicinity of Rockefeller Center he turned and went toward his hotel. The narrow street was dark and completely empty, but the fears implanted in him by Feinstein now seemed to belong to a diaspora mentality, transposed from the Old World to the New. Here he was walking all alone in the very heart of sin city and nothing was happening. And, in any case, even if there were some danger cars passed from time to time and lit up the street. Criminals have a sixth sense. They look at you and can tell if you have money. A strange tiredness flowed through his limbs, but he calculated that within ten to fifteen minutes he would reach the hotel. Walking had become difficult, but he recalled something Bronka said whenever she was ill. When I wake up in the morning and see the sun shining I credit it to my own stubborn efforts. By a wooden fence near a construction site he noticed a woman with a bag in her hand. As he got closer he saw that she was black and he did not have it in him to pass her by without acknowledging her. Her face wore a vacant smile as if it had frozen in the middle of a spasm. He didn't hear what she said but understood the intent. Perhaps if she had been white he would have nodded and gone on his way, but just because she was black he found the need to make clear, as far as possible in words and beyond that through the tone of his voice, that he had no scorn, only pity. The woman did not understand what he wanted to say. She thought he was trying to bargain. An angry pride stirred within her and she called him a stupid ass, a man of his age should be glad he wasn't being asked twice as much. He was sorry he had started this idiotic conversation with her, since he lacked the essential vocabulary, and he stepped back a little, as if making to leave. She came up so close to him that her pointed breasts almost touched his chest, and asked if he was afraid. He stammered that he was not afraid, but that he had never paid for a woman's favors. With a scornful smile she said that there was always a first time and that pretty soon it would be too late for him to start anything new. He realized that she was making fun of him and tried to break it off. Then she emitted a few foul expressions. The vulgarity saddened him profoundly. He lowered his head and turned to go. She got very angry when she realized that she had been wasting her time on him. She shouted at him as if he had been trying to put something over on her by enjoying her company without paying. Something that showed in his face, maybe the fear, maybe the pain, inspired a weird gaiety in her. She screamed at the top of her lungs and savored his embarrassment. Two cars drew up with a hair-raising squeal of tires, bathed them in light, and then abandoned them to the darkness. He quickened his pace, and she walked behind shouting at him through the empty street. He felt like a soldier running the gantlet. He was no more than a building's width from the brightly lit avenue when he suddenly noticed two motionless figures leaning against the wooden fence. From up close he saw the expression of scorn on their faces, as if they were playing at funny faces. One was white and his face was emaciated and sickly; the other was black, stout, and his thick lips suggested innocence and curious expectancy. They were not blocking his path, but he was afraid that if he passed them he would be struck from behind. He slowed down as he passed and one said to the other: wise guy. Their movements were clearer than their speech and when they stopped him they kept grumbling under their breath, as if they blamed him for bringing them to this. Now that he saw them eye to eye his fear left him. He was proud of himself for acting without panic as he had been instructed. He gave them his wallet and turned his pockets inside out. They expressed their disappointment with hostile words. He hoped that the danger was past, that they had satisfied their need for violence by cursing. Had he been able to find words he would even have apologized for having gone to the movies and depriving them of three and a half dollars more. The white man threw the wallet to the ground, and the black searched him. The black man's face was close to his own and he could not suppress a little smile when it was all over. And then suddenly the black man thrust a fist in his face, and in the fraction of a second before he fell he managed to hate the white man's cruel, distorted smile with all his might.

In the police car he was asked to give a description of his attackers, but the patrolman paid no attention to what he said. The police sergeant noticed that his visa had expired. A clerk took down his testimony with complete indifference and spoke on the telephone a few times and ignored him completely. A doctor examined him with a dour expression, as if he were about to claim damages that he was not entitled to. In the end they made him sign a document whose contents he did not understand. An officer put some questions to him in grumpy fashion. He had no idea what he was supposed to be apologetic about. Finally, they came right out with it: an old man does not wander along a dark street at night unless he's looking for trouble. There are no surprises in New York.

The driver who took him back to the hotel spoke to him in Yiddish. He apologized for his colleagues. Maybe they had not treated him nicely. The police was overworked. You had to be careful. New York was not Tel Aviv. All the crazies came here from all over the world to be swallowed up in the sewer of America.

When he had shut the door behind him he was overcome

with fear. A growing agitation welled up inside him. It was to no avail that he told himself it was all over, that he had come out of it unharmed, that there was nothing to get excited about, and that he must not get angry. But he was angry at the policemen who had treated him with such indifference and at Feinstein and at Anna Steinhardt and at himself. He hated the man at the airport and the muggers and the telephone. As if they had all ganged up on him.

The rage grew and grew and seemed to draw him into a whirlpool. He fell onto the bed sinking into the foam and felt as if two strong hands were strangling him. He told himself again and again that there was nothing to get excited about. Here he was back at the hotel, on his bed. Nobody was after him. And even so the rage continued to mount: two youngsters against a helpless old man. And that cruelty for the sake of cruelty! And they didn't even know he was Jewish!

Now he was angry with himself at having been duped into coming to America. And now he wasn't even sure that Anna Steinhardt really existed. Sylvia had set him a trap and taken her revenge. It was she who had wanted him to die in a foreign land, alone, without his children, without his grandchildren, without his wife, without all his friends.

He was still lucid enough to reject the thoughts about death—this was only a delayed reaction to a real danger and the humiliating sense of helplessness—but when the telephone rang in his room he imagined he was dreaming. His arms were as heavy as stones. He thought about the workers risking their lives on the steel beams as if he had dredged them up from the depths of his memory, as a thing that had occurred to him years before. And the telephone rang and rang, but he only looked at it with wide-open eyes.

About the Author

Nathan Shaham was born in Tel Aviv in 1925. He is the son of Eliezer Steinman, the noted Hebrew author and essayist. A member of Kibbutz Bet Alfa since 1945, he has worked as an editor in the Sifriyat Poalim publishing house and has also edited a bimonthly magazine. He was also vice-chairman of the Israel Broadcasting Authority. From 1977 to 1980 he served as Israel's cultural attaché in the United States. He is the author of twenty-six books in Hebrew, including ten novels, three collections of short fiction, several children's books, and travel accounts, as well as nine plays, several of which have been translated and performed abroad. He is the recipient of five literary awards in Israel.